Grammar School

4 Dimensions of Editing and Revising:

Everything a Student Needs for a Lifetime of Writing Success

Teach BIG provides the explanations behind the concepts addressed in your curriculum, regardless of which curriculum is used in your classroom.

This book contains a word for word breakdown of every sentence, every time. It spans the gamut of grammar, editing, and revising skills.

"We all need to go back to Grammar School every once in a while."

- Randi Whitney

By Randi Whitney

Grammar School: BEST Practices in Editing and Revising for All Curriculum Types

ISBN: 978-1-966301-30-1

Published by BIG Time Publishing Company

For permissions or inquiries, contact:

BIG Time Publishing Company
3502 Columbia Memorial Parkway, Kemah, TX 77565, 281-549-4466
randiwhitney.com

This book is a work of non-fiction. Any references to real events, people, or organizations are intended only to provide context and support the author's perspective and are used with permission when applicable.

First Edition: 2025
Printed in the United States of America

Randi Whitney's Library Card!

Enjoy all the books across multiple genres by Randi Whitney

Children's Books

- Buffalo Nickel Ranch
- Who Let the Goat Out
- I Love Buggy Rides
- The Messes We Make
- The Annual Cookie Tree
- It's Valentines, of Course of Course
- The Community Can
- Be Three
- Leaving Tracks
- The Blue Egg
- The Class with Heart
- Leave Something Take Something
- Tomato Boy
- Every Letter Counts
- Chocolate Chip Cookies
- Louis, Louis

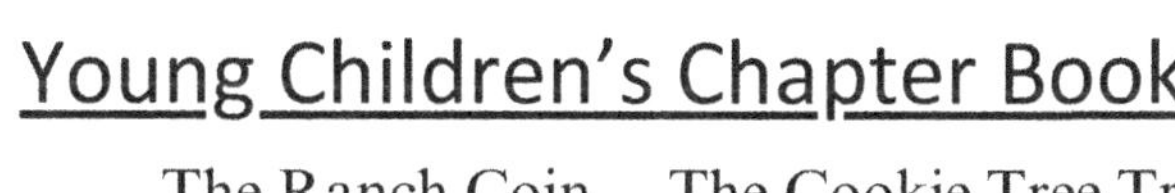

Young Children's Chapter Books

- The Ranch Coin
- Buggy Rides
- The Great Goatsby
- The Community Colection
- The Cookie Tree Tradition
- The Biggest Mess
- The Green Egg
- The Lost Medal

Early Reader Picture Books

- The Other Side of the Nickel
- The Goat's Gate

Educational Books

- Reading for Retrieval
- Writing for Purpose
- Teach BIG: Believe in Greatness – Bring Best Practices Back
- Teach BIG: Believe in Greatness – Study Guide
- 4 Dimensions of Comprehension
- Grammatical Matters
- Lexicon Mysteries Solved
- Fluency Flows
- GAP Phonics: Preventing and Closing Gaps

Mystery/Thriller Novels

- A Good Witness
- The Knock
- The Teacher Retreat
- Twisted Poison

Christian Novels

- The Last Day
- The First Day

Motivational Books

- Don't Spend Your CAN Years CAN'Ting

Preteen Christian Chapter Books

- The Bookcase: Matthew
- The Bookcase: Mark
- The Bookcase: Luke
- The Bookcase: John
- The Bookcase: Acts
- The Bookcase: Romans

randiwhitney.com
teachbig.com

Table of Contents

Section 1: Grammar Foundations

Section 2: Capitalization

Section 3: Punctuation

Section 4: Editing

Section 5: Revising

Section 6: The Virtual Learner

Dear Fellow Grammatarians,

I write to you with a heart full of passion for teaching all things grammar, editing, and revising. If you're holding this book, you are someone who understands the importance of language—the precision it brings to expression, the clarity it offers to thought, and the power it bestows upon our students. You are in the trenches every day, balancing countless expectations while trying to instill the magic of words into your learners. I know the road can feel overwhelming at times.

In today's educational landscape, with ever-changing standards and growing pressures, it can be difficult to carve out the time and space for grammar instruction that is both engaging and meaningful. The truth is, grammar, editing, and revising often get pushed aside for the sake of "more pressing" skills. Yet we know these skills are not just important—they are foundational. Without them, our students' voices can't shine, and their ideas won't take the shape they were meant to.

This book was created to be more than a set of lesson plans or quick exercises. It's a ***resource*** *and a* ***companion*** *designed to fit into whatever curriculum you are using. Whether you teach from a district-mandated program or use a more flexible framework, these strategies will integrate seamlessly to enrich your existing materials. Consider it a toolbelt—a collection of ready-to-use lessons, creative activities, and tangible techniques to help make grammar instruction accessible, memorable, and fun.*

I know the challenges you face, but I also know the joy that comes when a student finally ***gets it****—when they understand the structure of a well-written sentence or see the power of revising their own work. This is what keeps us coming back to the classroom, day after day. Together, we can make grammar less about memorization and more about empowerment.*

Thank you for your tireless dedication and passion. I hope this book brings new energy into your classroom and reminds you that your work matters—every single word of it.

Let's teach them to write boldly, to revise with intention, and to see the beauty in the language that surrounds them.

With gratitude and excitement,
Randi Whitney
Your Fellow Grammatarian

By utilizing the following guidelines, *Grammar School* will become your go-to resource for teaching grammar, editing, and revising. With personalized tools, targeted lessons, and engaging activities, you'll transform your students into confident writers and editors while meeting your teaching goals.

Guidelines for Using *Grammar School* Effectively

Grammar School is designed to be a flexible resource that empowers teachers to bring grammar, editing, and revising to life in their classrooms. Whether you're a new teacher or a veteran educator, here's how to personalize this book for your grade level, state standards, and classroom needs.

---

1. Align with Your State Standards

Goal: Ensure that your teaching aligns with your required curriculum.
How:

- **Step 1:** Print or access your state standards for language arts.
- **Step 2:** Use color-coded stickers or highlighters to mark the concepts that appear in the book that match your grade-level standards.
- **Example:** If "compound-complex sentences" is part of your 6th-grade standards, place a green sticker next to that section in the book for easy reference.

---

2. Use Teacher Training Scripts for Clarity

Goal: Enhance your own understanding and find the perfect language for teaching difficult concepts.
How:

- Flag or highlight the *Teacher Training Scripts* for areas where you need help explaining abstract ideas (e.g., identifying dangling modifiers or differentiating dependent clauses).
- Practice reading the scripts aloud before teaching to build confidence.
- Use these scripts during professional development sessions to share strategies with colleagues.

---

3. Identify Mentor Texts for Classroom Use

Goal: Provide real-world examples to your students.
How:

- Create a section in your teacher's binder to catalog the *mentor texts* provided in the book.

- Flag passages that align with the concepts you're teaching, such as subject-verb agreement or vivid sentence construction.
- Print and laminate select mentor texts for use in centers or small groups.

4. Label Poster Pages and Handouts

Goal: Make visual aids easily accessible for student reference.
How:

- Flag pages that contain *ready-to-copy posters or anchor charts* and make multiple copies for your classroom wall or writing center.
- Encourage students to paste smaller versions into their writing notebooks for quick reference.
- Use laminated versions for small-group grammar workshops.

---

5. Create a Personal Reference Guide for Each Unit

Goal: Save time and streamline your planning process.
How:

- Keep a tabbed binder for each section of the book: **Grammar, Capitalization, Punctuation, Editing, and Revising.**
- Add your own notes about which activities worked well for specific student groups.
- Personalize assessments by jotting down which practice questions best match your students' needs.

---

6. Use Color-Coding for Quick Access

Goal: Make frequently used resources easy to find.
How:

- Use **sticky tabs** for lesson plans, assessments, and scripts.
- Color-code your sticky tabs:
    - **Blue:** Grammar concepts
    - **Green:** Revising strategies
    - **Yellow:** Mentor texts
    - **Red:** Editing assessments

7. Build Small-Group and Station Rotations

Goal: Differentiate instruction for diverse learners.
How:

- Designate sections of the book for small-group activities.
- Build *station rotations* around the different types of revising and editing strategies using the lesson plans provided.
- Rotate between stations for **peer review, sentence reconstruction, and punctuation correction games.**

---

8. Integrate Songs, Chants, and Dramas into Daily Practice

Goal: Make grammar fun and memorable.
How:

- Identify the *songs, chants, and readers' theater scripts* that align with your unit.
- Use the chants as part of your daily grammar warm-ups.
- Perform reader's theater scripts in small groups for a creative approach to teaching sentence construction.

---

9. Organize Mock Assessment Questions for Test Prep

Goal: Help students become confident and competent in editing and revising.
How:

- Create a test-prep folder for the *mock assessment questions* provided in the book.
- Use these questions in warm-ups, quizzes, and review games.
- Track student progress and adjust lessons as needed based on assessment results.

---

10. Collaborate and Share

Goal: Build a community of learning among your colleagues.
How:

- Use *Grammar School* as a resource during team meetings or professional development.
- Share effective lesson plans and teaching scripts with other teachers.
- Collaborate on classroom projects using ideas from the book.

The Importance of Effective Editing in Written Communication

Effective written communication is one of the most valuable skills in both personal and professional life, and at the heart of this skill lies the ability to edit well. Editing is more than correcting errors—it's the process of refining a message to ensure clarity, precision, and impact. Being an effective editor transforms a writer into a powerful communicator, capable of expressing ideas with confidence and influence. In the editing process, attention to detail, an understanding of language mechanics, and the ability to apply stylistic nuances combine to create writing that resonates with its audience.

An essential foundation for successful editing is a deep understanding of the mechanics of language, including **parts of speech, capitalization, punctuation, and sentence variety**. Each of these elements plays a vital role in shaping the meaning and effectiveness of written communication:

1. **Parts of Speech**: A strong grasp of nouns, verbs, adjectives, adverbs, and other parts of speech allows writers to construct sentences with precision and purpose. Knowing how to use these tools ensures that ideas are conveyed clearly and that the relationships between words are logical and compelling.
2. **Capitalization**: Proper capitalization is more than a stylistic choice—it provides cues to the reader, indicating the beginning of sentences, proper nouns, and significant concepts. Misusing capitalization can lead to confusion or a lack of professionalism, undermining the credibility of the writer.
3. **Punctuation**: Punctuation is the roadmap of writing, guiding readers through the text with clarity and flow. From commas and semicolons to periods and quotation marks, punctuation ensures that meaning is unambiguous and ideas are connected effectively. A single misplaced punctuation mark can change the entire meaning of a sentence.
4. **Sentence Variety**: Writing that incorporates a mix of sentence structures—simple, compound, complex, and compound-complex—engages the reader and enhances readability. Varying sentence length and style prevents monotony and allows writers to emphasize key points and create a rhythm that mirrors the intended tone of the message.

Effective editing is not just about finding and fixing mistakes; it's about recognizing opportunities to elevate a piece of writing. An editor's role is to shape the text into its best possible form, ensuring it is grammatically sound, stylistically appropriate, and tailored to its audience. For this reason, mastering editing skills is imperative for anyone who seeks to become an excellent written communicator.

This chapter of *Grammar School* focuses on the critical skills required for effective editing. Through a thorough exploration of language mechanics and practical strategies, it equips readers with the tools to transform their writing from good to exceptional. By understanding and utilizing the essential elements of grammar and style, writers will gain the confidence and competence to craft clear, professional, and impactful communication in any context.

Challenges in Learning Parts of Speech for New Readers and Writers

For new readers and writers, acquiring the knowledge of parts of speech can be overwhelming because each part serves a different function in a sentence. While some parts of speech are easier to grasp, others create confusion due to their similar roles or abstract nature. These challenges can impact students' ability to build strong sentences, comprehend texts, and express their thoughts clearly in writing.

Parts of Speech That Are Typically Easier

1. **Nouns ( )** – *Naming words* are often the first part of speech that young learners identify and use. Since nouns represent tangible objects (like *dog, book, or chair*) or familiar people (like *mom or teacher*), they are concrete and easy to visualize.
2. **Verbs ( )** – *Action words* such as *run, eat, and play* also come naturally to children because they relate to physical activities or everyday actions. Linking verbs (*is, are*) may take a little more explanation, but once mastered, they become essential in forming complete sentences.
3. **Adjectives ( )** – Describing words like *big, blue, and happy* are easier to grasp because they are directly tied to nouns. Learners enjoy using adjectives to add detail and color to their writing, making it a fun part of speech to learn.

Parts of Speech That Are More Challenging

1. **Adverbs ( )** – Adverbs can be tricky because they modify verbs, adjectives, or other adverbs, often answering *how, when, where*, or *to what extent*. The challenge lies in recognizing the difference between adjectives and adverbs. For instance, distinguishing between *quick* (adjective) and *quickly* (adverb) requires practice and explanation.
   Example:
   The fast dog (adjective) ran quickly (adverb).
   Students may confuse the function of the two, thinking both modify nouns.
2. **Pronouns ( )** – While basic pronouns (*he, she, it, they*) are simple, **antecedent agreement** can confuse students. Replacing nouns with the correct pronoun requires understanding number (singular vs. plural) and gender consistency.
   Example:
   The student lost their book. (*Student* is singular, but *their* is plural, creating confusion.)
3. **Prepositions ( )** – Prepositions can be hard to grasp because they often introduce abstract relationships of **time, place, or direction**. Recognizing prepositional phrases and understanding how they provide context requires a more advanced level of

sentence comprehension.
Example: *The cat is under the table.*

4. **Conjunctions ( )** – Coordinating conjunctions (*and, but, or*) are easier to learn because they connect simple ideas. However, **subordinating conjunctions** (*because, although, if*) and **correlative conjunctions** (*either...or, neither...nor*) add complexity that may confuse new learners.
5. **Interjections ( )** – Although interjections (*Wow! Hey! Ouch!*) are fun and expressive, students may struggle to understand how they differ from other parts of speech since they don't fit into the sentence structure as logically as nouns or verbs do.

Common Confusions

- **Adjective vs. Adverb** – Both describe things, but adjectives modify nouns while adverbs modify verbs, adjectives, or other adverbs.
  Confusion Example: *The dog runs fast (adverb), not fastly.*
- **Noun vs. Pronoun** – Students may struggle to understand when to use a pronoun to replace a noun and how to ensure agreement.
- **Preposition vs. Adverb** – Prepositions introduce phrases, but adverbs can also indicate location or time, causing confusion.
  Example:
  He ran outside (adverb). vs. *He ran outside the house (prepositional phrase).*

Why Mastering Parts of Speech Is Important

Understanding parts of speech is the foundation for grammar, sentence construction, and clear communication. It allows students to:

- **Write more complex sentences** with varied structure.
- **Improve reading comprehension** by recognizing how words function within sentences.
- **Avoid errors in grammar** such as subject-verb disagreement or misusing modifiers.

Although some parts of speech present more challenges than others, with practice, students can master even the most complex concepts. **Multisensory strategies** like Sentence Weather Symbols help demystify these concepts and make learning fun and engaging. The key is **consistent reinforcement** and **real-world practice**, ensuring students become confident readers and writers over time.

Research Regarding the Connection Between Knowledge of Parts of Speech and Literacy Development

Yes, there is significant research connecting the understanding of parts of speech to the effectiveness of reading comprehension and writing skills. Studies in **linguistics, cognitive psychology, and literacy education** consistently show that a deep understanding of grammar—including parts of speech—improves both reading fluency and writing coherence. This connection lies in how grammar provides the **structural framework** for language, helping students recognize patterns in reading and construct clear, logical sentences in writing.

Research Evidence and Key Findings

1. **Grammar Knowledge as a Predictor of Reading Comprehension**
   Cain & Nash (2011) conducted a study that showed students with a stronger grasp of grammar, particularly the roles of nouns, verbs, and conjunctions, performed significantly better on reading comprehension tasks. Recognizing parts of speech helps students predict sentence patterns and make meaning from text more efficiently.
   - **Example:** Understanding conjunctions (*and, but, because*) allows readers to grasp the relationship between ideas in complex sentences, improving comprehension.
   - **Conclusion:** Knowing how parts of speech function helps students parse sentence structures and better understand the meaning of longer, more complex texts.
2. **Grammar Knowledge Enhances Writing Clarity and Organization**
   A study by **Myhill et al. (2012)** found that students who received explicit instruction on parts of speech and sentence construction demonstrated greater improvements in their writing than those who focused solely on content. By understanding how words like **adjectives, adverbs,** and **prepositions** shape meaning, students produced clearer, more engaging writing.
   - **Example:** A student who understands how adverbs modify verbs (*She sang beautifully*) can create more vivid, descriptive writing.
   - **Conclusion:** Grammatical awareness allows students to construct sentences with more variety and precision, improving overall communication.

3. **Parts of Speech and Sentence Fluency**
   Research in **developmental linguistics** shows that early mastery of parts of speech improves **sentence fluency**. According to **Nippold (2009)**, students who can identify parts of speech are better equipped to avoid common sentence-level errors such as run-

on sentences, fragments, and misplaced modifiers. This fluency in sentence construction translates to more polished and readable writing.

- **Example:** A student who understands subject-verb agreement and noun-pronoun consistency is less likely to write confusing or grammatically incorrect sentences.
- **Conclusion:** Knowledge of parts of speech helps students build grammatically sound sentences, making their writing easier to understand and more enjoyable to read.

Why Parts of Speech Matter for Writers and Readers

1. **Better Sentence Parsing in Reading** – Readers with a solid understanding of parts of speech can quickly recognize sentence structures, making it easier to predict meaning and context.
   - **Example:** Recognizing prepositions and conjunctions helps readers break complex sentences into manageable parts.
   - **Sentence:** *The boy who was standing by the tree ran quickly toward the house because it started to rain.*
     Students who understand prepositions (*by, toward*) and conjunctions (*because*) can break down this sentence into smaller chunks, improving comprehension.
2. **Enhanced Writing Skills** – Knowing the difference between adjectives and adverbs, or understanding when to use a conjunction, gives students more tools for writing effectively.
   - **Example:** Instead of writing multiple short sentences—*The cat is big. The cat is fluffy.*—a student can combine ideas: *The big, fluffy cat sleeps on the couch.*
3. **Improved Vocabulary Acquisition** – Students who are familiar with the functions of parts of speech are better equipped to decode and use new words. This is especially helpful for **English language learners (ELLs)** and students with limited vocabulary

Practical Applications in the Classroom

- **Diagramming sentences** to reinforce grammar and writing skills.
- **Multisensory activities** like Sentence Weather Symbols to make abstract concepts tangible.
- **Peer editing** exercises focusing on identifying parts of speech to improve sentence structure.

Conclusion

The research is clear: **Understanding parts of speech enhances reading comprehension, writing clarity, and overall literacy development**. By teaching students the roles that different words play in a sentence, we give them the tools they need to be more confident, effective communicators. This foundation in grammar not only improves academic success but also fosters lifelong language skills that will serve students well beyond the classroom.

Why Grammar Instruction Should Occur at Multiple Levels:

Whole Group, Small Group, Paired Team, and Individual

Teaching grammar effectively requires a **multifaceted approach** that leverages various group sizes and settings to meet the diverse needs of students. Each learning environment—whole group, small group, paired team, and individual—serves a distinct purpose in helping students **understand, apply, and internalize grammar concepts**. By using all four, teachers ensure that students can move from receiving direct instruction to actively practicing and applying their learning in meaningful ways.

Whole Group Instruction: Building a Shared Foundation

Purpose:
Whole group instruction introduces grammar concepts in a **structured and consistent manner**. This ensures all students have the same baseline understanding and allows the teacher to **model grammar rules** and **demonstrate sentence construction**.

Why It's Important:

- Provides a common framework for all students.
- Encourages collaborative discussion and engagement.
- Allows the teacher to use visual aids (e.g., Sentence Weather Symbols, anchor charts) and **interactive activities** like songs or chants to make grammar memorable.
- Immediate clarification of misconceptions is possible.

Example:
During a whole group lesson, the teacher introduces **adjectives** and models how they describe nouns using visual aids. The class works together to identify adjectives in sample sentences.

Small Group Instruction: Targeted Support and Practice

Purpose:
In small groups, students receive **targeted instruction based on their specific needs**. This setting allows teachers to differentiate, offering more practice to struggling learners while extending learning for those who excel.

Why It's Important:

- Provides personalized feedback and support.
- Encourages active participation from students who may hesitate in a larger group.
- Allows for tailored activities based on skill level or focus area (e.g., mastering verb tense, improving sentence variety).

Example:
A small group of students struggling with **prepositional phrases** might receive guided practice where they physically move around the room, labeling objects with prepositions like *on*, *under*, or *next to*.

Paired Team Instruction: Peer Collaboration and Reinforcement

Purpose:
Paired learning encourages **peer collaboration**, where students can practice grammar concepts together, offering feedback and reinforcing their understanding. This setting builds **social skills and accountability** while encouraging **peer teaching**.

Why It's Important:

- Provides a safe space for students to explore new concepts without the pressure of the whole class.
- Strengthens learning through discussion and shared problem-solving.
- Builds confidence as students explain concepts to one another.

Example:
In pairs, students combine sentences to practice **conjunctions**. One student writes two short sentences, and their partner helps combine them using the correct conjunction (*and, but, because*).

Individual Instruction: Mastery and Independent Application

Purpose:
Individual work allows students to **apply their knowledge independently**, ensuring they have mastered the concept. This is the most critical step in grammar instruction, as it shows whether students can use grammar correctly without external guidance.

Why It's Important:

- Encourages self-assessment and accountability.
- Develops critical thinking and problem-solving skills.
- Helps identify gaps in understanding that might not appear in group settings.

Example:
Students independently edit a passage, identifying errors in **capitalization, punctuation, verb tense,** or **subject-verb agreement**. This activity serves as both practice and assessment.

Why a Blended Approach Works Best

Combining whole group, small group, paired team, and individual instruction ensures that grammar learning is **layered and reinforced** through multiple experiences.

- **Whole group instruction** sets the foundation.
- **Small group instruction** offers targeted support.
- **Paired team instruction** fosters collaboration and shared learning.
- **Individual instruction** promotes mastery and independent thinking.

Together, these methods address the diverse learning needs of every student, providing a comprehensive grammar education that builds confident readers and writers. This balanced approach not only helps students **understand grammar rules** but also enables them to **apply those rules in writing** and **communicate more effectively**.

How to Fit Grammar Mini-Lessons into a Typical School Day

A typical school day offers **many small pockets of time** that can be used for **short, focused grammar mini-lessons**. These **"tiny time minutes"** provide opportunities to reinforce concepts without interrupting the flow of other lessons. Integrating grammar instruction throughout the day ensures consistent exposure and maximizes learning.

Chronological List of Grammar Opportunities Throughout the Day

1. Morning Warm-Up (8:00–8:15 a.m.)

Mini-Lesson: *Daily Grammar Sentence*
Example: Write a sentence on the board that contains an error in punctuation, subject-verb agreement, or word choice. Ask students to identify and correct the mistake.

- **Focus:** Sentence structure, punctuation, or verb tense
- **Why it works:** Helps students start the day with critical thinking and attention to detail.

Teacher Script:
"Good morning, class! Let's kick off our day with a sentence check. Can you find the mistake in this sentence: 'The cat sleep on the chair.' What needs to change?"

---

2. Transition Time Between Subjects (9:30–9:35 a.m.)

Mini-Lesson: *Quick Part-of-Speech Review*
Example: Ask students to name a noun, verb, or adjective from the last subject lesson.

- **Focus:** Reinforcing parts of speech in context
- **Why it works:** Connects grammar to other subject areas and keeps grammar practice brief but meaningful.

Teacher Script:
"Before we switch to math, who can tell me a noun from our science lesson? Great! How about a verb? Remember, nouns are things, and verbs show action!"

3. Mid-Morning Reading Block (10:15–10:30 a.m.)

Mini-Lesson: *Grammar in Context (Using Mentor Sentences)*
Example: While reading a story, pause to point out a well-crafted sentence and analyze its grammar.

- **Focus:** Sentence variety, conjunctions, or prepositional phrases
- **Why it works:** Helps students see grammar as part of authentic writing.

Teacher Script:
"Listen to this sentence: 'The wind howled through the night, but the little house stood strong.' Notice how the conjunction but connects two ideas? It makes the sentence more interesting and clear."

---

4. Writing Workshop (11:00–11:45 a.m.)

Mini-Lesson: *Sentence Expansion Practice*
Example: Encourage students to take a simple sentence and expand it using adjectives, adverbs, or prepositional phrases.

- **Focus:** Adding detail and improving sentence variety
- **Why it works:** Provides immediate application of grammar skills during independent writing.

Teacher Script:
"Let's take the sentence 'The dog ran.' How can we make this sentence more descriptive? Add an adjective, an adverb, or a prepositional phrase. How about 'The big dog ran quickly across the field'?"

---

5. After Lunch (12:45–1:00 p.m.)

Mini-Lesson: *Grammar Chant or Song*
Example: Use a song about parts of speech or sentence structure to get students moving and focused after lunch.

- **Focus:** Reinforcing previously taught concepts
- **Why it works:** Movement and music help students refocus and retain information.

Teacher Script:
"Let's wake up our brains with our grammar song! Remember the chant: 'Who, what, what, when, where!' This will help us remember how to build a sentence."

---

6. End-of-Day Reflection (2:45–3:00 p.m.)

Mini-Lesson: *Grammar Journal Reflection*
Example: Ask students to write a sentence or two summarizing their day and then check it for grammar errors.

- **Focus:** Sentence structure, capitalization, and punctuation
- **Why it works:** Encourages students to reflect while practicing grammar in a meaningful context.

Teacher Script:
"Before we leave, write a quick sentence about the best part of your day. After you've written it, check for capitalization, punctuation, and verb tense. Share with a partner if you'd like!"

Benefits of Using Tiny Time Minutes for Grammar

1. **Reinforcement Without Overwhelm** – Mini-lessons keep grammar concepts fresh without overwhelming students.
2. **Cross-Subject Integration** – Helps students see that grammar applies across all subjects, not just language arts.
3. **Consistent Practice** – Frequent short lessons promote long-term retention.
4. **Engagement and Variety** – Keeps learning interactive and fun.

By using these **tiny moments throughout the day**, teachers can **build strong grammar foundations** without taking away from core instructional time. Over time, these small bursts of practice can have a significant impact on students' reading and writing skills.

Station Rotation: Maximizing Small Group Instruction

Station rotation is an effective way to teach grammar in small groups while keeping students engaged and moving around the classroom. There are two primary types of station rotations:

1. Same Skill, Different Aspects of the Concept

In this model, each station focuses on a **different aspect of the same grammar skill.** This helps students develop a deeper understanding of the concept from multiple angles.

Example: Teaching Adjectives

- **Station 1:** Identifying adjectives in sentences (Highlighting or circling adjectives in sample texts).
- **Station 2:** Expanding sentences using adjectives (Students take a simple sentence and add descriptive words).
- **Station 3:** Sorting adjectives by type (Comparative, superlative, descriptive).
- **Station 4:** Writing with adjectives (Students write short descriptive paragraphs using at least five adjectives).

Why It Works:

- Reinforces the same concept through various learning modes (visual, auditory, and hands-on).
- Helps students build mastery through repeated exposure in different contexts.

---

2. Different Skills at Each Station

In this model, each station focuses on a **completely different grammar skill** or part of speech. This approach works well for **review sessions** or when students need targeted practice in multiple areas.

Example: Multi-Skill Grammar Review

- **Station 1:** Nouns and Pronouns (Identifying and using them correctly).
- **Station 2:** Verb Tenses (Practicing present, past, and future tense).
- **Station 3:** Conjunctions (Combining sentences using coordinating and subordinating conjunctions).
- **Station 4:** Prepositions (Building sentences with prepositional phrases).

Why It Works:

- Covers a broader range of skills in one session, helping students make connections between different parts of speech.
- Allows for targeted practice and quick assessments of multiple concepts.

How to Implement Effective Small Group Station Rotations

1. **Plan with Clear Objectives**: Ensure each station has a specific goal, whether it's introducing a new concept, reinforcing a skill, or assessing understanding.
2. **Use Engaging Activities**: Stations should include a mix of **hands-on tasks, collaborative work, and individual practice** to keep students interested.
3. **Rotate Consistently**: Keep station times short (10–15 minutes), allowing students to experience multiple stations in one session.
4. **Monitor and Guide**: While students rotate, the teacher works with one group, providing focused instruction while ensuring the other stations are running smoothly.

Conclusion

Small group instruction and station rotation models are essential for teaching grammar concepts effectively. By **personalizing instruction and offering multiple ways to engage with the material**, these methods ensure that students develop a comprehensive understanding of grammar. Whether honing in on a single concept or addressing multiple skills, small groups provide the **focused attention and targeted practice** that students need to become confident readers and writers.

Teaching Grammar Through Content Areas: A Smarter, Not Harder Approach

Teaching grammar through **social studies, science, fine arts, and physical education** is a highly effective way to **integrate learning** and make grammar more meaningful. When students encounter grammar concepts in the context of real-world subjects, they gain a **deeper understanding** of both the content and the mechanics of language. **Writing across the curriculum** allows for seamless learning experiences that reinforce grammar while enhancing content knowledge.

Why Teaching Grammar Across Content Areas Matters

1. **Makes Grammar Relevant and Authentic**
   - Grammar in isolation can feel abstract and disconnected. By weaving it into content areas, students see grammar as a **functional tool** rather than a set of arbitrary rules.
   - For example, teaching **cause-and-effect sentence structures** in a science experiment helps students connect grammar to their academic experiences.
   - In social studies, learning how to write descriptive sentences about historical events allows students to practice **adjectives** while reinforcing their understanding of the past.
2. **Supports Deeper Content Learning**
   - Writing across the curriculum encourages students to engage with content in new ways. When students are asked to write and reflect on what they've learned, they are **internalizing the subject matter** more deeply.
   - **Example:** In a science class, students might write a summary of how photosynthesis works, focusing on using precise verbs and prepositional phrases to describe each step.
3. **Reinforces Grammar Through Repetition in Various Contexts**
   - Grammar concepts become more ingrained when students encounter them repeatedly in different contexts. A student who practices **verb tense** in both language arts and science will retain it more effectively than if it were taught only once.
   - **Example:** Learning past-tense verbs when describing a historical event in social studies reinforces the same concept covered in an English class.
4. **Encourages Critical Thinking and Communication**
   - Writing across the curriculum develops **communication and critical thinking skills**, which are essential for academic success.
   - **Grammar and writing structure** allow students to organize their thoughts and present their ideas clearly, which is crucial in every subject.

Content Areas and Grammar Integration

Social Studies

- Focus on **descriptive language** when writing about historical figures or events.
- Use **complex sentences** to show cause and effect, such as explaining the impact of a major event.
- **Grammar Focus:** Adjectives, prepositional phrases, and conjunctions.

Science

- Teach **sequence and procedural writing** in science experiments.
- Use **precise verbs** and adverbs to describe scientific processes.
- **Grammar Focus:** Verb tenses (present for processes, past for discoveries), prepositions (location and direction), and adverbs (describing how something occurs).

Fine Arts

- Write reflections on art projects using **sensory adjectives** and **figurative language**.
- Create **narratives** about musical compositions or dramatic performances.
- **Grammar Focus:** Adjectives, conjunctions, and sentence variety.

Physical Education

- Focus on **action verbs** and **adverbs** when writing about physical activities.
- Write short summaries of game rules or fitness routines, emphasizing **sequence and clarity**.
- **Grammar Focus:** Action verbs, adverbs of manner and time, and prepositional phrases.

Grammar and Content: A Two-Way Relationship

Grammar Can Be Taught Through Content: When students write about social studies, science, or physical education, the focus is on both the **content** and the **grammar structure** needed to communicate it effectively.
Content Can Be Taught Through Grammar: Grammar lessons can incorporate content-specific examples, allowing students to learn both at once. For example, when teaching **complex sentences**, use a sentence about an important historical event or scientific process.

Why This Is a Smarter, Not Harder Approach

- **Time-Efficient:** Teaching grammar through content areas saves instructional time. Instead of separate grammar lessons, teachers embed grammar into content instruction, addressing multiple objectives simultaneously.
- **Holistic Learning:** Integrating grammar with content fosters a **holistic learning experience**, where students see the connections between different subjects.
- **Increased Retention:** Students remember concepts better when they are applied in meaningful contexts.
- **Improved Writing Across Disciplines:** Writing across the curriculum builds stronger writing skills in all areas, helping students become more effective communicators in science, social studies, and beyond.

Conclusion

Grammar and content learning shouldn't exist in silos. By weaving grammar into content areas—and vice versa—teachers provide students with a richer, more engaging learning experience. This approach ensures students don't just learn grammar rules; they **apply those rules** to communicate complex ideas across multiple disciplines. In doing so, students develop the **skills and confidence** they need to become thoughtful readers, writers, and thinkers.

Section 1

GRAMMAR

Scope and Sequence for "Grammar School

Section 1: Order to Introduce Parts of Speech

Chapter 1: Nouns

- Common, proper, singular, plural, possessive, concrete, abstract, and collective nouns.

Chapter 2: Pronouns

- Subjective and objective, personal, possessive, reflexive, intensive, relative, demonstrative, interrogative, indefinite, and antecedent agreement.

Chapter 3: Verbs

- Action, linking, helping verbs, tenses (past, present, future, perfect tenses, progressive tense), verb phrases, subject-verb agreement, active/passive verbs, and irregular verbs.

Chapter 4: Adjectives

- Descriptive, demonstrative, comparative, superlative, articles.

Chapter 5: Adverbs

- Types of adverbs (manner, place, time, degree, frequency), conjunctive adverbs, and comparison of adverbs.

Chapter 6: Prepositions

- Prepositional phrases, objects of prepositions, and their influence on subject-verb agreement.

Chapter 7: Conjunctions

- Coordinating, subordinating, correlative conjunctions, conjunctive adverbs.

Chapter 8: Interjections

- Expressions of emotion, punctuation with interjections.

Chapter 9: Sentence Construction

Chapter 10: Sentence Weather

Grammar School Diagnostic Questionnaire

Look at the questions that follow. See if you know the answers within the moment of seeing the question-and-answer choices. In other words if you have to think for very long to recall the necessary role or if you have to look it up, do not give yourself credit.

Instructions: This diagnostic assessment is designed to measure your understanding of grammar concepts covered in Chapters 1 through 10. For each chapter, answer the multiple-choice questions provided. Each question focuses on a different key point within the chapter.

Select the best answer for each question.

If you score 80% or above, you are on your way to mastery!

Use the scoring rubric at the end to evaluate your readiness.

Chapter 1: Nouns

Which of the following is a proper noun?

A) river
B) Mississippi River
C) water
D) lake

Identify the plural form of "child":
A) childs
B) children
C) childs'
D) childrens

Which sentence contains an abstract noun?
A) The dog barked loudly.
B) She admired his courage.
C) The team played soccer.
D) The apples were delicious.

Select the collective noun:
A) books
B) family
C) happiness
D) mountain

Which of the following shows correct possessive noun usage?
A) The cats toy is broken.
B) The cat's toy is broken.
C) The cat toy's broken.
D) The cats' toy broken.

Chapter 2: Pronouns

Choose the sentence with a correctly used reflexive pronoun:
A) Myself finished the project.
B) He gave himself a break.
C) She herself gave the gift to I.
D) They completed the task by theirselves.

What is the antecedent of the pronoun in this sentence? "The girl lost her book."
A) her
B) book
C) girl
D) lost

Which sentence uses a demonstrative pronoun correctly?
A) This are my books.
B) These is her house.
C) That is my favorite movie.
D) Those book is on the table.

Identify the indefinite pronoun:
A) Everyone enjoyed the show.
B) The car is parked outside.
C) That belongs to me.
D) He ran fast.

Which sentence correctly shows pronoun-antecedent agreement?
A) Each student must bring their book.
B) The students must bring his book.
C) The teacher gave their advice to the class.
D) Every runner needs his or her water bottle.

Chapter 3: Verbs

Choose the sentence written in the future progressive tense:
A) She is running in the marathon.
B) She was running in the marathon.
C) She will be running in the marathon.
D) She ran in the marathon.

Identify the irregular verb in the past tense:
A) She walked to school.
B) He brung his lunch.
C) They ate dinner early.
D) We talked about it.

Which sentence uses an active verb?
A) The cake was baked by Sarah.
B) Sarah baked the cake.
C) The cake is being baked.
D) The cake will have been baked.

Select the correct linking verb:
A) He ran fast.
B) She feels happy.
C) They are playing.
D) I will sing.

Choose the sentence with correct subject-verb agreement:
A) The team were winning.
B) The team is winning.
C) The teams was winning.
D) The teams are winning.

Chapter 4: Adjectives

Identify the sentence with a superlative adjective:
A) She is tall.
B) She is taller than her sister.
C) She is the tallest in her class.
D) She is as tall as her brother.

Which sentence correctly uses an article?
A) He saw a elephant at the zoo.
B) She bought an apple from the store.
C) I need the water bottle.
D) Both B and C.

Choose the descriptive adjective:
A) This is her house.
B) The bright sun shone all day.
C) I need that book.
D) She has many friends.

Identify the demonstrative adjective:
A) Those flowers are beautiful.
B) This is my favorite movie.
C) They went to the park.
D) He gave it to her.

Select the sentence with a comparative adjective:
A) This pizza is delicious.
B) This pizza is more delicious than that one.
C) This is the most delicious pizza.
D) This pizza is good.

Chapter 5: Adverbs

Which sentence contains an adverb of manner?
A) She sings beautifully.
B) They often go to the park.
C) He arrived late.
D) We will leave tomorrow.

Identify the conjunctive adverb:
A) She will come; however, she will be late.
B) He is tired but happy.
C) They stayed because it was raining.
D) The train arrived late.

Choose the sentence with an adverb of frequency:
A) He rarely eats breakfast.
B) She sang softly.
C) They walked outside.
D) I will see you tomorrow.

Which sentence contains an adverb of degree?
A) He is very excited.
B) She runs quickly.
C) They are arriving soon.
D) The room is upstairs.

Select the sentence with an adverb of place:
A) He ran here.
B) They went yesterday.
C) She speaks fluently.
D) I will finish later.

Chapter 6: Prepositions

Identify the prepositional phrase in the sentence: "The dog slept under the table."
A) The dog slept
B) under the table
C) slept under
D) the table

Which sentence uses a preposition correctly?
A) She ran to the park.
B) He jumped on top the car.
C) The book is under of the chair.
D) I will go in the morning.

Select the sentence that shows how a prepositional phrase influences subject-verb agreement:
A) The basket of apples is full.
B) The basket of apples are full.
C) The baskets of apple is full.
D) The baskets of apple are full.

Which word is the object of the preposition in this sentence? "They walked through the park."
A) walked
B) through
C) the
D) park

Choose the sentence with the correct preposition usage:
A) The cat is beside the chair.
B) The cat is besides the chair.
C) The cat is bysides the chair.
D) The cat is in side the chair.

Chapter 7: Conjunctions

Identify the coordinating conjunction in this sentence: "She wanted to stay, but she had to leave."
A) stay
B) but
C) had
D) leave

Which sentence uses a subordinating conjunction?
A) He ran and jumped.
B) She left because it was late.
C) I like apples or bananas.
D) They stayed but wanted to go.

Choose the sentence with correlative conjunctions:
A) Both the cat and the dog are sleeping.
B) She went to the park.
C) He plays, but she sings.
D) The book is on the table.

Select the sentence that uses a conjunctive adverb:
A) He arrived late; however, he finished on time.
B) I went to the store and bought milk.
C) The dog barked, but no one heard.
D) She went inside because it rained.

Which sentence correctly uses a conjunction to combine ideas?
A) I wanted to go, but it was raining.
B) I wanted to go, it was raining.
C) I wanted to go but, it was raining.
D) I wanted to go but it was, raining.

Chapter 8: Interjections

Choose the sentence with a correctly used interjection:
A) Wow! That was amazing.
B) Oh no, I forgot my wallet!
C) Hey, are you coming?
D) All of the above.

Identify the interjection in this sentence: "Oops, I made a mistake."
A) mistake
B) I
C) made
D) Oops

Select the sentence with proper punctuation for the interjection:
A) Well I guess that's fine.
B) Well, I guess that's fine.
C) Well. I guess that's fine.
D) Well I guess, that's fine.

Which sentence uses an interjection to express excitement?
A) Hooray! We won the game.
B) Oh, that's interesting.
C) Hmm, let me think.
D) Ah, I see what you mean.

Choose the interjection that expresses disappointment:
A) Wow!
B) Oh no!
C) Yay!
D) Oops!

Chapter 9: Sentence Construction

Identify the sentence fragment:
A) Running through the park, she smiled.
B) Because he was late.
C) They went home and slept.
D) The sun set and the stars appeared.

Which sentence correctly combines subjects and predicates?
A) She is singing and dance.
B) They run and play in the yard.
C) He eats and drinking water.
D) The dog barked but ran.

Choose the sentence with a compound-complex structure:
A) I went to the store, and I bought milk because we were out.
B) She likes to read and write stories.
C) He ran fast but tripped.
D) The sun shines and warms the earth.

Select the sentence that correctly uses modifiers:
A) She wore a red, dress.
B) The quickly dog ran to the park.
C) The brightly shining stars lit up the night.
D) I am happily very tired.

Identify the run-on sentence:
A) I love to read books it's my favorite hobby.
B) She likes apples, and he likes oranges.
C) Because I was late, I missed the meeting.
D) He sings well, but he doesn't dance.

Chapter 10: Phrases versus Clauses

Identify the noun phrase in this sentence: "The tall tree swayed in the wind."
A) tall tree
B) The tall tree
C) swayed in the wind
D) in the wind

Which sentence contains a prepositional phrase?
A) She runs every morning.
B) They played in the garden.
C) He sings beautifully.
D) I enjoy reading books.

Choose the sentence that correctly distinguishes between a phrase and a clause:
A) The dog ran after the ball, barking loudly.
B) She wants to eat.
C) Although it was late, they stayed.
D) Running through the park is fun.

Identify the sentence with an adverbial phrase:
A) She sings with great joy.
B) The dog barked loudly.
C) He runs fast.
D) I'll see you tomorrow.

Select the sentence where a prepositional phrase affects subject-verb agreement:
A) The basket of fruits is full.
B) The basket of fruits are full.
C) The fruits in the basket is full.
D) The fruits in the basket are full.

Scoring Rubric:

80% or higher: Mastery level; course not required.
50% to 79%: Partial understanding; recommended to take the course.
Below 50%: Needs improvement; strongly recommended to take the course.

Here's the **answer key** to the diagnostic assessment with explanations for both correct and incorrect answers:

Chapter 1: Nouns

1. Which of the following is a proper noun?
Correct Answer: B) Mississippi River

- *Why it's correct:* Proper nouns name specific people, places, or things. "Mississippi River" is a specific river, so it's proper.
- *Why others are wrong:*
    - A) "river" is a common noun.
    - C) "water" is a common noun referring to a general substance.
    - D) "lake" is a common noun.

2. Identify the plural form of "child":
Correct Answer: B) children

- *Why it's correct:* "Children" is the correct irregular plural form of "child."
- *Why others are wrong:*
    - A) "childs" is not a word.
    - C) "childs'" is a possessive form, not plural.
    - D) "childrens" adds an unnecessary plural marker.

3. Which sentence contains an abstract noun?
Correct Answer: B) She admired his courage.

- *Why it's correct:* "Courage" is an abstract noun representing an idea or quality.
- *Why others are wrong:*
    - A) "dog" and "barked" are concrete nouns/actions.
    - C) "team" and "soccer" are concrete.
    - D) "apples" is a tangible, concrete noun.

4. Select the collective noun:
Correct Answer: B) family

- *Why it's correct:* "Family" represents a group acting as one unit.
- *Why others are wrong:*
    - A) "books" is plural, not collective.
    - C) "happiness" is an abstract noun.
    - D) "mountain" is a singular concrete noun.

5. Which of the following shows correct possessive noun usage?
Correct Answer: B) The cat's toy is broken.

- *Why it's correct:* The apostrophe before "s" correctly indicates possession.
- *Why others are wrong:*

- A) "cats" is plural without indicating possession.
- C) "cat toy's" misplaces the apostrophe.
- D) "cats'" is plural possessive but doesn't match the singular "cat."

Chapter 2: Pronouns

1. Choose the sentence with a correctly used reflexive pronoun:
Correct Answer: B) He gave himself a break.

- *Why it's correct:* "Himself" correctly reflects back to the subject "He."
- *Why others are wrong:*
  - A) "Myself" cannot be the subject.
  - C) "I" should be "me."
  - D) "theirselves" is not a correct word.

2. What is the antecedent of the pronoun in this sentence?
Correct Answer: C) girl

- *Why it's correct:* "Her" refers to "girl."
- *Why others are wrong:*
  - A) "her" is the pronoun, not the antecedent.
  - B) "book" is the object.
  - D) "lost" is a verb.

3. Which sentence uses a demonstrative pronoun correctly?
Correct Answer: C) That is my favorite movie.

- *Why it's correct:* "That" correctly demonstrates a singular object.
- *Why others are wrong:*
  - A) "This are" should be "These are."
  - B) "These is" should be "This is."
  - D) "Those book" should be "Those books."

4. Identify the indefinite pronoun:
Correct Answer: A) Everyone enjoyed the show.

- *Why it's correct:* "Everyone" is an indefinite pronoun referring to an unspecified group.
- *Why others are wrong:*
  - B, C, and D use specific nouns or pronouns.

5. Which sentence correctly shows pronoun-antecedent agreement?
Correct Answer: D) Every runner needs his or her water bottle.

- *Why it's correct:* "His or her" matches the singular "runner."
- *Why others are wrong:*
    - A) "their" is plural, not singular.
    - B) "his" doesn't account for gender inclusivity.
    - C) "their" is plural, not singular.

Chapter 3: Verbs

1. Choose the sentence written in the future progressive tense:
Correct Answer: C) She will be running in the marathon.

- *Why it's correct:* Future progressive tense uses "will be" + verb-ing.
- *Why others are wrong:*
    - A) Present progressive tense.
    - B) Past progressive tense.
    - D) Simple past tense.

2. Identify the irregular verb in the past tense:
Correct Answer: C) They ate dinner early.

- *Why it's correct:* "Ate" is the past tense of "eat."
- *Why others are wrong:*
    - A and D use regular verbs.
    - B) "brung" is incorrect; the past tense is "brought."

3. Which sentence uses an active verb?
Correct Answer: B) Sarah baked the cake.

- *Why it's correct:* The subject performs the action.
- *Why others are wrong:*
    - A, C, and D use passive voice.

4. Select the correct linking verb:
Correct Answer: B) She feels happy.

- *Why it's correct:* "Feels" links the subject to a description.
- *Why others are wrong:*
    - A, C, and D use action verbs.

5. Choose the sentence with correct subject-verb agreement:
Correct Answer: B) The team is winning.

- *Why it's correct:* "Team" is singular, so "is" agrees.
- *Why others are wrong:*
  - A) "were" is plural.
  - C and D) Subject-verb mismatch.

Chapter 4: Adjectives

1. Identify the sentence with a superlative adjective:
Correct Answer: C) She is the tallest in her class.

- *Why it's correct:* "Tallest" compares one subject to all others, making it superlative.
- *Why others are wrong:*
  - A) "Tall" is positive, not superlative.
  - B) "Taller" is comparative, not superlative.
  - D) "As tall as" shows equality, not comparison.

2. Which sentence correctly uses an article?
Correct Answer: D) Both B and C.

- *Why it's correct:*
  - B) "an apple" is correct because "apple" starts with a vowel sound.
  - C) "the water bottle" is correct for specific reference.
- *Why others are wrong:*
  - A) "a elephant" is incorrect; "an elephant" is correct.

3. Choose the descriptive adjective:
Correct Answer: B) The bright sun shone all day.

- *Why it's correct:* "Bright" describes the noun "sun."
- *Why others are wrong:*
  - A, C, and D use possessive, demonstrative, or quantity words, not descriptive adjectives.

4. Identify the demonstrative adjective:
Correct Answer: A) Those flowers are beautiful.

- *Why it's correct:* "Those" points to specific flowers, making it a demonstrative adjective.
- *Why others are wrong:*
  - B) "This" is a demonstrative pronoun, not an adjective here.
  - C and D lack demonstrative adjectives.

5. Select the sentence with a comparative adjective:
Correct Answer: B) This pizza is more delicious than that one.

- *Why it's correct:* "More delicious" compares two things.
- *Why others are wrong:*
  - A) "Delicious" is positive.
  - C) "Most delicious" is superlative.
  - D) "Good" doesn't compare.

Chapter 5: Adverbs

1. Which sentence contains an adverb of manner?
Correct Answer: A) She sings beautifully.

- *Why it's correct:* "Beautifully" describes how she sings.
- *Why others are wrong:*
  - B, C, and D refer to time or frequency, not manner.

2. Identify the conjunctive adverb:
Correct Answer: A) She will come; however, she will be late.

- *Why it's correct:* "However" connects two clauses and shows contrast.
- *Why others are wrong:*
  - B, C, and D use coordinating or subordinating conjunctions.

3. Choose the sentence with an adverb of frequency:
Correct Answer: A) He rarely eats breakfast.

- *Why it's correct:* "Rarely" describes how often he eats.
- *Why others are wrong:*
  - B) Describes manner.
  - C) Describes place.
  - D) Describes time.

4. Which sentence contains an adverb of degree?
Correct Answer: A) He is very excited.

- *Why it's correct:* "Very" modifies the adjective "excited" by showing intensity.
- *Why others are wrong:*
  - B, C, and D do not contain degree adverbs.

5. Select the sentence with an adverb of place:
Correct Answer: A) He ran here.

- *Why it's correct:* "Here" specifies the location.
- *Why others are wrong:*
    - B, C, and D describe time or manner.

Chapter 6: Prepositions

1. Identify the prepositional phrase:
Correct Answer: B) under the table

- *Why it's correct:* "Under the table" begins with a preposition and includes its object.
- *Why others are wrong:*
    - A, C, and D are incomplete or incorrect phrases.

2. Which sentence uses a preposition correctly?
Correct Answer: A) She ran to the park.

- *Why it's correct:* "To" correctly links the action to the place.
- *Why others are wrong:*
    - B, C, and D use incorrect prepositions or phrasing.

3. Select the sentence that shows how a prepositional phrase influences subject-verb agreement:
Correct Answer: A) The basket of apples is full.

- *Why it's correct:* "Basket" (singular) is the subject, so "is" matches.
- *Why others are wrong:*
    - B) Uses "are" with a singular subject.
    - C and D) Show incorrect pluralization or agreement.

4. Which word is the object of the preposition?
Correct Answer: D) park

- *Why it's correct:* "Park" is the object of the preposition "through."
- *Why others are wrong:*
    - A, B, and C are not the objects of the preposition.

5. Choose the sentence with the correct preposition usage:
Correct Answer: A) The cat is beside the chair.

- *Why it's correct:* "Beside" is correct and logical.
- *Why others are wrong:*
    - B, C, and D use incorrect or nonexistent prepositions.

Chapter 7: Conjunctions

1. Identify the coordinating conjunction:
Correct Answer: B) but

- *Why it's correct:* "But" joins two independent clauses.
- *Why others are wrong:*
    - A, C, and D are not conjunctions.

2. Which sentence uses a subordinating conjunction?
Correct Answer: B) She left because it was late.

- *Why it's correct:* "Because" introduces a dependent clause.
- *Why others are wrong:*
    - A, C, and D use coordinating or no conjunctions.

3. Choose the sentence with correlative conjunctions:
Correct Answer: A) Both the cat and the dog are sleeping.

- *Why it's correct:* "Both...and" are correlative conjunctions.
- *Why others are wrong:*
    - B, C, and D do not use correlative conjunctions.

4. Select the sentence that uses a conjunctive adverb:
Correct Answer: A) He arrived late; however, he finished on time.

- *Why it's correct:* "However" connects two independent clauses.
- *Why others are wrong:*
    - B, C, and D use other types of conjunctions.

5. Which sentence correctly uses a conjunction to combine ideas?
Correct Answer: A) I wanted to go, but it was raining.

- *Why it's correct:* "But" properly combines the two ideas.
- *Why others are wrong:*
    - B, C, and D use incorrect punctuation or structure.

Chapter 8: Interjections

1. Choose the sentence with a correctly used interjection:
Correct Answer: D) All of the above.

- *Why it's correct:* All sentences use interjections appropriately.

2. Identify the interjection:
Correct Answer: D) Oops

- *Why it's correct:* "Oops" expresses a reaction.
- *Why others are wrong:*
  - A, B, and C are not interjections.

3. Select the sentence with proper punctuation for the interjection:
Correct Answer: B) Well, I guess that's fine.

- *Why it's correct:* The interjection "Well" is correctly separated by a comma.
- *Why others are wrong:*
  - A, C, and D use incorrect punctuation.

4. Which sentence uses an interjection to express excitement?
Correct Answer: A) Hooray! We won the game.

- *Why it's correct:* "Hooray" expresses excitement.
- *Why others are wrong:*
  - B, C, and D use interjections for other emotions.

5. Choose the interjection that expresses disappointment:
Correct Answer: B) Oh no!

- *Why it's correct:* "Oh no!" conveys disappointment.
- *Why others are wrong:*
  - A, C, and D express other emotions.

Chapter 1:

Nouns

The Building Blocks of Language

Nouns are the foundation of every sentence we speak, read, or write. Without nouns, it would be impossible to name people, places, things, or ideas. They help us identify and organize the world around us, providing clarity and precision in our communication. Understanding nouns from every angle is essential for becoming a strong writer and an effective communicator. Nouns aren't just about naming; they are about **describing**, **specifying**, and even **bringing life** to our words.

Types of Nouns

1. **Common Nouns** – These are general names for people, places, or things. They are not capitalized unless they begin a sentence.
   Example: *dog, city, teacher, book*
2. **Proper Nouns** – These are specific names for particular people, places, or things. They are always capitalized.
   Example: *Charlie, Paris, Mount Everest, Friday*
3. **Concrete Nouns** – These nouns can be perceived by the five senses. You can see, hear, touch, smell, or taste them.
   Example: *apple, car, thunder, perfume*
4. **Abstract Nouns** – These nouns represent ideas, qualities, or emotions—things you cannot perceive with the senses.
   Example: *freedom, love, courage, honesty*
5. **Collective Nouns** – These refer to a group of people or things as a single unit.
   Example: *team, flock, audience, class*
6. **Countable Nouns** – These nouns can be counted and have singular and plural forms.
   Example: *chair, dog, book (chairs, dogs, books)*
7. **Uncountable Nouns** – These nouns cannot be counted individually and do not have a plural form.
   Example: *water, air, rice, information*
8. **Possessive Nouns** – These show ownership or possession.
   Example: *Sara's book, the dog's collar*

Why Understanding Nouns Matters

Nouns are more than just words—they shape the meaning and structure of every sentence. Knowing how to identify different types of nouns helps writers avoid mistakes and create sentences that are precise and clear. Misusing or failing to understand nouns can lead to vague or awkward sentences. For example, using **concrete nouns** can help add vivid detail, while understanding **possessive nouns** clarifies ownership.

In this chapter, we'll explore all aspects of nouns and practice identifying and using them effectively. You'll learn how to transform basic sentences into engaging and detailed ones by selecting the right nouns. Get ready to take a deep dive into the world of nouns—you'll soon see how mastering them will elevate your writing and communication skills!

Teacher Training Script: Introduction to Chapter 1 – Nouns

*"Welcome, everyone! Today we're diving into the world of **nouns**, the building blocks of every sentence. Think of a noun like a **cornerstone in a house**. You can't build a house without a solid foundation, and you can't build a sentence without nouns. They give structure to our thoughts and help us name the people, places, and things around us. Imagine trying to describe your favorite vacation without naming the beach, the sun, or the ocean—it would be impossible!"*

"But nouns aren't just labels—they can be vivid and specific, helping your reader picture exactly what you mean. Some nouns are concrete and touchable, like apple or mountain. Others are more abstract, representing feelings or ideas, like freedom or love. Our job is to master all kinds of nouns, so we can choose the right ones for every sentence. Ready to build your grammar foundation? Let's go!"

List of 10 Examples for Each Type of Noun

Common Nouns

1. teacher
2. dog
3. book
4. table
5. chair
6. river
7. garden
8. ball
9. car
10. sandwich

Proper Nouns

1. Charlie
2. London
3. Starbucks
4. Monday
5. Mount Everest
6. Paris
7. Harry Potter
8. Nike

9. Thanksgiving
10. Mars

Concrete Nouns

1. apple
2. pencil
3. guitar
4. perfume
5. mountain
6. thunder
7. cake
8. table
9. clock
10. river

Abstract Nouns

1. courage
2. friendship
3. honesty
4. freedom
5. love
6. joy
7. sadness
8. trust
9. fear
10. kindness

Collective Nouns

1. team
2. class
3. flock
4. audience
5. committee
6. crew
7. herd
8. choir
9. swarm
10. family

All About Singular and Plural Nouns

Nouns are words that name a person, place, thing, or idea. **Singular nouns** refer to **one** person, place, thing, or idea, while **plural nouns** refer to **more than one**. Understanding how to use and form singular and plural nouns is essential for clear communication in both speaking and writing.

Singular Nouns

A singular noun represents just **one** object or entity.
Examples:

- Dog
- Child
- Book
- City
- Idea

When to Use Singular Nouns:

- Describing one item: *I saw a dog.*
- Referring to one person or thing: *The child is playing.*
- Expressing individual concepts or ideas: *Love is powerful.*

Plural Nouns

Plural nouns refer to **two or more** people, places, things, or ideas.
General Rule: Add **-s** to form the plural of most nouns.
Examples:

- Dog → Dogs
- Book → Books
- Chair → Chairs

Special Rules for Plural Nouns

1. **Nouns Ending in -s, -sh, -ch, -x, or -z:**
   Add **-es** to make them plural.
   Examples:
   - Bus → Buses
   - Box → Boxes
   - Dish → Dishes
2. **Nouns Ending in -y:**
   - If the noun ends in a consonant + **-y**, change **-y** to **-ies**.
     Examples:
     - Baby → Babies
     - City → Cities
   - If the noun ends in a vowel + **-y**, just add **-s**.
     Examples:
     - Boy → Boys
     - Toy → Toys
3. **Nouns Ending in -f or -fe:**
   Change **-f** or **-fe** to **-ves** for certain nouns.
   Examples:
   - Leaf → Leaves
   - Knife → Knives
4. **Irregular Plural Nouns:**
   Some nouns don't follow standard rules for forming plurals.
   Examples:
   - Child → Children
   - Man → Men
   - Foot → Feet
   - Mouse → Mice
   - Tooth → Teeth
5. **Nouns That Stay the Same in Singular and Plural Forms:**
   Some nouns don't change at all when pluralized.
   Examples:
   - Sheep → Sheep
   - Deer → Deer
   - Series → Series
6. **Plural of Compound Nouns:**
   For compound nouns, pluralize the most important part.
   Examples:
   - Mother-in-law → Mothers-in-law
   - Passer-by → Passers-by

Case Scenarios for Singular and Plural Nouns

1. **Subject and Verb Agreement**
   Singular nouns require singular verbs, and plural nouns require plural verbs.
   Examples:
   - Singular: The cat **jumps** on the table.
   - Plural: The cats **jump** on the table.
2. **Possessive Nouns**
   Singular Possessive: Add **'s** to show possession.
   Example: The dog's leash (The leash belongs to one dog.)
   Plural Possessive: Add **s'** for most plural nouns.
   Example: The dogs' leashes (The leashes belong to multiple dogs.)
3. **Countable vs. Uncountable Nouns**
   Some nouns can be pluralized (countable), while others cannot (uncountable).
   Examples of Countable Nouns: Book → Books, Car → Cars
   Examples of Uncountable Nouns: Water, Rice, Information

Common Errors with Singular and Plural Nouns

- **Using the wrong plural form:** *Childs* instead of *Children.*
- **Incorrect verb agreement:** *The books is on the table* instead of *The books are on the table.*
- **Possessive confusion:** *The teachers classroom* instead of *The teacher's classroom.*

By mastering singular and plural noun forms, students improve their sentence construction, clarity, and grammatical accuracy.

Common Collective Nouns with their corresponding singular forms

Collective Noun	**Singular Form**
Army	Soldier
Audience	Spectator
Band	Musician
Bouquet	Flower
Class	Student
Committee	Member
Company	Employee
Council	Councilor
Crew	Sailor
Family	Relative
Fleet	Ship
Flock	Bird/Sheep
Group	Individual
Herd	Cow/Elephant
Jury	Juror
Litter	Puppy
Mob	Person
Orchestra	Musician
Pack	Dog/Wolf/Card
Panel	Expert/Participant
Parliament	Owl
School	Fish
Set	Object/Item
Staff	Employee
Swarm	Bee
Team	Player

Fun and interactive activities and games to help students learn and master the most common collective nouns. These activities incorporate movement, teamwork, and creativity to make learning memorable and engaging.

---

1. Collective Noun Charades

Objective: Reinforce understanding of collective nouns through acting and guessing.

- **Materials:** Cards with collective nouns written on them (e.g., *flock, team, herd*).
- **How to Play:**
    1. One student picks a card and silently acts out the noun (e.g., *flock of birds* by flapping arms).
    2. The class guesses the collective noun and corresponding singular noun.
    3. The first correct guesser gets to go next.

Variation: Use animal-themed charades (e.g., *pack of wolves*) or jobs (*staff of employees*).

---

2. Matching Game

Objective: Match collective nouns to their corresponding singular forms.

- **Materials:** Create matching cards—one set with collective nouns and another with their singular forms.
- **How to Play:**
    1. Spread the cards face down.
    2. Students take turns flipping two cards to find matching pairs (e.g., *litter* and *puppy*).
    3. The student who collects the most pairs wins.

Tip: Add visuals for younger students for easier recognition.

3. Collective Noun Bingo

Objective: Familiarize students with common collective nouns.

- **Materials:** Bingo cards with collective nouns in different boxes.
- **How to Play:**
    1. The teacher calls out the singular noun (e.g., *bee*), and students mark the corresponding collective noun (*swarm*) on their cards.
    2. The first to get five in a row (horizontally, vertically, or diagonally) calls "Bingo!"

---

4. Sentence Building Relay

Objective: Practice using collective nouns in sentences.

- **Materials:** Sentence strips with blanks for collective nouns (e.g., "A ______ of fish swam past us.") and a list of collective nouns.
- **How to Play:**
    1. Divide the class into teams.
    2. Teams race to fill in the blanks with the correct collective nouns.
    3. The team that completes the sentences correctly first wins.

---

5. Collective Noun Pictionary

Objective: Develop familiarity with collective nouns through drawing.

- **Materials:** Whiteboard or large sheets of paper, markers, and a list of collective nouns.
- **How to Play:**
    1. One student draws a picture representing a collective noun (e.g., *a herd of cows*).
    2. The rest of the class guesses the collective noun.

Variation: Use a timer to make it more competitive.

6. Scavenger Hunt

Objective: Spot and identify collective nouns in context.

- **How to Play:**
  1. Hide sentence cards with collective nouns around the classroom.
  2. Students work in pairs or teams to find the cards and write down the collective nouns.
  3. They earn points for each correct noun they identify and explain.

---

7. Story Time Challenge

Objective: Encourage creative writing using collective nouns.

- **How to Play:**
  1. Give students a list of collective nouns.
  2. Challenge them to write a short story using at least 5 collective nouns.
  3. Students share their stories with the class.

---

8. Human Collective Noun

Objective: Demonstrate the concept of collective nouns physically.

- **How to Play:**
  1. Assign each student a role (e.g., *one student is a bird, and the rest form a flock*).
  2. The teacher calls out a collective noun (*"Be a swarm of bees!"*), and students act it out.
  3. Discuss how each role fits into the group.

9. Collective Noun Quiz Show

Objective: Review and reinforce collective nouns in a quiz format.

- **Materials:** List of collective noun questions.
- **How to Play:**
    1. Divide students into teams.
    2. Ask questions like *"What is a group of musicians called?"*
    3. Teams earn points for correct answers.

---

10. Collective Noun Poster Project

Objective: Create visual representations of collective nouns.

- **How to Play:**
    1. Assign each student a collective noun (e.g., *bouquet* or *fleet*).
    2. Students create a poster illustrating their noun and write a sentence using it.
    3. Display the posters around the room for a "Collective Noun Gallery Walk."

Why These Activities Matter

- **Multi-Sensory Learning:** Combining movement, visuals, and interaction reinforces memory.
- **Collaboration:** Encourages teamwork and peer learning.
- **Creativity:** Helps students see language as fun and flexible.

"The Power of Nouns"

In every sentence, bold and true,
Nouns will always appear to you.
A person, place, thing, or thought,
Nouns name it all, they must be taught!

Proper nouns stand tall and bright,
Like *Paris* glowing in the night.
Concrete nouns, you touch and see,
Like *apple*, *river*, or *tall oak tree.*

***Abstract nouns**, they feel so grand—*
Love and courage take your hand.
***Collective nouns** bring groups to play,*
Like flock of birds at break of day.

Tackle nouns and you will find,
Your words will always shine in time!

Drama: "The Noun News Report"

Characters:

- **Narrator**
- **Common Noun Reporter**
- **Proper Noun Reporter**
- **Concrete Noun Analyst**
- **Abstract Noun Specialist**
- **Collective Noun Anchor**
- **Countable Noun Scientist**
- **Uncountable Noun Meteorologist**
- **Possessive Noun Detective**
- **Student 1**
- **Student 2**

Narrator: *Welcome to today's broadcast on Noun News Network! We have our team of experts here to help explain the many types of nouns you encounter every day. Let's start with our Common Noun Reporter.*

Common Noun Reporter: *Thank you, Narrator! Common nouns are everywhere. I report on words like teacher, dog, car, and book. These are the nouns you use in everyday speech to describe general things.*

Proper Noun Reporter: *And I cover proper nouns—those special, capitalized names like Charlie, London, and Mount Everest. Remember, every proper noun is unique!*

Concrete Noun Analyst: *I'm all about the five senses! I analyze nouns you can see, hear, touch, taste, or smell—like apple, river, and thunder. Concrete nouns make sentences more vivid.*

Abstract Noun Specialist: *I work with feelings and ideas—abstract nouns like love, courage, and freedom. You can't touch these, but they're just as real.*

Collective Noun Anchor: *Collective nouns bring groups together! Think of class, team, and family. They represent many things as one unit.*

Countable Noun Scientist: *My focus is on countable nouns—nouns you can count, like chair, dog, and book. You can make them plural, like chairs or dogs.*

Uncountable Noun Meteorologist: *Unlike my countable colleague, I forecast uncountable nouns like water, air, and rice. These nouns don't have plurals.*

Possessive Noun Detective: *And I solve mysteries of ownership! Possessive nouns show who owns what—like Sara's book or the dog's collar.*

Student 1: *Wow! I never knew there were so many kinds of nouns!*

Student 2: *Me neither! But now it all makes sense. Nouns help us name everything around us!*

Narrator: *And that's the Noun News Report! Remember—mastering nouns will make your writing stronger and your sentences clearer!*

10 Ways to Ask Questions About Nouns Without Using the Word "Nouns"

1. *What words do we use to name people, places, and things?*
2. *What do we call words that represent objects we can see or touch?*
3. *Which words in this sentence describe an idea or emotion?*
4. *How do we identify ownership in a sentence?*
5. *What are the names for groups of people or things?*
6. *What kind of words are capitalized when they refer to a specific person or place?*
7. *Which words tell us about something that can't be counted individually?*
8. *How do you turn a word into something plural that you can count?*
9. *What type of words can be used for something you experience with your senses?*
10. *What part of a sentence tells you who or what it's about?*

Lesson Plan 1: "Noun Scavenger Hunt Adventure" (Active Small-Group Activity)

Objective:
Students will identify and categorize different types of nouns by participating in a classroom scavenger hunt.

Materials:

- Noun Category Cards: Common Nouns, Proper Nouns, Concrete Nouns, Abstract Nouns, Collective Nouns
- Clipboards and pencils
- Sticky notes or small cards for labeling nouns in the room

Introduction (5 minutes)
Teacher script: "Today, we're going on a Noun Scavenger Hunt! Nouns are everywhere—people, places, things, and ideas. Your mission is to find as many nouns as possible around the room. You'll work with your team to search for different types of nouns and label them. Let's see how many you can discover!"

Activity (15–20 minutes)

1. Divide the class into small groups.
2. Each group receives a clipboard with a checklist of noun categories.
3. Students explore the classroom, identifying and labeling objects and items that represent different types of nouns.
    - **Example:** Label a globe (concrete noun), kindness from a classroom rule poster (abstract noun), or students (collective noun).
4. Each group must find at least one noun for each category.

Sample Categories:

- **Common Noun**: chair, desk
- **Proper Noun**: Monday, Ms. Johnson
- **Concrete Noun**: book, whiteboard
- **Abstract Noun**: bravery, happiness
- **Collective Noun**: class, team

Wrap-Up (5–10 minutes)
Teacher script: "Great job, hunters! Let's share what we found. Remember, nouns are all around us. Every time you write, think about how using different types of nouns can make your writing more interesting and clear!"

Assessment:

Each group presents their labeled nouns to the class, explaining why each noun fits its category. The teacher checks for correct categorization and encourages peer feedback.

Lesson Plan 2: "Noun Role Play Showdown" (Drama-Based Whole-Group Activity)

Objective:
Students will learn to differentiate between various types of nouns by acting out scenarios and identifying nouns in context.

Materials:

- Prewritten role-play cards with scenarios (e.g., a classroom, a grocery store, a park)
- Noun List (included below)
- Noun Type Signs: Common, Proper, Concrete, Abstract, Collective

---

Introduction (5 minutes)
Teacher script: "We're turning our classroom into a stage! Today, you'll act out scenes while your classmates guess and identify the nouns in your performance. Each scene will be full of nouns—people, places, things, and even ideas. Let's see who can spot the most!"

Activity (15–20 minutes)

1. Divide the class into small groups. Assign each group a role-play scenario.
2. Groups have 5 minutes to prepare a short performance. They must include at least one noun from each category in their scene.
   - **Example Scene:** A family picnic at the park. Nouns could include: family (collective), park (common), blanket (concrete), love (abstract), Saturday (proper).
3. After each performance, the audience identifies and categorizes the nouns.
   - **Teacher prompts:** *"What concrete noun did they use? Can you find an abstract noun in their scene?"*

Sample Scenarios:

- Grocery shopping
- A birthday party
- A day at the zoo
- Preparing for a school play
- Watching a football game

Wrap-Up (5 minutes)
Teacher script: "Fantastic performances! You just proved that nouns are everywhere—in the

people we meet, the places we visit, and even the emotions we feel. Keep practicing identifying different types of nouns in your reading and writing!"

Assessment:
Each group receives feedback based on their inclusion of various types of nouns. The teacher asks reflective questions: *"Which noun was hardest to find? Did any group surprise you with their creative use of an abstract or collective noun?"*

Observable/Actionable Assessment Tool: Noun Sorting Game

Objective:
Assess students' understanding of noun categories through an interactive sorting game.

Materials:

- 50 noun cards (pre-made with words from different categories)
- Large sorting mats labeled: Common, Proper, Concrete, Abstract, Collective

Instructions:

1. Set up five sorting stations around the classroom.
2. Students rotate through each station, picking noun cards and placing them in the correct category on the sorting mat.
3. After sorting, students discuss their choices with their peers at each station.

Teacher Assessment Checklist:

- Accuracy in sorting nouns
- Ability to explain and justify their choices
- Engagement and participation during the activity

Chapter 2:

Pronouns

The Essential Substitutes

Pronouns are powerful tools in language, allowing us to avoid repetition and improve sentence flow. Imagine a story without them: *"John went to John's house so John could feed John's cat."* It sounds awkward and repetitive! Pronouns make this sentence far more natural: *"John went to his house so he could feed his cat."* These tiny words act as substitutes for nouns, making writing clearer, smoother, and more engaging.

But pronouns come in many forms, each serving a specific purpose. Knowing how to use them effectively is essential for avoiding common mistakes and ensuring your writing is polished and precise. It's also crucial to maintain **antecedent agreement**, which means every pronoun must clearly refer to its noun (the antecedent) in both **number (singular/plural)** and **gender (male, female, neutral)**. **Antecedent discord** can cause confusion, leaving readers wondering who or what you're talking about.

Types of Pronouns

1. **Subjective Pronouns** – Act as the subject of the sentence.
   Examples: *I, you, he, she, it, we, they*
   Example Sentence: *She enjoys reading.*
2. **Objective Pronouns** – Function as the object of a verb or preposition.
   Examples: *me, you, him, her, it, us, them*
   Example Sentence: *Give the book to her.*
3. **Possessive Pronouns** – Show ownership or possession.
   Examples: *mine, yours, his, hers, ours, theirs*
   Example Sentence: *That bike is mine.*
4. **Reflexive Pronouns** – Refer back to the subject of the sentence.
   Examples: *myself, yourself, himself, herself, itself, ourselves, themselves*
   Example Sentence: *He taught himself to play the guitar.*
5. **Demonstrative Pronouns** – Point to specific things.
   Examples: *this, that, these, those*
   Example Sentence: *These are my favorite books.*

6. **Relative Pronouns** – Connect clauses or phrases to a noun or pronoun.
   Examples: *who, whom, whose, which, that*
   Example Sentence: *The girl who won the race is my friend.*
7. **Interrogative Pronouns** – Used to ask questions.
   Examples: *who, whom, whose, which, what*
   Example Sentence: *Who is at the door?*
8. **Indefinite Pronouns** – Refer to nonspecific people or things.
   Examples: *anyone, everybody, something, none, many*
   Example Sentence: *Everyone is invited to the party.*

The Importance of Antecedent Agreement

For pronouns to work properly, they must match their antecedent in both number and gender. **Antecedent agreement** ensures your writing is clear and logical. When there is **antecedent discord**, your reader may get confused.

Example of Correct Agreement:

- **Correct:** *The student forgot his backpack.* (The singular pronoun *his* refers to *student.*)
- **Incorrect:** *The student forgot their backpack.* (The plural pronoun *their* does not agree with the singular noun *student.*)

Sometimes, antecedent discord leads to **ambiguity** when it's unclear what the pronoun refers to:
Example:
When Sarah called Jenna, she didn't answer. (Who didn't answer—Sarah or Jenna?)

How to Prevent Antecedent Discord

1. **Be Clear:** Keep pronouns close to their antecedents.
2. **Use Specific Nouns:** Repeat the noun for clarity if there's any risk of confusion.
   Example: *John told Peter that John would be late.*
3. **Match Number and Gender:** Always ensure the pronoun agrees with the antecedent.

Why Pronouns Matter

Mastering pronouns isn't just about avoiding errors—it's about improving the clarity and flow of your writing. Without pronouns, sentences would become repetitive and clunky. With them, your writing becomes natural and easy to follow. In this chapter, we'll explore each type of pronoun, tackle the challenges of antecedent agreement, and learn how to make our writing clearer, smoother, and more professional.

Teacher Training Script: Introduction to Chapter 2 - Pronouns

"Today, we're talking about pronouns—the tiny but powerful words that help us clean up our sentences and avoid repetition. Imagine telling a story without pronouns: 'John went to John's house so John could feed John's cat.' It feels clunky and awkward! Pronouns step in like superheroes to save us from repetition and confusion. Now, the sentence reads: 'John went to his house so he could feed his cat.' It's smoother, clearer, and easier to understand!"

"But not all pronouns are created equal. There are different types for different jobs—some stand in for subjects, others show possession, and some even ask questions. One important rule is to always match your pronoun with its noun, called an ***antecedent****. This keeps your writing clear and logical. If there's a mismatch, it's like giving the wrong key to the wrong lock—things stop working! Let's explore the world of pronouns together and learn how to make them our secret weapon for great writing."*

List of 10 Examples for Each Type of Pronoun

Subjective Pronouns

1. I
2. you
3. he
4. she
5. it
6. we
7. they
8. you (plural)
9. who
10. whoever

Objective Pronouns

1. me
2. you
3. him
4. her
5. it
6. us
7. them
8. whom
9. whomever
10. you (plural)

Possessive Pronouns

1. mine
2. yours
3. his
4. hers
5. its
6. ours
7. theirs
8. whose
9. yours (plural)
10. one's

Reflexive Pronouns

1. myself
2. yourself
3. himself
4. herself
5. itself
6. ourselves
7. yourselves
8. themselves
9. oneself
10. itself

Demonstrative Pronouns

1. this
2. that
3. these
4. those
5. such
6. here
7. there
8. yonder
9. now
10. then

Relative Pronouns

1. who
2. whom
3. whose
4. which
5. that
6. whoever
7. whomever
8. whichever
9. what
10. whatsoever

Interrogative Pronouns

1. who
2. whom
3. whose
4. which
5. what
6. whoever
7. whomever
8. whichever
9. why
10. how

Indefinite Pronouns

1. anyone
2. everyone
3. someone
4. nobody
5. nothing
6. everything
7. something
8. many
9. few
10. all

Demonstrative Pronouns: This, That, These, Those

Demonstrative pronouns are words that point to specific nouns in a sentence. They help clarify which person, place, thing, or idea is being referred to. The four main demonstrative pronouns in English are **this, that, these,** and **those**. They are categorized based on **distance** (near or far) and **number** (singular or plural).

Demonstrative Pronoun Breakdown:

Pronoun	Singular/Plural	Distance	Example Sentence
This	Singular	Near (close to the speaker)	*This is my favorite book.*
That	Singular	Far (away from the speaker)	*That is the house I grew up in.*
These	Plural	Near (close to the speaker)	*These are the keys to the car.*
Those	Plural	Far (away from the speaker)	*Those are the mountains we climbed.*

Detailed Explanation and Examples:

1. **This (Singular, Near)**
    - Refers to one thing or person that is **close** to the speaker in time or space.
    - **Example:** *This apple is delicious.* (The apple is near the speaker.)
    - **Time Example:** *This morning was very productive.* (Refers to the current morning.)
2. **That (Singular, Far)**
    - Refers to one thing or person that is **far away** from the speaker in time or space.
    - **Example:** *That building is very tall.* (The building is at a distance.)
    - **Time Example:** *That summer was unforgettable.* (Refers to a past summer.)
3. **These (Plural, Near)**
    - Refers to multiple things or people that are **close** to the speaker.
    - **Example:** *These shoes are new.* (The shoes are near the speaker.)
4. **Those (Plural, Far)**
    - Refers to multiple things or people that are **far away** from the speaker.
    - **Example:** *Those stars are so bright.* (The stars are distant.)

Common Mistakes with Demonstrative Pronouns:

1. **Confusing this/that and these/those with their corresponding adjectives.**
   Demonstrative pronouns replace a noun, while demonstrative adjectives modify a noun.
    - **Demonstrative Pronoun:** *That is mine.*
    - **Demonstrative Adjective:** *That book is mine.*
2. **Using the incorrect pronoun for number or distance.**
    - Incorrect: *This books are on the table.*
    - Correct: *These books are on the table.*

Why Are Demonstrative Pronouns Important?

Demonstrative pronouns make communication clearer and more concise. Instead of repeating a noun, you can use a demonstrative pronoun to point it out, making your writing and speech more fluent and natural. Understanding these pronouns helps avoid ambiguity and makes descriptions more precise.

Relative Pronouns: A Detailed Guide

Relative pronouns are words that **introduce relative clauses**. They connect a dependent clause to a noun or pronoun in the main clause, providing **extra information** about that noun. Relative pronouns help make writing more descriptive and cohesive.

The **main relative pronouns** are:
who, whom, whose, which, that
Other less common ones include: **where, when, why** (used in specific contexts to refer to places, times, or reasons).

Types of Relative Pronouns and Their Uses

1. **Who** – Refers to people (subject of the clause)
   - **Example:** The student **who** won the competition is in my class.
   - Explanation: "Who" introduces a clause that describes "student." It acts as the subject of the relative clause.
2. **Whom** – Refers to people (object of the clause)
   - **Example:** The teacher **whom** you met yesterday is my mentor.
   - Explanation: "Whom" is the object of the verb "met." It's more formal and often replaced by "who" in spoken English.
3. **Whose** – Shows possession (for people, animals, or things)
   - **Example:** The dog **whose** collar is red loves to play fetch.
   - Explanation: "Whose" indicates that the dog owns the collar.
4. **Which** – Refers to animals or things
   - **Example:** The book **which** I borrowed is fascinating.
   - Explanation: "Which" introduces a clause that gives more information about "book."
5. **That** – Refers to people, animals, or things (often used in defining clauses)
   - **Example:** The house **that** we bought needs renovation.
   - Explanation: "That" introduces essential information about "house."
6. **Where** – Refers to places
   - **Example:** The town **where** I grew up is beautiful.
   - Explanation: "Where" introduces a clause that describes "town."
7. **When** – Refers to times
   - **Example:** Summer is the season **when** we go to the beach.
   - Explanation: "When" introduces a clause that describes "summer."
8. **Why** – Refers to reasons
   - **Example:** The reason **why** he left early is unclear.
   - Explanation: "Why" explains the reason for leaving.

Common Difficulties and Confusion Among Students

1. **Confusion Between "Who" and "Whom"**
    - **Challenge:** "Who" and "whom" are often mixed up because "whom" sounds old-fashioned.
    - **Solution:** Teach students to replace the pronoun with "he" (subject) or "him" (object). If "him" fits, use "whom"; if "he" fits, use "who."
      Example: You met **whom**? ("You met him.") Correct use of "whom."
2. **Overuse of "That"**
    - **Challenge:** Students use "that" for everything, even when "which" or "who" is more appropriate.
    - **Solution:** Encourage students to use "that" only for essential information (restrictive clauses) and "which" for non-essential information (non-restrictive clauses).
      Example:
    - Restrictive: The car **that** I bought is red.
    - Non-restrictive: The car, **which** I bought last year, is red.
3. **Misplaced Relative Clauses**
    - **Challenge:** Students often place relative clauses too far from the noun they modify, creating ambiguity.
      Example: Incorrect: The boy kicked the ball **who** was wearing a blue shirt.
    - **Solution:** The relative clause should be next to the noun it modifies: **The boy who was wearing a blue shirt kicked the ball.**
4. **"Whose" for Things**
    - **Challenge:** Students hesitate to use "whose" for objects, thinking it only applies to people.
    - **Solution:** Clarify that "whose" is acceptable for showing possession for objects as well.
      Example: The house **whose** roof is leaking needs repairs.

Helpful Tips for Teaching Relative Pronouns

1. **Relative Pronoun Sorting Game** – Have students match sentences with the correct relative pronoun.
2. **Color-Coding Sentences** – Highlight the antecedent in one color and the relative clause in another to show the connection.
3. **Create Silly Sentences** – Encourage students to write silly sentences using each relative pronoun, making the learning process fun and memorable.
4. **Peer Review** – Have students identify and correct relative pronoun errors in their peers' writing.

The Importance of Proximity in Pronoun-Noun Relationships

When using pronouns, **clarity is essential**. The closer a pronoun is to the noun it refers to (its **antecedent**), the easier it is for readers to follow the sentence's meaning. When a pronoun and its antecedent are **far apart**, readers may become confused, especially if there are multiple nouns in the sentence or paragraph. This confusion can lead to **misunderstanding or ambiguity**, forcing the reader to stop and reread.

Example of Clear Pronoun Usage (Close Proximity)

Sarah grabbed her notebook and sat down to study. She opened it and began reviewing her notes.

- In this example, the antecedent **Sarah** is close to the pronoun **she**, making it clear who "she" refers to.

Example of Ambiguous Pronoun Usage (Distant Antecedent)

Sarah grabbed her notebook, put it on the table, and helped her brother organize the books on the shelf. **She** then decided to go for a walk.

- In this example, the reader might wonder if **she** refers to **Sarah** or **her brother**, creating ambiguity.

Techniques to Help Students Identify Pronoun Referents

1. **Proximity Check**
   - Encourage students to check how close the pronoun is to the antecedent. If several nouns appear between the antecedent and the pronoun, students should consider revising for clarity.
     Example:
     Instead of: *After the teacher handed out the test, several students asked her questions about it.*
     Revise to: *Several students asked the teacher questions about the test after she handed it out.*
2. **Underline and Circle Method**
   - **Underline** the noun and **circle** the pronoun it refers to. This visual technique helps students trace the connection and confirm whether it's logical and clear.

3. **Eliminate Ambiguity by Replacing the Pronoun**
    - If the sentence is ambiguous, replace the pronoun with the noun for clarity.
      Example:
      Instead of: *She said it was her favorite class.*
      Revise to: *Emily said that science was her favorite class.*
4. **Color-Coding Pronouns and Antecedents**
    - Use different colors for each pronoun and its corresponding antecedent. This technique works well in longer passages and helps students spot mismatches or unclear references.
5. **Question the Sentence**
    - Ask guiding questions to help students determine the antecedent:
        - **Who is performing the action?**
        - **What object or idea is being discussed?**

Practice Activities for Clarity

1. **Pronoun Hunt**
    - Provide students with a paragraph and ask them to underline all the pronouns. Then, have them draw arrows to the nouns they refer to. Discuss any unclear pronoun references and revise the paragraph together.
2. **Rewrite for Clarity**
    - Give students sentences with unclear pronoun references and ask them to rewrite the sentences for improved clarity.
3. **Pronoun Matching Game**
    - Create sentence strips with nouns and pronouns. Have students physically match each pronoun to the correct antecedent, reinforcing the importance of proximity.

Conclusion

Teaching students to keep pronouns close to their antecedents ensures clearer communication. When proximity is maintained, writing becomes more polished and understandable. Using targeted strategies such as proximity checks, underlining, and rewriting helps students develop strong revision habits and improve their sentence structure.

Examples of Pronoun Proximity

Example 1:

Original (Distant Pronoun):
Sophia baked a cake for her friends, set the table, turned on the music, and cleaned the kitchen. Then, she served it.

- *Who does "it" refer to? The cake or the table?*

Revised (Close Proximity):
Sophia baked a cake for her friends. Then, she served the cake after setting the table, turning on the music, and cleaning the kitchen.

Example 2:

Original (Distant Pronoun):
The children visited the museum, walked through the park, and stopped at the library for storytime. They loved it.

- *What does "it" refer to—museum, park, or library?*

Revised (Close Proximity):
The children visited the museum. They loved the museum, then walked through the park and stopped at the library for storytime.

Example 3:

Original (Distant Pronoun):
Michael gave his dog a bath, cleaned the dog's kennel, and prepared dinner. It made him tired.

- *What made him tired—the bath, cleaning, or cooking?*

Revised (Close Proximity):
Michael gave his dog a bath, which made him tired. Afterward, he cleaned the dog's kennel and prepared dinner.

Example 4:

Original (Distant Pronoun):
Lily opened her backpack, took out her notebook, grabbed a snack from the counter, and placed it on the table. She forgot it there.

- *What did Lily forget—the notebook, the snack, or the backpack?*

Revised (Close Proximity):
Lily grabbed a snack from the counter and placed it on the table. She forgot the snack there.

Example 5:

Original (Distant Pronoun):
The coach called a timeout, gave instructions to the team, and adjusted the scoreboard. Then, he turned it off.

- *What does "it" refer to—timeout, instructions, or scoreboard?*

Revised (Close Proximity):
The coach adjusted the scoreboard and then turned it off after calling a timeout and giving instructions to the team.

Why Proximity Matters:

These examples show how keeping pronouns close to their antecedents reduces confusion. By bringing the pronoun nearer to its related noun, the sentence becomes clearer and easier to understand, improving overall communication.

Practicing Pronoun Proximity

Confusing Pronoun-Noun Passage:

Sarah and Emma went to the park with their dogs and younger brothers. They played fetch while they chased each other around the pond. When Sarah took her dog to get water, Emma called her brother to join them. He didn't want to leave his spot on the bench, but they insisted. Later, the dogs ran after him near the trees while Emma laughed at them. Sarah grabbed her dog and told her to stop, but it didn't listen. Eventually, they all walked back to the car, tired but happy, although Emma forgot her bag on the bench.

Pronoun-Noun Clarification Chart:

Pronoun	Noun it Refers To
They	Sarah and Emma (first instance)
They	The dogs (second instance)
Her	Sarah (her dog)
Them	Sarah and Emma (joining them)
He	Emma's brother
They	Sarah and Emma (insisting he leave the bench)
Him	Emma's brother
Them	The dogs (chasing him)
Her	Sarah (grabbing her dog)
It	Sarah's dog
They	Sarah, Emma, and their dogs and brothers
Her	Emma (her bag)

Explanation:

In the passage, the pronouns are deliberately scattered and vague, making it difficult to determine which noun they reference. The chart provides clarity, helping readers track how each pronoun relates back to its antecedent. This exercise demonstrates the importance of maintaining proximity and clarity with pronoun use

"The Power of Pronouns"

Pronouns are tiny but mighty strong,
They shorten sentences, moving along.
Instead of repeating nouns you have said,
Use a pronouns he, she, or it instead!

***Subjective** ones act like stars of the show—*
I, you, we, they, leading sentences to flow.
Objective ones follow verbs with delight:
Give it to me or *take her to the right.*

***Possessive** pronouns—oh, what a treat!*
Mine, yours, and theirs keep things neat.
***Reflexive** ones bounce right back to the start:*
He taught himself how to master the art.

With **demonstrative** pronouns, you point and say,
This is mine! or *That's yours today!*
***Indefinite** pronouns don't name one or two,*
But everyone knows somebody like you!

Pronouns are helpers: clarify and guide,
Keeping your writing neat and supplied.

Drama: "Pronoun Superheroes"

Characters:

- **Narrator**
- **Subjective Pronoun Hero**
- **Objective Pronoun Hero**
- **Possessive Pronoun Hero**
- **Reflexive Pronoun Hero**
- **Demonstrative Pronoun Hero**
- **Relative Pronoun Hero**
- **Interrogative Pronoun Hero**
- **Indefinite Pronoun Hero**
- **Student 1**
- **Student 2**

Narrator: *Welcome to Grammar City, where our heroes—the Pronoun Superheroes—are here to save sentences from clunky repetition and confusion! First up, let's meet Subjective Pronoun Hero!*

Subjective Pronoun Hero: *I'm the subject of the sentence, always ready to lead. Use me when you need a word like I, you, he, she, it, we, or they. Without me, sentences would be lost!*

Objective Pronoun Hero: *I follow the action, receiving what happens! Words like me, him, her, and us are my specialty. Remember, if there's action, I'm there!*

Possessive Pronoun Hero: *Ownership is my game! Mine, yours, his, and hers help show who owns what. No need to repeat the noun—just call on me!*

Reflexive Pronoun Hero: *I bounce back to the subject! If you see myself, herself, or themselves, it's my time to shine. I always reflect back to the star of the sentence!*

Demonstrative Pronoun Hero: *Point it out with this, that, these, and those. I'm like the pointer finger of grammar, showing you what's what!*

Relative Pronoun Hero: *I connect ideas, holding sentences together with who, whom, whose, which, and that. You can count on me for smooth transitions!*

Interrogative Pronoun Hero: *I'm the question master! Words like who, what, and which bring curiosity and answers to the table.*

Indefinite Pronoun Hero: *I'm a little mysterious, but helpful all the same. Words like everyone, something, or many are my go-to tools!*

Student 1: *Wow! I never knew pronouns had so many different types and jobs!*

Student 2: *Me neither! But now it's clear how they make sentences easier and less repetitive.*

Narrator: *And that's how our Pronoun Superheroes save Grammar City every day! Remember—choose the right pronoun, and your sentences will always flow beautifully!*

10 Ways to Ask Questions About Pronouns Without Using the Word "Pronoun"

1. *What words can replace names in a sentence?*
2. *How do we avoid repeating the same noun in a sentence?*
3. *What words show possession without repeating the noun?*
4. *Which words refer back to the subject of the sentence?*
5. *What kind of words point to specific things like this or that?*
6. *How do you connect clauses with a word like who or which?*
7. *What words can you use to ask a question about a person or thing?*
8. *Which words refer to an unknown or nonspecific amount of something?*
9. *How do you show ownership in a sentence without using the noun again?*
10. *What kind of word replaces a noun in front of a verb?*

Lesson Plan 1: "Pronoun Switch-Up" (Interactive Whole-Group Activity)

Objective:
Students will identify and use different types of pronouns (subjective, objective, possessive, reflexive, demonstrative, and indefinite) by actively replacing nouns in sentences with appropriate pronouns.

Materials:

- Prewritten sentences on chart paper or a digital board
- Index cards with nouns written on them
- Pronoun posters for reference

Introduction (5 minutes)
Teacher script: "Today, we're learning about pronouns—the words that step in to take the place of nouns. Pronouns are like stand-ins for the main actors in a play. Imagine saying, 'My dog loves my dog's toy, and my dog takes my dog's toy everywhere.' That's repetitive! Instead, you can say, 'My dog loves ***his*** *toy, and* ***he*** *takes it everywhere.' Let's practice switching nouns for pronouns and see how much smoother our sentences can be!"*

Activity (15–20 minutes)

1. **Modeling:**
   Read a sentence from the board: *"Lisa saw Lisa's reflection in the mirror."*
   Ask: *"How can we make this sentence less repetitive?"*
   Students suggest replacing **Lisa** with **she** and **Lisa's** with **her** to create *"Lisa saw her reflection in the mirror."*
2. **Group Activity:**
   - Distribute noun cards to students.
   - Each student takes a turn reading a sentence aloud and replacing the underlined noun with an appropriate pronoun.
   - Other students give thumbs up if they agree with the replacement or suggest corrections if needed.

Example Sentences for Practice:

- *Jack and Jill went up the hill to fetch Jack and Jill's pail of water.*
- *The teacher gave the students the teacher's advice.*
- *Sarah washed Sarah's car before Sarah went to the party.*

Wrap-Up (5 minutes)
Teacher script: "Great job! Remember, pronouns make our sentences smoother and easier to

understand. Always make sure your pronoun matches the noun it's replacing in number and gender. Keep an eye out for pronouns when you read!"

Assessment:

Students form pairs and write one sentence with a repeated noun, then rewrite it using pronouns. They read both versions aloud to the class. The teacher listens for correct pronoun usage.

Lesson Plan 2: "Pronoun Relay Race" (Kinesthetic Small-Group Activity)

Objective:
Students will categorize and identify different types of pronouns by participating in a fast-paced relay race.

Materials:

- Cards labeled with various pronouns (subjective, objective, possessive, reflexive, demonstrative, indefinite)
- Hula hoops or boxes labeled with pronoun categories (Subjective, Objective, Possessive, Reflexive, Demonstrative, Indefinite)
- Stopwatch or timer

Introduction (5 minutes)
Teacher script: "Today, we're getting active with pronouns! Pronouns have different jobs—some stand in as the subject of a sentence, like I, he, or they. Others show possession, like mine, yours, or their. Your goal is to correctly sort these pronouns into the right categories as fast as you can!"

Activity (15–20 minutes)

1. **Set Up:**
   Place hula hoops or boxes in different corners of the room, each labeled with a pronoun category.
2. **Instructions:**
   - Divide the class into small groups.
   - Each group lines up at a starting point.
   - One student at a time picks a pronoun card, runs to the correct category, and places the card in the hoop or box.
   - The next student in line repeats the process.
   - Continue until all pronoun cards are sorted.
3. **Debrief:**
   Go through the cards in each category as a class. Discuss any incorrect placements and why the pronoun belongs in a different category.

Pronoun Card Examples:

- **Subjective:** I, he, she, they, we
- **Objective:** me, him, her, us, them
- **Possessive:** mine, yours, his, hers, ours, theirs
- **Reflexive:** myself, yourself, himself, herself, themselves

- **Demonstrative:** this, that, these, those
- **Indefinite:** someone, anyone, nobody, everything, many

Wrap-Up (5 minutes)
Teacher script: "Fantastic work, everyone! Pronouns help our sentences stay smooth and clear. Keep practicing, and you'll be a pronoun expert in no time!"

Assessment:
Students stand by their assigned pronoun category and explain what kind of pronouns they placed there. The teacher checks for accuracy and understanding through group discussion.

Actionable/Observable Assessment Tool: Pronoun Sorting Showdown

Objective:
Assess students' ability to categorize and explain different types of pronouns in a hands-on competition.

Instructions:

1. **Set Up Stations:** Create five sorting stations with categories: Subjective, Objective, Possessive, Reflexive, Demonstrative, and Indefinite pronouns.
2. **Activity:**
   - Students rotate in pairs to each station.
   - At each station, they draw pronoun cards and place them in the correct category.
   - After sorting, each pair explains their reasoning to a teacher or peer.
3. **Scoring:** Points are awarded for accuracy and explanations.

Chapter 3:

Verbs

The Heartbeat of Every Sentence

Verbs are the driving force behind every sentence. They give sentences life by showing **action**, expressing **state of being**, or helping us understand **when** something happened. Without verbs, communication would be incomplete and lifeless. Imagine trying to describe your day without using a single verb—it would be impossible!

Understanding all the different types of verbs, their tenses, and how they work together is crucial for mastering sentence construction. Verbs connect every part of a sentence, helping us describe actions clearly and accurately. But not all verbs function the same way. Some show **action**, while others simply link ideas or help other verbs convey a specific meaning. Let's explore all the essential aspects of verbs.

Types of Verbs

1. **Action Verbs** – These verbs express physical or mental actions. They tell us what someone or something is doing.
   Examples: *run, think, dance, believe, jump*
   Example Sentence: *She runs every morning.*
2. **Linking Verbs** – These verbs don't show action; instead, they connect the subject to additional information about it. The most common linking verb is **to be** (am, is, are, was, were).
   Examples: *seem, become, feel, appear*
   Example Sentence: *He seems tired.*
3. **Helping Verbs** – These verbs work with action or linking verbs to create verb phrases and show tense, mood, or voice.
   Examples: *is, have, will, can, should, may*
   Example Sentence: *She is running in the race.*
4. **Active Verbs vs. Passive Verbs**
   - **Active Voice:** The subject performs the action.
     Example: *The cat chased the mouse.*

- **Passive Voice:** The subject receives the action.
  Example: *The mouse was chased by the cat.*

5. **Irregular Verbs** – These verbs don't follow the standard rule of adding "-ed" to form the past tense.
   Examples: *go → went, eat → ate, sing → sang*
   Example Sentence: *I went to the store yesterday.*

Verb Tenses

Verb tense tells us **when** an action takes place. Using the right tense ensures clarity and consistency in writing.

1. **Past Tense:** Describes actions that have already happened.
   Example: *She walked to the park.*
2. **Present Tense:** Describes actions happening now.
   Example: *She walks to the park.*
3. **Future Tense:** Describes actions that will happen.
   Example: *She will walk to the park.*

Perfect Tenses

Perfect tenses show completed actions at different times.

- **Present Perfect:** *She has walked to the park.*
- **Past Perfect:** *She had walked to the park.*
- **Future Perfect:** *She will have walked to the park.*

Progressive Tenses

Progressive tenses show ongoing or continuous actions.

- **Present Progressive:** *She is walking.*
- **Past Progressive:** *She was walking.*
- **Future Progressive:** *She will be walking.*

Verb Phrases

A **verb phrase** consists of one main verb and one or more helping verbs. Verb phrases help clarify tense, mood, or voice.
Example: *She has been studying for hours.*

Subject-Verb Agreement

For a sentence to be correct, the **subject** and **verb** must agree in number (singular or plural). This rule ensures that sentences make sense and flow properly.

- **Correct:** *The dog runs fast.* (singular subject and verb)
- **Incorrect:** *The dog run fast.* (singular subject with plural verb)
- **Correct:** *The dogs run fast.* (plural subject and verb)

Why is subject-verb agreement important? If the subject and verb don't match, the sentence becomes awkward and confusing for the reader.

Why Verbs Matter

Mastering verbs is crucial for building strong sentences. Verbs control the **action**, **time**, and **tone** of your writing. Understanding verb types, tenses, and subject-verb agreement will help you write with accuracy and confidence. In this chapter, we'll dive deep into the world of verbs and practice using them in every form—so get ready to bring your writing to life!

Teacher Training Script: Introduction to Chapter 3 – Verbs

"Today, we're exploring ***verbs****—the heartbeat of every sentence. Imagine your sentence as a body. The noun is like the bones—it gives structure and form. But without verbs, there would be no movement, no life. Verbs are the heart, pumping action, time, and energy into every sentence."*

"Some verbs show action—run, jump, think. Others are like bridges that connect the subject to a description—am, is, seems. And some work behind the scenes, helping other verbs clarify tense and meaning—will, have, can. Verbs also tell us ***when*** *something happens, whether it's in the past, present, or future. Mastering verbs will help you build sentences that are clear, powerful, and alive!"*

List of 10 Examples for Each Type of Verb

Action Verbs

1. run
2. jump
3. think
4. dance
5. sing
6. believe
7. write
8. play
9. eat
10. dream

Linking Verbs:

1. am
2. is
3. are
4. was
5. were
6. be
7. being
8. been
9. become
10. seem

Helping Verbs

1. is
2. has
3. have
4. will
5. can
6. should
7. could
8. may
9. must
10. shall

Active Verbs, Present Tense

1. build
2. paint
3. fix
4. drive
5. read
6. catch
7. fly
8. throw
9. plant
10. bake

Irregular Verbs (Past Forms)

1. go → went
2. eat → ate
3. sing → sang
4. drink → drank
5. write → wrote
6. bring → brought
7. buy → bought
8. catch → caught
9. teach → taught
10. run → ran

Verb Tense Chart: Simple, Progressive, and Perfect Tenses

Tense	Definition	Example Sentence	Helping/Linking Verbs	Notes
Simple Past	Describes a completed action in the past	I walked to school yesterday.	None	Often ends in **-ed** for regular verbs
Simple Present	Describes a current action or fact	I walk to school every day.	None	Add **-s** for third-person singular
Simple Future	Describes an action that will happen	I will walk to school tomorrow.	**will**	Always uses **will** or **shall**
Progressive Past	Ongoing action in the past	I was walking to school.	**was, were**	Uses **-ing** form of the verb
Progressive Present	Ongoing action happening now	I am walking to school.	**am, is, are**	Emphasizes ongoing nature
Progressive Future	Ongoing action in the future	I will be walking to school.	**will be**	Combines **will** with **be + -ing**
Perfect Past	Action completed before another past action	I had walked to school before the rain started.	**had**	Commonly used for sequences of past events
Perfect Present	Action completed at an unspecified time before now	I have walked to school many times.	**have, has**	Emphasizes experience or result
Perfect Future	Action that will be completed before a specific time in the future	I will have walked to school by noon.	**will have**	Combines **will have** with past participle

Summary of Helping/Linking Verbs by Tense

- **Past:** was, were, had
- **Present:** am, is, are, have, has
- **Future:** will, shall, will be, will have

The History of Irregular Verbs

Irregular verbs are a fascinating aspect of the English language with roots that stretch back to Old English and its Germanic origins. Unlike regular verbs, which form their past tense by adding "-ed," irregular verbs follow older patterns of conjugation that were common in early Germanic languages. Over time, while many verbs shifted to the regular "-ed" ending, some retained their original forms—these are what we call **irregular verbs**.

In Old English, verbs were classified into **strong** and **weak** verbs:

- **Strong verbs** changed their vowels to indicate tense (e.g., sing → sang → sung).
- **Weak verbs** used a suffix, similar to today's regular verbs (e.g., walk → walked).

As the English language evolved, many strong verbs became weak, but some commonly used verbs (like **go, come, eat, see, bring, take,** and **run**) kept their irregular forms. These verbs have remained irregular due to their frequent use in everyday speech, preserving the older linguistic patterns.

Please reference the ***Phonics Forever*** book by Randi Whitney for rationale regarding pronunciation that do not follow regular patterns such as VCC patterns.

Helpful Hints for Learning Irregular Verbs

1. **Group Similar Verbs Together**
   Irregular verbs can be easier to learn when grouped by similar patterns. For example:
   - Verbs that change their vowel sounds in a similar way:
     sing → sang → sung
     drink → drank → drunk
2. **Use Mnemonic Devices**
   Create short stories or phrases to remember verb patterns. For example:
   "I drink juice every morning, drank juice yesterday, and have drunk it many times."
3. **Practice with Visuals and Charts**
   Use a visual table or chart to compare the present, past, and past participle forms of irregular verbs. This gives students a clear reference to reinforce memory.

Three Engaging Activities to Practice Irregular Verbs

1. **Irregular Verb Bingo**
   - **Objective:** Reinforce recognition of present, past, and past participle forms.
   - **Materials:** Bingo cards with different verb forms (e.g., *sing, sang, sung*).
   - **Instructions:** Call out a verb (e.g., *past tense of drink*), and students mark the correct verb on their card. The first to get five in a row wins!
2. **Verb Charades**
   - **Objective:** Help students internalize irregular verbs through movement and acting.
   - **Instructions:** Write various irregular verbs on slips of paper (e.g., *run, swim, fly*). Students act out the verb in its past form (e.g., *ran*) without speaking, while classmates guess the verb and its correct past tense.
3. **Irregular Verb Storytelling**
   - **Objective:** Encourage students to use irregular verbs in context.
   - **Instructions:** Provide a list of irregular verbs and ask students to write a short story, incorporating at least 10 verbs in their past tense forms. Students share their stories with the class, and peers highlight the verbs they hear.

---

50 most common irregular verbs, organized alphabetically into five columns with ten words each. You can copy and paste this easily.

Column 1	Column 2	Column 3	Column 4	Column 5
Be	Draw	Hold	Ride	Speak
Become	Drink	Keep	Ring	Spend
Begin	Drive	Know	Rise	Stand
Break	Eat	Lead	Run	Steal
Bring	Fall	Leave	Say	Swim
Build	Feel	Lose	See	Take
Buy	Find	Make	Sell	Teach
Catch	Fly	Meet	Send	Tell
Choose	Forget	Pay	Set	Think
Come	Give	Put	Sit	Write

30 irregular verbs, showing the present, past, and future tense forms

Verb	Present	Past	Future
Be	am/is/are	was/were	will be
Begin	begin	began	will begin
Break	break	broke	will break
Bring	bring	brought	will bring
Build	build	built	will build
Buy	buy	bought	will buy
Catch	catch	caught	will catch
Choose	choose	chose	will choose
Come	come	came	will come
Do	do/does	did	will do
Drink	drink	drank	will drink
Drive	drive	drove	will drive
Eat	eat	ate	will eat
Fall	fall	fell	will fall
Feel	feel	felt	will feel
Find	find	found	will find
Fly	fly	flew	will fly
Get	get	got	will get
Give	give	gave	will give
Go	go	went	will go
Have	have/has	had	will have
Hear	hear	heard	will hear
Hold	hold	held	will hold
Keep	keep	kept	will keep
Know	know	knew	will know
Leave	leave	left	will leave
Lose	lose	lost	will lose
Make	make	made	will make
Read	read (pronounced reed)	read (pronounced red)	will read
Say	say	said	will say

Conclusion: Learning irregular verbs is essential for fluency in English, as these verbs are some of the most commonly used in both speech and writing. By providing students with strategies to recognize patterns, offering visual tools, and incorporating fun activities like storytelling and games, you can make learning irregular verbs an engaging and memorable experience.

Active vs. Passive Voice: Understanding the Difference

The **voice** of a sentence refers to the relationship between the subject and the verb. In English, verbs can be expressed in **active** or **passive** voice. While both voices are grammatically correct, they serve different purposes in writing. Knowing when to use each—and how to identify them—is crucial for writing clearly and effectively.

What is Active Voice?

In an **active voice** sentence, the subject performs the action of the verb. It is **direct, clear, and more engaging**.

Structure:
Subject → Verb → Object

Examples:

- The dog (subject) chased (verb) the ball (object).
- The teacher (subject) praised (verb) the student (object).

Why Active Voice Matters:

- It makes writing clearer and more concise.
- It helps maintain a stronger, more authoritative tone.
- Often used in fiction, journalism, and persuasive writing to keep the reader engaged.

What is Passive Voice?

In a **passive voice** sentence, the subject receives the action. The object of the action is moved to the front, and the subject is either placed later in the sentence or omitted altogether. Passive voice typically uses a form of the verb "to be" (is, was, were) with a past participle.

Structure:
Object → Form of "to be" → Past Participle → (by Subject)

Examples:

- The ball was chased by the dog.
- The student was praised by the teacher.

Why Passive Voice Exists:

- Useful when the performer of the action is unknown or unimportant: *The window was broken last night.*
- Common in scientific or technical writing to focus on the action or result rather than the person performing it: *The experiment was conducted over three days.*

Active vs. Passive: Why Knowing the Difference is Important

1. **Clarity and Strength:** Active voice is more straightforward and concise. Passive voice can make writing vague or wordy.
2. **Reader Engagement:** Active sentences are more energetic, while passive sentences can feel detached.
3. **Focus on the Subject:** Active voice highlights the subject performing the action, while passive voice can hide the doer. This can cause confusion or reduce accountability in writing.
4. **Genre-Specific Needs:** Understanding both voices allows writers to adapt to different writing styles (creative, academic, scientific).

How to Identify Active vs. Passive Voice

1. **Look for a form of "to be" followed by a past participle:**
    - *The cake was baked by John* (passive) vs. *John baked the cake* (active).
2. **Ask yourself:** *Is the subject doing the action, or is the subject receiving the action?*
3. **Check for a "by" phrase:** Passive voice often contains a phrase starting with "by" that identifies the performer.

Methods for Teaching Active vs. Passive Voice

1. Sentence Transformation

Have students practice rewriting passive sentences in active voice and vice versa.
Example:

- Passive: *The homework was completed by Maria.*
- Active: *Maria completed the homework.*

2. Highlighting or Circling

Provide a passage and have students highlight the forms of "to be" and the past participle. Ask them to identify whether each sentence is active or passive.

3. Act It Out

In a small group, assign students roles (subject, verb, object). Have them physically move to represent the structure of an active or passive sentence. This helps kinesthetic learners grasp the concept.

4. Anchor Charts and Visuals

Create visual aids that compare active and passive structures with examples. Use color-coding to highlight key differences.

5. Real-World Writing Practice

Ask students to write a short news article or story in active voice and then convert it to passive voice. This shows them how the tone and focus of writing change.

Examples for Practice

Identify Active or Passive:

1. The door was opened by Sarah.
2. Sarah opened the door.
3. The experiment was conducted by the scientists.
4. The scientists conducted the experiment.

Rewrite Passive Sentences in Active Voice:

1. *The book was read by the child.*
   → The child read the book.
2. *The cake was eaten by the guests.*
   → The guests ate the cake.

By understanding and practicing the difference between active and passive voice, students will develop stronger, clearer writing skills. Mastering these concepts empowers them to communicate with purpose and precision in any form of writing.

Active and Passive Learning in Grammar Instruction

When teaching grammar, it's essential to balance both **active** and **passive** learning strategies. **Active learning** involves **direct, hands-on instruction** and **immediate engagement** from students, while **passive learning** creates a supportive **environment rich in visual reminders and resources**. Both approaches play a vital role in helping students internalize grammar concepts and develop stronger reading and writing skills.

Active Learning in Grammar

Active learning is teacher-driven and student-centered, focusing on explicit instruction followed by active student participation. This approach ensures that students **practice, apply, and reinforce grammar concepts** in meaningful ways.

Key Elements of Active Learning

- **Explicit Teaching:** The teacher introduces grammar concepts in clear, focused lessons, ensuring that students understand each part of speech, sentence structure, and grammar rule.
- **Guided Practice:** Students work through examples with teacher support, often receiving immediate feedback.
- **Collaborative Activities:** Grammar learning is enriched through small group discussions, paired activities, and whole-class participation.
- **Kinesthetic and Creative Engagement:** Activities like **Readers Theater, interactive poetry, songs, chants, and movement-based learning** help make grammar fun and memorable.
- **Immediate Response and Reflection:** Students actively correct errors, answer questions, and reflect on their understanding during each lesson.

Examples of Active Learning Activities:

1. **Readers Theater:** Students act out scripts using Sentence Weather Symbols to represent parts of speech in context.
2. **Interactive Poetry:** Students create poems focusing on adjectives, adverbs, and conjunctions, acting out their parts of speech with motions.
3. **Songs and Chants:** Grammar chants reinforce sentence construction, verb tense, and subject-verb agreement through repetition and rhythm.
4. **Sentence Rearranging Races:** Students compete to rearrange scrambled sentences for proper grammar and clarity.

Why Active Learning Works:

- Encourages **engagement and critical thinking**.
- Provides **immediate practice and feedback**.
- Appeals to multiple learning styles (visual, auditory, kinesthetic).
- Builds **collaboration and social skills** in group settings.

Passive Learning in Grammar

Passive learning focuses on creating a **grammar-rich environment** that provides students with consistent, visual exposure to grammar rules and concepts. Although students don't interact directly during passive learning, their surroundings offer constant reinforcement, building **subconscious familiarity** over time.

Key Elements of Passive Learning

- **Classroom Displays:** Posters and anchor charts for parts of speech, punctuation rules, and sentence structures serve as daily visual reminders.
- **Writer's Notebook Resources:** Students can reference grammar tips, commonly confused words, and verb tense charts stored in their notebooks.
- **Word Walls and Anchor Charts:** Visuals that feature frequently used adjectives, conjunctions, and prepositions help reinforce word choice.
- **Consistent Visual Cues:** Items such as Sentence Weather Symbols displayed around the room create visual associations with each part of speech.
- **Sentence Samples:** Well-crafted sentences posted on the wall serve as examples of proper grammar usage, giving students something to emulate.

Examples of Passive Learning Resources:

1. **Grammar Posters:** Visual aids for verb tense, subject-verb agreement, and punctuation rules.
2. **Sentence Weather Wall:** A chart displaying symbols for each part of speech (☁ for nouns, ☀ for adjectives, 💧 for verbs) helps reinforce identification skills.
3. **Word Banks:** Lists of descriptive adjectives, adverbs, and strong verbs for students to reference during writing tasks.
4. **Daily Grammar Sentence:** A sentence written on the board each day that models proper grammar and structure.

Why Passive Learning Works:

- Builds **long-term memory** through visual exposure.
- Helps students recognize patterns in grammar without direct instruction.
- Provides a **non-threatening learning environment** for academically challenged learners.
- Offers quick, **accessible resources** for students to reference during independent work.

Balancing Active and Passive Learning

An effective grammar curriculum combines both approaches:

- **Active learning** for direct instruction and immediate application.
- **Passive learning** for continuous reinforcement and subconscious absorption.

For example, a teacher might **introduce conjunctions with a song and movement activity (active learning)**, then reinforce the concept with a **classroom poster and sample sentences on the board (passive learning)**.
By combining these methods, students gain a deep, well-rounded understanding of grammar concepts, preparing them for **stronger reading comprehension and more polished writing**.

"The Heart of Every Sentence"

A sentence starts with a name or two,
But verbs come next to tell what they do!
They jump, they run, they think, they play—
Verbs bring action to every day.

***Linking** verbs just show the state,*
Am, is, was, were—they communicate.
***Helping** verbs like will and can,*
Support the main verb, hand in hand.

Tenses tell us time so well,
***Past or present, future** they spell.*
Verbs bring writing to life so bright—
Without them, nothing feels quite right!

Drama: "Verb Time Travelers"

Characters:

- **Narrator**
- **Action Verb Explorer**
- **Linking Verb Guide**
- **Helping Verb Helper**
- **Past Tense Detective**
- **Present Tense Professor**
- **Future Tense Scientist**
- **Subject-Verb Agreement Enforcer**
- **Irregular Verb Wizard**
- **Student 1**
- **Student 2**

Narrator: *Welcome to the Verb Time Travel Adventure! Today, we're going to learn how verbs take us through time—past, present, and future—and bring sentences to life. Meet Action Verb Explorer!*

Action Verb Explorer: *I'm the one who shows all the action—run, jump, think, and dream. If you want movement in your sentence, I'm your verb!*

Linking Verb Guide: *I'm not about action—I connect things. I link the subject to information: He is happy or They seem tired. Think of me as the bridge!*

Helping Verb Helper: *I'm the assistant! I help verbs express tense and mood—will, has, have, can. You'll see me in verb phrases like She is running or They have gone. I make sure things are clear.*

Past Tense Detective: *Let's head back in time! If the action already happened, I'll show you with verbs like walked, danced, sang. I'm the past tense master!*

Present Tense Professor: *I live in the here and now! My verbs show what's happening right this second—walks, dances, sings. I keep things current!*

Future Tense Scientist: *Want to know what will happen? That's my job! Add will or shall to your verb—She will dance or He will walk. Welcome to the future!*

Subject-Verb Agreement Enforcer: *I make sure subjects and verbs always match. If you have a singular subject like dog, use runs. If it's plural like dogs, use run. Agreement keeps your sentence in line!*

Irregular Verb Wizard: *I'm the tricky one! My past tense forms don't follow the rules—go becomes went, and sing becomes sang. Learn my forms, and you'll be a grammar wizard, too!*

Student 1: *Wow! Verbs can do so many things!*

Student 2: *They're like time travelers! Now I understand how they work.*

Narrator: *Remember—verbs are the heart of every sentence. They give life, time, and meaning to your words. Use them wisely, and your writing will always be strong!*

10 Ways to Ask Questions About Verbs Without Using the Word "Verb"

1. *What word in the sentence shows action?*
2. *Which word tells us what the subject is doing?*
3. *What word connects the subject to a description?*
4. *How do we know when the action happened in this sentence?*
5. *Which word helps express the tense in this sentence?*
6. *What word shows the state of being?*
7. *Which word tells us what will happen in the future?*
8. *What word tells us about continuous or ongoing action?*
9. *How can you tell if this sentence is in past tense?*
10. *What word is helping the main action word?*

Lesson Plan 1: "Verb Charades" (Kinesthetic Whole-Group Activity)

Objective:
Students will identify and differentiate between action, linking, and helping verbs through an engaging game of charades.

Materials:

- Verb Charades cards (pre-made with various action, linking, and helping verbs)
- Timer
- Verb Chart on the board labeled: Action, Linking, Helping

Introduction (5 minutes)
Teacher script: "Today, we're diving into the exciting world of verbs—the heartbeat of every sentence! Verbs show action, link ideas, or help other verbs express meaning. Think of verbs as the 'movers and shakers' of our language. Our goal today is to act out different verbs and classify them as action, linking, or helping. Let's get moving!"

Activity (15–20 minutes)

1. **Explain the Types of Verbs:**
   Action Verbs: "These show physical or mental actions. Words like run, jump, or think are action verbs."
   Linking Verbs: "These connect the subject to more information about itself—is, seem, and become are common linking verbs."
   Helping Verbs: "These 'help' the main verb show tense, mood, or voice—has, will, and can are helping verbs."
2. **Game Instructions:**
   - Divide the class into small teams.
   - One student draws a Verb Charades card and acts it out without speaking.
   - Their team guesses the verb and classifies it as action, linking, or helping.
   - Teams earn points for correctly identifying and classifying the verb.

Sample Charades Cards:

- Action Verbs: dance, swim, write, sleep, eat
- Linking Verbs: is, are, seem, feel, become
- Helping Verbs: has, will, can, should, might

Wrap-Up (5 minutes)
Teacher script: "You all did a fantastic job acting out verbs! Remember, action verbs show

what's happening, linking verbs connect ideas, and helping verbs give us more details about the action. Keep an eye out for verbs in everything you read!"

Assessment:
Students form pairs and take turns identifying verbs in a short passage read aloud by the teacher. They categorize each verb as action, linking, or helping.

Lesson Plan 2: "Verb Tense Relay Race" (Small-Group, Kinesthetic Activity)

Objective:
Students will understand verb tenses (past, present, future, and perfect tenses) by participating in a high-energy relay race.

Materials:

- Verb Tense Task Cards (with sentences in various tenses)
- Three labeled stations: Past Tense, Present Tense, Future Tense
- Stopwatch or timer

Introduction (5 minutes)
Teacher script: "Verbs not only tell us what's happening—they also tell us ***when*** *it's happening! Today, we're exploring verb tenses: past, present, and future. Imagine saying, 'I jump,' versus 'I jumped,' versus 'I will jump.' Verb tenses give your reader a timeline of events. We're going to practice recognizing verb tenses with a relay race!"*

Activity (15–20 minutes)

1. **Explain Verb Tenses:**
   Past Tense: "This describes actions that have already happened—I jumped."
   Present Tense: "This describes actions happening right now—I jump."
   Future Tense: "This describes actions that will happen—I will jump."
2. **Relay Instructions:**
   - Divide students into small teams.
   - Set up three stations labeled Past, Present, and Future.
   - Each team picks a runner who draws a Verb Tense Task Card (with a sentence) and races to the correct station.
   - Teams earn points for placing their card in the correct tense category.

Sample Task Cards:

- *I ran to the store.* (Past)
- *We are eating lunch.* (Present)
- *She will visit her grandma.* (Future)
- *They have played soccer.* (Perfect Tense)

Wrap-Up (5 minutes)
Teacher script: "Great job racing through verb tenses! Remember, past tense is for things that already happened, present tense is for what's happening now, and future tense is for what will happen. Keep practicing your verb tenses—you're on your way to becoming verb experts!"

Assessment:
Each team writes a short story in three parts: one paragraph in the past tense, one in the present tense, and one in the future tense. Teams present their stories to the class, and the teacher checks for correct tense usage.

Actionable/Observable Assessment Tool: Verb Sorting Game

Objective:
Assess students' ability to identify and categorize verbs based on type (action, linking, helping) and tense (past, present, future).

Instructions:

1. **Set Up Stations:** Create verb sorting stations with labeled categories (Action, Linking, Helping) and (Past, Present, Future).
2. **Activity:**
    - Students rotate in small groups to each station.
    - At each station, they draw verb cards and place them in the correct category.
    - After sorting, each group explains their choices.
3. **Scoring:** Points are awarded for accuracy and explanations.

Chapter 4:

Adjectives

The Words that Add Color, Detail, and Life

Adjectives are the artists of language. They paint vibrant pictures in our minds by adding detail, color, and texture to nouns and pronouns. Without adjectives, language would be bland and uninspired. Imagine trying to describe your favorite dessert without words like *sweet, creamy, or delicious*. Adjectives help us convey more precise and vivid information about the world around us, making our writing clear, descriptive, and engaging.

Adjectives serve an important function in sentences by **modifying nouns and pronouns**. They tell us **what kind, which one, how many,** or **how much** about the noun. These versatile words can appear in various places within a sentence and can even form **adjective phrases** for added complexity. Let's explore the many types and functions of adjectives.

Types of Adjectives

1. **Descriptive Adjectives**
   These are the most common adjectives, providing detail and describing qualities or characteristics.
   Examples: *blue, tall, spicy, happy*
   Example Sentence: *She wore a blue dress.*
2. **Demonstrative Adjectives**
   These adjectives point to specific nouns. The four demonstrative adjectives are **this, that, these,** and **those**.
   Examples: *this book, those shoes*
   Example Sentence: *I prefer that movie over this one.*
3. **Comparative Adjectives**
   Comparative adjectives compare two nouns or pronouns, often ending in **-er** or using the word **more**.
   Examples: *faster, taller, more interesting*
   Example Sentence: *My car is faster than yours.*
4. **Superlative Adjectives**
   Superlative adjectives compare three or more nouns, often ending in **-est** or using the

word **most**.
Examples: *fastest, tallest, most interesting*
Example Sentence: *This is the fastest route to school.*

5. **Articles (a, an, the)**
   Articles are a special category of adjectives that introduce nouns.
   - **A** and **an** are indefinite articles, referring to any one of a group.
     Example: *a cat, an apple*
   - **The** is the definite article, referring to a specific noun.
     Example: *the house*

Adjective Phrases

An **adjective phrase** is a group of words that functions as an adjective, modifying a noun or pronoun. These phrases usually start with a preposition or participle.
Examples:

- *The book on the shelf is mine.* (The phrase *on the shelf* describes *book.*)
- *The girl wearing a red hat waved at me.* (The phrase *wearing a red hat* describes *girl.*)

Where Adjectives Appear in a Sentence

Adjectives can appear in several places within a sentence:

1. **Before a Noun (Attributive Position):** This is the most common position for adjectives.
   Example: *The hungry dog barked.*
2. **After a Linking Verb (Predicative Position):** The adjective acts as a complement to the subject.
   Example: *The dog is hungry.*
3. **In an Adjective Phrase:** The adjective is part of a larger phrase that describes a noun.
   Example: *The house with the red door belongs to me.*

Functions of Adjectives

Adjectives enhance writing by providing detail and specificity. They help answer important questions about nouns and pronouns:

- **What kind?** *A fluffy cat*
- **Which one?** *Those apples*
- **How many?** *Three books*
- **How much?** *Some sugar*

Adjectives help writers evoke emotions and create vivid imagery. For example, consider the difference between these sentences:

- *He sat on a chair.*
- *He sat on a soft, comfortable chair.*

The second sentence is much more descriptive and allows the reader to visualize the scene.

Why Adjectives Matter

Adjectives are essential for effective communication. They make language more interesting and expressive, allowing us to share experiences and ideas in a richer way. Understanding how to use adjectives correctly—including where they appear and how to form comparative and superlative forms—can improve both writing and speaking.

In this chapter, we'll explore adjectives in detail, practice identifying them, and learn how to use them to bring your writing to life. Prepare to discover the magic of adjectives and how they can transform ordinary sentences into extraordinary ones!

Teacher Training Script: Introduction to Chapter 4 – Adjectives

"Today, we're diving into the world of adjectives—the artists of language. Imagine writing without adjectives. It would be like drawing in black and white when you could use a rainbow of colors! Adjectives paint our words with detail, emotion, and texture. They tell us what kind, which one, how many, or how much about a noun or pronoun, making our sentences vivid and memorable."

"Think about your favorite dessert. Without adjectives, you'd just say 'I ate dessert.' But adjectives let you say, 'I ate a creamy, chocolatey, delicious dessert.' Now we can almost taste it! Adjectives make writing more interesting, whether you're describing a tall tree, a sweet kitten, or a warm summer breeze. Let's explore how these magical words bring language to life!"

List of 10 Examples for Each Type of Adjective

Demonstrative	Descriptive	Comparative	Superlative
this	beautiful	more beautiful	most beautiful
that	soft	softer	softest
these	colorful	more colorful	most colorful
those	important	more important	most important
such	bright	brighter	brightest
certain	delicious	more delicious	most delicious
either	quiet	quieter	quietest
neither	friendly	friendlier	friendliest
any	expensive	more expensive	most expensive
which	careful	more careful	most careful

Notes:

- **Descriptive Adjectives** describe qualities or characteristics.
- **Comparative Adjectives** compare **two nouns** (e.g., *softer pillow*).
- **Superlative Adjectives** show the **highest degree** among **three or more nouns** (e.g., *softest pillow*).

Special Adjectives known as Articles

When to Use "A" or "An"

The choice between **"a"** and **"an"** depends on the sound that begins the next word, not the spelling.

1. **Use "A"** before words that begin with a consonant sound:
    - Example: a dog, a teacher, a house
2. **Use "An"** before words that begin with a vowel sound (a, e, i, o, u):
    - Example: an apple, an elephant, an umbrella

Important Note: It's all about the **sound**, not the letter. Some words that begin with a consonant letter are pronounced with a vowel sound, and vice versa:

- **An hour** (the "h" is silent, so it sounds like a vowel)
- **A university** (the "u" sounds like "yoo," which is a consonant sound)
-

How to Pronounce "The"

The word "the" can be pronounced with either a **long E (/ði:/)** or a **schwa sound (/ðə/)**, depending on what follows it.

1. **Use "thee" (/ði:/)** when the next word starts with a vowel sound:
    - Example: *thee* apple, *thee* elephant, *thee* unusual idea
      This pronunciation emphasizes the word and makes speech flow more smoothly.
2. **Use "thuh" (/ðə/)** when the next word starts with a consonant sound:
    - Example: *thuh* book, *thuh* dog, *thuh* teacher

Optional Rule for Emphasis:
You can use **"thee"** for emphasis in formal speech, regardless of the sound:

- *He is THEE best singer.* (to emphasize "best")

"The Magic of Adjectives"

Adjectives bring color to every line,
They make your writing bold and fine.
They tell us what kind, which one, how much,
Adding detail with a brilliant touch.

Descriptive *ones paint a picture bright—*
Tall trees sway in the golden light.
Comparative *words help things compete,*
Bigger, faster, or less sweet.

Superlatives *stand out in a crowd—*
The biggest, best, and most are proud.
With ***articles*** *like a and the,*
Adjectives make writing poetry!

Drama: "Adjective Adventures"

Characters:

- **Narrator**
- **Descriptive Adjective Artist**
- **Demonstrative Adjective Pointer**
- **Comparative Adjective Competitor**
- **Superlative Adjective Judge**
- **Article Guide**
- **Adjective Phrase Explorer**
- **Student 1**
- **Student 2**
- **Teacher**
- **Audience Member**

Narrator: *Welcome to Adjective Adventures! Today, we'll explore how adjectives bring language to life. First, let's meet Descriptive Adjective Artist!*

Descriptive Adjective Artist: *I'm the painter of words! I add detail and description—blue, spicy, soft, and loud. Without me, sentences would be plain and boring!*

Demonstrative Adjective Pointer: *I'm your guide! I point out specific nouns—this, that, these, and those. I make sure you know exactly which one!*

Comparative Adjective Competitor: *I'm all about comparison! My job is to show which noun is bigger, faster, or stronger. If you're comparing two things, you need me!*

Superlative Adjective Judge: *When it's time to declare a winner, I'm here! I show who's the best or the biggest. Words like fastest, tallest, and most interesting are my specialty!*

Article Guide: *Don't forget me! I'm an important type of adjective too. Words like a, an, and the help introduce nouns and make sentences complete.*

Adjective Phrase Explorer: *I lead the adventure into adjective phrases! These phrases give even more detail—like the house with the red door or the girl wearing a red hat.*

Student 1: *Wow! I didn't realize adjectives did so much!*

Student 2: *Me neither! But now I know how they can bring writing to life!*

Teacher: *Remember—adjectives are your secret weapon for vivid, detailed writing. Use them wisely, and your sentences will always shine!*

10 Ways to Ask Questions About Adjectives Without Using the Word "Adjective"

1. *What word tells us more about the noun?*
2. *Which word describes how something looks or feels?*
3. *How do we know how many or how much of something there is?*
4. *Which word tells us what kind of person, place, or thing it is?*
5. *What word compares two things in this sentence?*
6. *How can you tell which noun is the biggest or best?*
7. *What word points to a specific noun?*
8. *Which word shows the order or ranking of things?*
9. *What part of the sentence gives extra detail about the noun?*
10. *Which word tells us which one or whose it is?*

Lesson Plan 1: "Adjective Detective: Describing the Mystery Object" (Whole-Group, Interactive Activity)

Objective:
Students will identify and use descriptive, comparative, and superlative adjectives to describe objects and understand how adjectives add detail and precision to sentences.

Materials:

- A mystery bag filled with various objects (e.g., a soft scarf, a toy car, a shiny spoon, a large book)
- Adjective Chart (Descriptive, Comparative, Superlative)
- Whiteboard or chart paper for brainstorming adjectives

Introduction (5–10 minutes)
Teacher script: "Today, we're becoming Adjective Detectives! Our job is to find the perfect adjectives to describe mystery objects. Adjectives are words that tell us more about nouns—they describe size, color, texture, shape, and more. Imagine writing without adjectives. Instead of saying, 'The big, fluffy dog barked,' you'd just say, 'The dog barked.' That's not very exciting! Let's add some adjectives and bring our sentences to life."

Activity (15–20 minutes)

1. **Mystery Bag:**
   - One at a time, pull an object from the mystery bag.
   - Ask students to observe the object and shout out adjectives to describe it. Write their suggestions on the board.
2. **Adjective Categorization:**
   - Guide students to categorize the adjectives as descriptive, comparative, or superlative.
   - **Example:**
     - Descriptive: *soft, blue, shiny*
     - Comparative: *softer, bluer, shinier*
     - Superlative: *softest, bluest, shiniest*
3. **Sentence Creation:**
   - Choose several adjectives and create a descriptive sentence about the object.
   - **Example:** *The soft, blue scarf is the warmest one in the bag.*

Wrap-Up (5 minutes)
Teacher script: "Great job, detectives! Remember, adjectives make writing more interesting and help your reader picture exactly what you mean. Keep using adjectives to add color and detail to your sentences!"

Assessment:
Students pick an object in the classroom, write down three adjectives to describe it (one for each category), and share their adjectives with the class.

Lesson Plan 2: "Adjective Relay Race" (Kinesthetic Small-Group Activity)

Objective:
Students will practice identifying adjectives and using them in sentences through an engaging relay race.

Materials:

- Adjective cards (with descriptive, comparative, and superlative adjectives)
- Sentences with blanks for adjectives (written on large chart paper or a digital board)
- Timer or stopwatch

Introduction (5–10 minutes)
Teacher script: "Get ready to move while learning about adjectives! Adjectives make our writing more vivid by describing nouns. They answer questions like: What kind? Which one? How many? Today, we'll race to fill in the blanks in sentences with the most fitting adjectives. Let's see how fast and creative you can be!"

Activity (15–20 minutes)

1. **Set Up:**
    - Divide the class into small teams.
    - Place adjective cards at one end of the room and sentence strips with blanks at the other end.
2. **Relay Instructions:**
    - One student from each team runs to the adjective card pile, selects a card, and runs back.
    - The team decides where the adjective fits in the blank sentence.
    - Repeat until all blanks are filled with adjectives.
    - **Example Sentence:** *The _____ cat is the _____ pet in the house.*
        - Possible adjectives: *fluffy, cutest*
3. **Check and Discuss:**
    - After all teams finish, review the sentences and discuss whether the adjectives make sense.

Wrap-Up (5 minutes)
Teacher script: "Amazing work! Remember, adjectives are powerful tools that make our writing fun and descriptive. Keep adding adjectives to your sentences to create vivid pictures for your readers!"

Assessment:
Each team presents their completed sentence to the class and explains why they chose their adjectives.

Actionable/Observable Assessment Tool: "Adjective Scavenger Hunt"

Objective:
Assess students' ability to identify and apply adjectives in a real-world context.

Instructions:

1. **Set Up:** Give students a checklist of adjective categories (e.g., size, color, texture, quantity, comparative, superlative).
2. **Activity:** Students search the classroom or outdoor area for objects that fit each category and write down a sentence describing the object using an appropriate adjective.
   - **Example:** *I found a shiny red apple.*
3. **Debrief:** Students share their sentences and reflect on how adjectives improved their descriptions.

Chapter 5:

Adverbs

The Words that Add Precision and Depth

Adverbs are the dynamic enhancers of language, adding precision, clarity, and depth to our sentences. While adjectives describe nouns, adverbs modify **verbs, adjectives, or other adverbs**. They answer questions like **how, when, where, how often,** or **to what degree** something happens. Imagine trying to describe how you run—without adverbs, you could only say *I run.* But with adverbs, you can be much more specific: *I run quickly, I run daily,* or *I run outdoors.*

Adverbs allow us to fine-tune our sentences and communicate in a more engaging, detailed, and clear way. Understanding the different types of adverbs and how they function will help you create sentences that flow naturally and convey your exact meaning.

Types of Adverbs

1. **Adverbs of Manner**
   These adverbs describe *how* an action is performed. They often end in **-ly** and provide vivid details.
   Examples: *quickly, gently, loudly, slowly*
   Example Sentence: *She sang beautifully.*
2. **Adverbs of Place**
   These adverbs tell us *where* an action takes place.
   Examples: *here, there, everywhere, nearby, inside, outside*
   Example Sentence: *The kids are playing outside.*
3. **Adverbs of Time**
   These adverbs indicate *when* an action occurs.
   Examples: *now, yesterday, soon, later, already*
   Example Sentence: *We will leave tomorrow.*
4. **Adverbs of Degree**
   These adverbs explain *to what extent* or *how much* something happens.
   Examples: *very, too, almost, completely, quite, extremely*
   Example Sentence: *The water was very cold.*

5. **Adverbs of Frequency**
   These adverbs describe *how often* something happens.
   Examples: *always, often, sometimes, rarely, never*
   Example Sentence: *He always arrives on time.*
6. **Conjunctive Adverbs**
   These special adverbs connect two independent clauses and show the relationship between them. They act like bridges in writing, improving the flow and coherence of ideas.
   Examples: *however, therefore, meanwhile, consequently, moreover*
   Example Sentence: *I wanted to join the team; however, I missed the tryouts.*
7. **Comparison of Adverbs**
   Adverbs can also be used to compare actions. Like adjectives, adverbs have **positive, comparative,** and **superlative** forms.
   - **Positive:** *He ran fast.*
   - **Comparative:** *He ran faster.*
   - **Superlative:** *He ran fastest.*

What Do Adverbs Modify?

Adverbs are unique because they can modify **verbs, adjectives, or other adverbs**, making them highly versatile in writing.

1. **Modifying Verbs:** They tell how, when, or where an action occurs.
   Example: *She speaks softly.* (modifies the verb *speaks*)
2. **Modifying Adjectives:** They add intensity or emphasis to an adjective.
   Example: *The movie was incredibly exciting.* (modifies the adjective *exciting*)
3. **Modifying Other Adverbs:** They adjust the degree of another adverb.
   Example: *He finished surprisingly quickly.* (modifies the adverb *quickly*)

Where Do Adverbs Appear in Sentences?

Adverbs can appear in different positions within a sentence:

1. **At the beginning:** *Yesterday, we went hiking.*
2. **In the middle (before or after the verb):** *She often reads before bed.*
3. **At the end:** *They played outside.*

The placement of an adverb can affect the emphasis and meaning of a sentence, so it's important to position them thoughtfully.

Why Adverbs Matter

Adverbs make language richer and more expressive. They help us explain actions in detail, clarify the intensity of emotions, and describe how things happen with precision. Without adverbs, writing can feel flat and incomplete.

Types of Adverbs

Adverbs of Manner	Adverbs of Time	Adverbs of Place	Adverbs of Frequency	Adverbs of Degree	Conjunctive Adverbs
quickly	yesterday	here	always	very	however
carefully	now	there	often	quite	therefore
happily	soon	everywhere	never	extremely	consequently
slowly	later	nearby	sometimes	almost	meanwhile
loudly	today	outside	rarely	too	nevertheless
softly	already	inside	frequently	entirely	moreover
angrily	tomorrow	behind	occasionally	fairly	furthermore
neatly	afterward	forward	usually	completely	nonetheless
bravely	recently	across	seldom	absolutely	subsequently
gently	early	upwards	periodically	rather	otherwise

Teacher Training Script: Introduction to Chapter 5 – Adverbs

"Welcome to the world of adverbs—the precision tools of language! If adjectives are the artists that color our nouns, adverbs are the editors who fine-tune everything. Imagine this: Without adverbs, you might say, 'I run.' But with adverbs, you can say, 'I run quickly,' or 'I run every morning.' Adverbs make your writing clearer, more descriptive, and full of life."

"Adverbs tell us how something happens, when it happens, where it happens, how often, or to what degree. They modify verbs, adjectives, or even other adverbs, acting like little amplifiers for your words. Think of them as the spice cabinet of language—just the right amount can turn a plain sentence into something extraordinary!"

List of 10 Examples for Each Type of Adverb

Adverbs of Manner

1. quickly
2. slowly
3. gently
4. loudly
5. quietly
6. beautifully
7. badly
8. carefully
9. easily
10. angrily

Adverbs of Place

1. here
2. there
3. outside
4. inside
5. nearby
6. everywhere
7. upstairs
8. downtown
9. abroad
10. anywhere

Adverbs of Time

1. now
2. yesterday
3. soon
4. later
5. already
6. tomorrow
7. recently
8. tonight
9. finally
10. immediately

Adverbs of Degree

1. very
2. too
3. almost
4. completely
5. quite
6. extremely
7. barely
8. entirely
9. nearly
10. totally

Adverbs of Frequency

1. always
2. often
3. sometimes
4. rarely
5. never
6. occasionally
7. usually
8. frequently
9. seldom
10. daily

Conjunctive Adverbs

1. however
2. therefore
3. meanwhile
4. consequently
5. furthermore
6. moreover
7. otherwise
8. similarly
9. indeed
10. nevertheless

"The Power of Adverbs"

Adverbs add sparkle, detail, and flair,
They tell us how, when, or where.
Quickly, softly, loudly they show,
How actions happen and make writing glow.

Adverbs of ***place*** *tell us here or there,*
While **time** *adverbs tell when, like now or where.*
Often and always, they let us know,
How ***frequently*** *actions come and go.*

Conjunctive *ones, like however and then,*
Connect ideas from start to end.
Adverbs are tools for writers like you—
Master them and your words shine through!

Drama: "The Adverb Adventure"

Characters:

- **Narrator**
- **Adverb of Manner**
- **Adverb of Place**
- **Adverb of Time**
- **Adverb of Degree**
- **Adverb of Frequency**
- **Conjunctive Adverb**
- **Verb Modifier**
- **Adjective Modifier**
- **Student 1**
- **Student 2**

Narrator: *Welcome to the Adverb Adventure! Today, we'll explore how adverbs bring detail and precision to sentences. Let's meet our team of adverb experts, starting with Adverb of Manner!*

Adverb of Manner: *I describe how actions happen—quickly, slowly, beautifully, badly. Want your writing to be more vivid? Just add me!*

Adverb of Place: *I tell you where something happens—here, there, outside, inside. Without me, you'd never know where the action is!*

Adverb of Time: *When does something happen? That's my job! Words like now, yesterday, soon, and later are in my toolkit.*

Adverb of Degree: *I'm the intensity expert! I help you express how much—very, too, almost, and completely are my favorite words.*

Adverb of Frequency: *Want to know how often something happens? Always, often, sometimes, and never are mine! I make sure you get the full picture.*

Conjunctive Adverb: *I'm the bridge between sentences—however, therefore, moreover, and meanwhile. I help ideas flow smoothly!*

Verb Modifier: *I modify verbs, telling you how, when, and where an action happens.*

Adjective Modifier: *And I modify adjectives, adding emphasis and detail—very hot, extremely tired, or completely surprised!*

Student 1: *I didn't realize how many different kinds of adverbs there are!*

Student 2: *Me neither! But now I can see how they make writing more interesting and clear!*

Narrator: *That's right! Adverbs are powerful tools. Use them wisely, and your sentences will shine!*

---

10 Ways to Ask Questions About Adverbs Without Using the Word "Adverb"

1. *What word tells us how the action is performed?*
2. *Which word explains where the action takes place?*
3. *How do we know when something happens in this sentence?*
4. *What word tells how often the event occurs?*
5. *Which word modifies the verb in this sentence?*
6. *What word shows the intensity or degree of the adjective?*
7. *How do we know the action is continuous or sudden?*
8. *Which word connects these two independent clauses?*
9. *What part of the sentence describes how much or how little?*
10. *How can you tell where the action happens in this sentence?*

Lesson Plan 1: "Adverb Adventure Game" (Whole-Group, Interactive Activity)

Objective:
Students will identify and categorize adverbs by exploring how they modify verbs, adjectives, and other adverbs.

Materials:

- Adverb Cards with different adverbs (divided by manner, place, time, degree, frequency)
- Verb Action Cards (with actions like run, jump, sing, speak, dance)
- Chart labeled with adverb categories: Manner (how), Place (where), Time (when), Degree (to what extent), Frequency (how often)

Introduction (5–10 minutes)
Teacher script: "Today, we're going on an Adverb Adventure! Adverbs are like little guides that give us more information about verbs, adjectives, and other adverbs. They tell us things like how, when, where, how much, and how often something happens. Without adverbs, our sentences would be dull and incomplete. Let's discover how adverbs make our writing come alive!"

Activity (15–20 minutes)

1. **Modeling:**
    - Write a simple sentence on the board: *The boy runs.*
    - Ask: *"How can we describe how the boy runs?"*
    - Add adverbs to the sentence: *The boy runs quickly. The boy runs outside. The boy runs daily.*
2. **Adverb Adventure Game Instructions:**
    - Divide the class into small groups.
    - Each group draws a Verb Action Card (e.g., run, sing, dance).
    - They select an Adverb Card and act out the verb using the adverb. For example: *run slowly, sing loudly, dance gracefully.*
    - The rest of the class guesses the adverb category and what adverb was used.
3. **Categorization:**
   After each group's performance, place the adverb in the correct category on the chart (Manner, Place, Time, Degree, Frequency).

Sample Adverb List:

- **Manner (how):** carefully, happily, loudly
- **Place (where):** outside, here, nearby
- **Time (when):** yesterday, soon, now
- **Degree (to what extent):** very, almost, completely
- **Frequency (how often):** always, sometimes, never

Wrap-Up (5 minutes)
Teacher script: "Great job, adventurers! Remember, adverbs add details and help your reader understand exactly how things happen. Keep an eye out for adverbs in your reading and writing!"

Assessment:
Students form pairs and create a sentence using a verb and adverb from different categories. They act it out for the class, and the teacher observes for correct usage and understanding.

Lesson Plan 2: "Adverb Relay Race" (Kinesthetic Small-Group Activity)

Objective:
Students will practice identifying adverbs and understanding how they modify verbs, adjectives, and other adverbs through a relay race.

Materials:

- Adverb Sentence Cards (sentences with blanks for adverbs)
- Adverb Cards (pre-made cards with various adverbs)
- Timer

Introduction (5–10 minutes)
Teacher script: "Get ready for the Adverb Relay Race! Adverbs help answer questions like how, when, where, how often, and to what extent. Today, you'll be racing to complete sentences with the best-fitting adverbs. Let's stretch our minds and our legs!"

Activity (15–20 minutes)

1. **Set Up:**
   - Divide the class into small teams.
   - Place the Adverb Sentence Cards at one end of the room and the Adverb Cards at the other end.
2. **Relay Instructions:**
   - The first student on each team runs to the Adverb Card pile, picks an adverb, and brings it back.
   - The team chooses which sentence to place the adverb in.
   - Repeat until all sentences have adverbs.

Sample Sentences:

- *The dog barked __________ (how).*
- *We will meet __________ (when).*
- *She looked __________ at the painting (to what extent).*

3. **Review and Discuss:**
   After the race, each team reads their completed sentences aloud. Discuss whether the chosen adverbs fit logically and improve the sentence.

Wrap-Up (5 minutes)
Teacher script: "Excellent racing! Remember, adverbs can change the meaning of a sentence in

powerful ways. Keep practicing how to use them, and your writing will become even more detailed and interesting!"

Assessment:
Each team creates a short story using five adverbs from different categories. They perform a dramatic reading of their story, emphasizing the adverbs. The teacher observes for variety and correct usage.

Actionable/Observable Assessment Tool: "Adverb Storytelling Challenge"

Objective:
Assess students' ability to use adverbs effectively in context by creating a short story.

Instructions:

1. **Story Creation:** Students work in small groups to write a story incorporating at least five adverbs from different categories (manner, time, place, degree, frequency).
2. **Performance:** Groups perform their story in front of the class, emphasizing the adverbs.
3. **Reflection:** The class discusses how the adverbs added meaning and detail to the story.

Chapter 6:

Prepositions

The Great Connectors

Prepositions are essential tools in the English language, acting as bridges that connect nouns or pronouns to other parts of a sentence. They show relationships of **direction, location, time, cause,** or **manner**, helping us express ideas with greater clarity. Imagine trying to give directions without prepositions—you couldn't say *"The book is on the table"* or *"I will meet you after class."* Prepositions make our writing precise and organized, guiding readers through sentences with ease.

A **prepositional phrase** begins with a preposition and ends with a **noun or pronoun** called the **object of the preposition**. Prepositional phrases provide important details that answer questions like **where, when, how,** or **why**. Understanding how prepositional phrases work is essential for writing sentences that are complete and logically structured.

Prepositions and Prepositional Phrases

A **prepositional phrase** consists of a **preposition,** its **object** (a noun or pronoun), and sometimes additional modifiers. These phrases never contain a subject or verb and cannot stand alone as a complete sentence.

Examples:

- *The book is on the table.* (preposition: *on*; object: *table*)
- *She went to the park.* (preposition: *to*; object: *park*)
- *We will meet after the game.* (preposition: *after*; object: *game*)

Prepositional Phrases vs. Clauses

It's important to distinguish between **phrases** and **clauses**.

- A **phrase** is a group of words that functions as a single part of speech but **does not contain both a subject and a verb.**
  Example: *on the table, before lunch, under the bed*
- A **clause** is a group of words that **contains both a subject and a verb.**
  Example: *I went to the store because I needed milk.* (The underlined portion is a dependent clause.)

Prepositional phrases can never be clauses because they don't contain a verb.

Prepositional Phrases and Subject-Verb Agreement

Prepositional phrases can sometimes confuse subject-verb agreement by appearing between the subject and verb. To maintain correct agreement, it's important to ignore the prepositional phrase and focus on the true subject.

Examples:

- *The group of students is excited.* (The subject *group* is singular, despite the plural noun *students*.)
- *A basket of apples was on the counter.* (The subject *basket* is singular.)

Without careful attention, it's easy to let the noun in the prepositional phrase influence the verb incorrectly.

Types of Prepositions

Prepositions express various relationships in a sentence:

1. **Prepositions of Place:** *on, in, under, between*
   - *The keys are on the table.*
2. **Prepositions of Time:** *after, before, during, at*
   - *We arrived before the movie started.*
3. **Prepositions of Direction or Movement:** *to, into, onto, toward*
   - *He walked into the room.*
4. **Prepositions of Cause or Reason:** *because of, due to, for*
   - *They canceled the game because of the rain.*

Why Prepositions Matter

Prepositions might seem small, but they are powerful. They add essential details that help readers understand relationships in time, space, and cause-and-effect. Mastering prepositions will allow you to write with precision and avoid common errors, especially in subject-verb agreement. In this chapter, you'll learn how to identify prepositional phrases, distinguish between phrases and clauses, and ensure your writing remains clear and grammatically correct.

Different types of prepositions organized by **Place**, **Time**, **Direction/Movement**, and **Cause/Reason**, with 10 examples in each column.

Prepositions of Place	Prepositions of Time	Prepositions of Direction/Movement	Prepositions of Cause/Reason
on	at	into	because of
in	on	onto	due to
under	in	toward	for
over	during	through	since
between	since	across	owing to
beside	until	along	thanks to
behind	before	out of	in view of
above	after	down	as a result of
below	by	up	on account of
near	within	past	for the sake of

Explanation:

1. **Prepositions of Place**: Indicate the position of something (e.g., *on the table, under the bed*).
2. **Prepositions of Time**: Refer to specific points or durations in time (e.g., *at 5 PM, during the meeting*).
3. **Prepositions of Direction/Movement**: Show movement from one place to another (e.g., *into the room, toward the exit*).
4. **Prepositions of Cause/Reason**: Indicate why something happened or the cause of an action (e.g., *because of the weather, due to traffic*).

Teacher Training Script: Introduction to Chapter 6 – Prepositions

"Today, we're diving into prepositions—the great connectors of language! Think of prepositions as ***bridges****. They connect nouns or pronouns to other parts of the sentence, helping us describe location, direction, time, and even cause. Without prepositions, sentences would be confusing and incomplete."*

"Imagine giving someone directions without prepositions: 'Meet me the park noon.' What's missing? Prepositions like at and by. They guide your reader like a GPS in a sentence, showing where, when, and why. Prepositions are always part of a prepositional phrase, which starts with a preposition and ends with a noun or pronoun, called the ***object of the preposition****. Let's explore how these connectors can transform your writing and make it clearer and more precise!"*

List of 10 Examples for Each Type of Preposition

Prepositions of Place

1. on
2. in
3. under
4. between
5. over
6. next to
7. behind
8. near
9. above
10. below

Prepositions of Time

1. after
2. before
3. during
4. at
5. since
6. by
7. until
8. within
9. throughout
10. from

Prepositions of Direction or Movement

1. to
2. into
3. onto
4. toward
5. through
6. across
7. along
8. out of
9. over
10. down

Prepositions of Cause or Reason

1. because of
2. due to
3. for
4. in spite of
5. on account of
6. thanks to
7. as a result of
8. owing to
9. out of
10. with

"The Power of Prepositions"

Prepositions are bridges, they guide with care,
Telling how, when, and where.
They connect words to form a phrase,
Helping our writing in so many ways.

Prepositions of **time** *tell when we'll meet,*
After, before, or at noon on the street.
Prepositions of **place** *show where we should go,*
In, on, or under—they help us know!

Cause *or* ***direction****, they're always on track,*
Without them, sentences they do lack.
Master these words, and you will see—
Your writing will flow with clarity!

Drama: "The Preposition Bridge Adventure"

Characters:

- **Narrator**
- **Preposition of Place**
- **Preposition of Time**
- **Preposition of Direction**
- **Preposition of Cause**
- **Object of the Preposition**
- **Prepositional Phrase Builder**
- **Clause Detective**
- **Student 1**
- **Student 2**

Narrator: *Welcome to "The Preposition Bridge Adventure!" Today, we'll explore how prepositions connect ideas in sentences. First up, let's meet Preposition of Place!*

Preposition of Place: *I show where things happen—on, in, under, between. Without me, you'd never know where anything is!*

Preposition of Time: *I tell you when things happen—before, after, during, at. Want to know when to meet? I'm your preposition!*

Preposition of Direction: *I'm all about movement! Words like into, onto, toward, and through help you describe where someone is going.*

Preposition of Cause: *I explain why things happen. Words like because of, due to, and thanks to are my favorites. Without me, cause and effect would be a mystery!*

Object of the Preposition: *I'm always at the end of the prepositional phrase. If you start with a preposition, you'll find me—table, park, rain. I give meaning to the phrase!*

Prepositional Phrase Builder: *I put it all together! A prepositional phrase starts with a preposition and ends with the object. Example: The book is on the table. I add detail to sentences!*

Clause Detective: *And don't confuse me with a clause! Clauses have both a subject and a verb. Prepositional phrases never have verbs!*

Student 1: *I never knew prepositions were so important!*

Student 2: *Me neither! But now I see how they help connect everything in a sentence.*

Narrator: *That's right! Prepositions are essential for clear communication. Use them well, and your writing will always make sense!*

---

10 Ways to Ask Questions About Prepositions Without Using the Word "Preposition"

1. *What word shows where something happens?*
2. *Which word explains when something takes place?*
3. *What word connects a noun to another word in the sentence?*
4. *How do we describe the reason for an action in this sentence?*
5. *Which word tells us how someone got from one place to another?*
6. *What word introduces a phrase that tells location?*
7. *How do we indicate time in this sentence?*
8. *What part of the sentence tells us the cause of an event?*
9. *Which word shows the direction of movement?*
10. *How do you describe where an object is located in relation to another object?*

Lesson Plan 1: "Preposition Obstacle Course" (Kinesthetic, Whole-Group Activity)

Objective:
Students will identify and use prepositions to describe positions, directions, and locations by participating in an interactive obstacle course.

Materials:

- Cones, chairs, boxes, or other classroom items to create an obstacle course
- Preposition Cards (with words like *under, over, between, beside, through*)
- A toy or small object to move through the course

Introduction (5 minutes)
Teacher script: "Today, we're going to explore prepositions! Prepositions are words that tell us where or when something happens. Words like under, over, beside, and through are prepositions. Imagine giving directions without prepositions—how would you know where to go? Let's bring prepositions to life by creating an obstacle course and using prepositions to describe the path!"

Activity (15–20 minutes)

1. **Set Up:** Create an obstacle course in the classroom with various items that students can move around, over, under, or through.
2. **Instructions:**
    - One student draws a Preposition Card (e.g., *under*).
    - The student guides a toy or small object through the course, acting out the preposition on their card (e.g., *"Move the toy under the chair"*).
    - The class guesses the preposition and where it fits in a sentence.
3. **Example Sentences:**
    - *The toy went* ***under*** *the table.*
    - *He ran* ***between*** *the chairs.*
    - *She crawled* ***through*** *the tunnel.*

Wrap-Up (5 minutes)
Teacher script: "Great job navigating our obstacle course! Remember, prepositions help us describe where things are or when things happen. Look for prepositions in your reading and try to use them in your writing!"

Assessment:
Students take turns creating their own prepositional phrases and using them to direct a partner through a smaller obstacle course. The teacher listens for correct preposition usage and observes how well students apply the concept.

Lesson Plan 2: "Prepositional Phrase Scavenger Hunt" (Small-Group, Active Learning)

Objective:
Students will identify prepositional phrases in real-world contexts and understand how they modify nouns and verbs.

Materials:

- Preposition List (on chart paper or digital display)
- Scavenger Hunt Checklist (categories for prepositional phrases that describe place, time, direction, cause, or manner)
- Clipboards and pencils

Introduction (5–10 minutes)
Teacher script: "Prepositional phrases help us add detail to our sentences. They start with a preposition and end with a noun or pronoun—the object of the preposition. Prepositional phrases answer questions like where, when, how, or why. Today, we're going on a scavenger hunt to find prepositional phrases in the classroom and beyond!"

Activity (15–20 minutes)

1. **Explain Prepositional Phrases:**
   - *"A prepositional phrase begins with a preposition and ends with a noun or pronoun. For example, in the sentence, 'The book is on the table,' the phrase 'on the table' tells us where the book is."*
2. **Scavenger Hunt Instructions:**
   - Divide students into small groups.
   - Each group searches the classroom to find objects and create sentences with prepositional phrases.
   - Groups record their phrases on the scavenger hunt checklist.

Example Sentences:

- *The clock is **above** the whiteboard.*
- *We met **after** lunch.*
- *The backpack is **beside** the desk.*

3. **Challenge:** Ask students to find at least one prepositional phrase for each category (place, time, direction, cause, manner).

Wrap-Up (5 minutes)
Teacher script: "Excellent work, explorers! You found so many prepositional phrases. Remember, these phrases give us extra information about nouns and verbs. Keep looking for prepositional phrases in your writing and see how they make your sentences more descriptive!"

Assessment:
Each group presents three sentences from their scavenger hunt, emphasizing the prepositional phrase and explaining what question it answers (where, when, how, or why). The teacher listens for accuracy and understanding.

Actionable/Observable Assessment Tool: "Preposition Toss Game"

Objective:
Assess students' understanding of prepositions and prepositional phrases through a hands-on game.

Instructions:

1. **Set Up:** Place several labeled targets around the room (e.g., *under the table, beside the chair, on the desk*).
2. **Activity:**
   - Students take turns tossing a beanbag toward a target and creating a sentence with a prepositional phrase based on where the beanbag lands.
   - **Example:** *"The beanbag landed beside the chair."*
3. **Reflection:** The class discusses how the prepositional phrases change the meaning of the sentence.

Prepositional Phrases: Modifying Nouns and Verbs

A **prepositional phrase** is a group of words that begins with a preposition and ends with a noun or pronoun (the **object of the preposition**). These phrases provide **additional details** about a noun or verb by answering questions like *which one?*, *what kind?*, *how?*, *when?*, or *where?*. They enhance writing by adding clarity and precision, helping readers visualize or understand the action more clearly.

Prepositional Phrases Modifying Nouns

When a prepositional phrase modifies a noun, it functions as an **adjective**, giving more information about that noun. It usually answers *which one?* or *what kind?*

Examples:

- The house **on the hill** is beautiful. *(The prepositional phrase "on the hill" describes "house," specifying which house.)*
- The book **with the red cover** belongs to me. *(The phrase "with the red cover" tells us more about "book.")*
- The students **in the library** are studying. *(The phrase "in the library" clarifies which students.)*

Why This Matters:
Prepositional phrases help **reduce ambiguity** and make sentences more informative. Without them, writing can feel incomplete or vague. For example:

- *The house is beautiful. → The house on the hill is beautiful.*

Prepositional Phrases Modifying Verbs

When a prepositional phrase modifies a verb, it functions as an **adverb**, providing details about **how, when, where, or why** the action happens.

Examples:

- She danced **with grace**. *(The phrase "with grace" tells how she danced.)*

- He arrived **at noon**. *(The phrase "at noon" tells when he arrived.)*
- They walked **to the park**. *(The phrase "to the park" tells where they walked.)*

Why This Matters:
Adverbial prepositional phrases help **clarify the action**, making it easier for readers to picture what is happening and when or where it is occurring.

Key Points to Remember

1. **Modifying Nouns:** Prepositional phrases act like adjectives, providing specific details about a noun.
2. **Modifying Verbs:** Prepositional phrases act like adverbs, explaining how, when, where, or why something happens.
3. **Avoid Ambiguity:** Proper placement of prepositional phrases ensures clarity in writing. Misplaced phrases can confuse readers.

Examples Showing the Difference

1. **Modifying a Noun:**
   - *The dog **under the table** is sleeping.* (Which dog? The one under the table.)
2. **Modifying a Verb:**
   - *The dog is sleeping **under the table**.* (Where is the dog sleeping? Under the table.)

By understanding how prepositional phrases modify both nouns and verbs, students can make their writing clearer, more vivid, and more accurate. This knowledge empowers them to create sentences that flow logically and convey more detailed information.

Chapter 7:

Conjunctions

The Bridge Builders of Language

Conjunctions are the glue that holds our sentences together. They connect words, phrases, and clauses, creating smoother transitions and logical flow in writing. Imagine trying to express complex ideas without conjunctions. Instead of *"I wanted to go to the store, but it started to rain,"* you would be stuck with *"I wanted to go to the store. It started to rain."* Conjunctions give us the tools to combine ideas, show relationships, and create more sophisticated sentences.

Conjunctions serve several important functions, from joining simple ideas to forming complex relationships between clauses. By mastering conjunctions, you can improve the clarity and variety of your sentences, making your writing more engaging and cohesive. There are four main types of conjunctions: **coordinating, subordinating, correlative,** and **conjunctive adverbs.** Each plays a unique role in sentence structure and meaning.

Types of Conjunctions

1. **Coordinating Conjunctions**
   Coordinating conjunctions join two equal parts of a sentence—whether they are words, phrases, or independent clauses. The acronym **FANBOYS** can help you remember them:
   - **F**or – shows reason (*I stayed home, for I was sick.*)
   - **A**nd – adds information (*She likes apples and oranges.*)
   - **N**or – joins negative alternatives (*He didn't call, nor did he write.*)
   - **B**ut – shows contrast (*I wanted to play, but it rained.*)
   - **O**r – presents options (*Do you want pizza or pasta?*)
   - **Y**et – introduces a surprising result (*She was tired, yet she kept running.*)
   - **S**o – shows cause and effect (*He studied hard, so he passed the test.*)

Example Sentence: *I wanted to go to the park, but it started raining.*

2. **Subordinating Conjunctions**
   Subordinating conjunctions connect an independent clause with a dependent (subordinate) clause, showing the relationship between the two. They answer questions like **why, when, where,** or **how** something happened.
   Examples: *because, although, since, while, after, if, unless*
   Example Sentence: *I stayed inside because it was raining.*

Subordinating conjunctions help create **complex sentences**, where one idea depends on another for meaning.
Example: *If you study hard, you will succeed.*

3. **Correlative Conjunctions**
   Correlative conjunctions work in pairs to link equal parts of a sentence.
   Examples: *either...or, neither...nor, both...and, not only...but also*
   Example Sentence: *You can either stay home or come with us.*

These conjunctions ensure balance and parallelism in a sentence.
Example: *She is not only smart but also kind.*

4. **Conjunctive Adverbs**
   Conjunctive adverbs connect two independent clauses while showing a relationship such as contrast, cause and effect, or addition. They often require a semicolon before them and a comma after.
   Examples: *however, therefore, moreover, nevertheless, consequently*
   Example Sentence: *I wanted to join the team; however, I missed the tryouts.*

Types of Sentences Conjunctions Help Create

1. **Simple Sentences:** Contain one independent clause.
   Example: *I like pizza.*
2. **Compound Sentences:** Contain two independent clauses joined by a coordinating conjunction.
   Example: *I like pizza, but I prefer pasta.*
3. **Complex Sentences:** Contain one independent clause and one or more dependent clauses.
   Example: *I stayed inside because it was raining.*
4. **Compound-Complex Sentences:** Contain at least two independent clauses and one or more dependent clauses.
   Example: *I stayed inside because it was raining, but I still had fun.*

Why Conjunctions Matter

Conjunctions are essential for writing and speaking with clarity and variety. They help us avoid choppy, disconnected sentences.

Conjunction Example Sentences

1. **Coordinating Conjunctions (For, And, Nor, But, Or, Yet, So)**
    1. I wanted to go to the park, **but** it started raining.
    2. She loves reading **and** writing stories.
    3. You can have pasta **or** pizza for dinner.
    4. He was tired, **so** he went to bed early.
    5. I called him twice, **yet** he didn't answer.

2. **Subordinating Conjunctions (Because, Since, If, When, Although)**
    6. We stayed inside **because** it was snowing.
    7. **Since** you've finished your homework, you can watch TV.
    8. **If** you study hard, you will pass the test.
    9. **Although** she was sick, she went to school.
    10. He was late for the meeting **because** he missed the bus.

3. **Correlative Conjunctions (Either...or, Neither...nor, Both...and, Not only...but also)**
    11. **Either** you finish your project now, **or** you'll have to stay late.
    12. **Neither** Sarah **nor** Emily could solve the riddle.
    13. **Both** the teacher **and** the students enjoyed the activity.
    14. He is **not only** smart **but also** kind.
    15. You can **either** walk to school **or** take the bus.

4. **Conjunctive Adverbs (However, Therefore, Consequently, Furthermore, Moreover)**
    16. I was tired; **however**, I continued working on my presentation.
    17. She didn't study; **consequently**, she failed the exam.
    18. The weather is cold; **therefore**, you should wear a coat.
    19. He was late; **moreover**, he forgot to bring his homework.
    20. She loves painting; **furthermore**, she is a talented musician.

Teacher Training Script: Introduction to Chapter 7 – Conjunctions

"Today, we're talking about conjunctions—the bridge builders of language. Think of a conjunction like a ***suspension bridge*** *connecting two sides of a river. Without it, we'd have two separate pieces with no flow between them. Conjunctions help combine words, phrases, and ideas, creating smooth, logical connections in our writing."*

"Imagine trying to describe your day without conjunctions: 'I woke up. I ate breakfast. I went to school.' It sounds robotic! With conjunctions, your sentence becomes much more natural: 'I woke up, ate breakfast, and went to school.' Conjunctions help us add variety and complexity to our sentences, turning simple ideas into detailed and engaging thoughts!"

List of 10 Examples for Each Type of Conjunction

Coordinating Conjunctions (FANBOYS)

1. for
2. and
3. nor
4. but
5. or
6. yet
7. so
8. plus
9. even
10. still

Subordinating Conjunctions

1. because
2. although
3. since
4. while
5. after
6. if
7. unless
8. before
9. when
10. whenever

Correlative Conjunctions

1. either...or
2. neither...nor
3. both...and
4. not only...but also
5. whether...or
6. as...as
7. such...that
8. rather...than
9. no sooner...than
10. just as...so

Conjunctive Adverbs

1. however
2. therefore
3. moreover
4. nevertheless
5. consequently
6. otherwise
7. meanwhile
8. furthermore
9. instead
10. likewise

Common Subordinating Conjunctions by Category

Category	Subordinating Conjunctions
1. Cause and Effect	because, since, as, so that, in order that
2. Time	after, before, when, while, until, as soon as, once
3. Opposition/Contrast	although, though, even though, whereas, while
4. Condition	if, unless, provided that, as long as, in case
5. Comparison	than, as...as, just as

Common Correlative Conjunctions and Their Functions

Correlative Conjunction Pair	Function/Usage	Example Sentence
either...or	Presents two options or alternatives	We can either go to the park or stay home.
neither...nor	Denotes two negative alternatives	Neither the teacher nor the students were happy.
not only...but also	Emphasizes an additional point	She is not only smart but also kind.
both...and	Combines two positive ideas	Both the movie and the book were amazing.
whether...or	Indicates a choice between two alternatives	I don't know whether he'll come or stay home.
as...as	Makes a comparison for equality	She is as fast as her brother.
just as...so	Draws a relationship between two similar actions	Just as I expected, so did the results match my theory.
the more...the more	Expresses a cause-effect relationship	The more you practice, the better you get.
rather...than	Indicates a preference	I'd rather walk than take the bus.
such...that	Shows a degree or consequence	He was such a good speaker that everyone clapped.

Why Correlative Conjunctions Matter

Correlative conjunctions help maintain parallel structure in sentences, ensuring clarity and balance. Incorrect use or lack of parallelism can make sentences awkward and confusing. Learning to use them effectively improves both writing and comprehension.

"The Bridge Builders"

Conjunctions are bridges, they help us combine,
Words and ideas, making writing divine.
Both small and large, they bring thoughts together,
Not only joining sentences **but also** making them better.

Coordinating ones—**and**, **but**, **so** true,
They link equal parts to give meaning to you.
Subordinating ones show cause and time,
Whether it's reason **or** sequence in rhyme.

Correlative pairs are quite the team,
Either...or, they make sentences gleam.
Neither clumsy phrasing **nor** broken flow,
Stops clear communication—watch your skills grow!

Conjunctive adverbs connect with grace,
Just as expected, **so** does meaning embrace.
Master conjunctions, and soon you will see,
Your writing will sparkle naturally!

Drama: "Conjunction Junction Live!"

Characters:

- **Narrator**
- **Coordinating Conjunction Coach**
- **Subordinating Conjunction Scientist**
- **Correlative Conjunction Duo**
- **Conjunctive Adverb Explorer**
- **Simple Sentence Builder**
- **Compound Sentence Creator**
- **Complex Sentence Crafter**
- **Student 1**
- **Student 2**

Narrator: *Welcome to Conjunction Junction Live! Today, we're learning how conjunctions connect ideas and make our writing flow smoothly. First up, let's meet Coordinating Conjunction Coach!*

Coordinating Conjunction Coach: *I'm here to help you combine equal parts! Words like and, but, or, and so are my favorites. Want to join two independent clauses? I'm your coach!*

Subordinating Conjunction Scientist: *I connect independent and dependent clauses, showing cause, time, and contrast—because, since, while, and after. I create complex sentences that explain why things happen!*

Correlative Conjunction Duo: *(speaking in unison) We work in pairs—either...or, neither...nor, both...and. We keep sentences balanced and parallel!*

Conjunctive Adverb Explorer: *I connect independent clauses with style—however, therefore, meanwhile. I add a semicolon before me and a comma after to guide your reader through the sentence.*

Simple Sentence Builder: *I'm a simple sentence—just one independent clause. I'm clear and straightforward!*

Compound Sentence Creator: *Add a coordinating conjunction, and I become a compound sentence! I link two independent clauses with and, but, or so.*

Complex Sentence Crafter: *When you add a subordinating conjunction like because or after, I become a complex sentence with one independent clause and one dependent clause.*

Student 1: *I didn't realize conjunctions did so much!*

Student 2: *Me neither! But now I see how they connect everything together.*

Narrator: *That's right! Conjunctions are the glue that holds our sentences together. Use them wisely, and your writing will flow beautifully!*

---

10 Ways to Ask Questions About Conjunctions Without Using the Word "Conjunction"

1. *What word connects these two parts of the sentence?*
2. *How do we join two independent clauses?*
3. *Which word shows the relationship between these ideas?*
4. *What word helps create a compound sentence?*
5. *How do we combine these two thoughts into one sentence?*
6. *Which word shows cause and effect in this sentence?*
7. *What word introduces the dependent clause?*
8. *How can we connect these contrasting ideas?*
9. *Which word shows a time relationship between the clauses?*
10. *What word balances these two options in the sentence?*

Lesson Plan 1: "Conjunction Connectors" (Whole-Group, Kinesthetic Activity)

Objective:
Students will identify coordinating, subordinating, and correlative conjunctions by creating sentences using physical movement to connect sentence parts.

Materials:

- Sentence strips with independent and dependent clauses written on them
- Large signs labeled with the types of conjunctions (Coordinating, Subordinating, Correlative)
- Conjunction Cards (each card with one conjunction: *and, but, because, although, either...or, neither...nor*, etc.)

Introduction (5–10 minutes)
Teacher script: "Today, we're learning about conjunctions—the words that help us connect ideas and make our writing flow. Think of conjunctions as bridges that join words, phrases, or sentences. Without conjunctions, sentences would sound choppy and disconnected. Let's discover how conjunctions help us create smoother sentences!"

Activity (15–20 minutes)

1. **Explain Types of Conjunctions:**
   - **Coordinating Conjunctions (FANBOYS):** *"For, and, nor, but, or, yet, so—these join equal parts like two independent clauses."*
   - **Subordinating Conjunctions:** *"Words like because, although, since, and while introduce dependent clauses and connect them to independent clauses."*
   - **Correlative Conjunctions:** *"These come in pairs—either...or, neither...nor, both...and—to link ideas with balance."*
2. **Conjunction Connectors Game:**
   - Divide the class into small groups.
   - Place sentence strips around the room—some are independent clauses, others are dependent clauses.
   - Students draw a Conjunction Card and find two sentence strips that can be connected with the conjunction on their card.
   - Once they've connected the sentence strips, they read the new sentence aloud and explain what kind of conjunction they used.

Example Sentences:

- *I wanted to go to the park, but it started raining.* (Coordinating)
- *We stayed inside because it was raining.* (Subordinating)
- *Either you finish your homework, or you can't go outside.* (Correlative)

Wrap-Up (5 minutes)
Teacher script: "Great work connecting ideas! Remember, conjunctions are powerful tools that help make your writing clear and smooth. Keep an eye out for conjunctions in your reading, and practice using them in your writing!"

Assessment:
Students create and perform a short skit using at least three types of conjunctions. The teacher listens for correct usage and observes how students connect ideas effectively.

Lesson Plan 2: "Conjunction Showdown" (Small-Group, Competitive Game)

Objective:
Students will practice identifying conjunctions and using them to combine sentences correctly.

Materials:

- Whiteboard or digital display for sentence prompts
- Buzzer or bell for each team
- Scoreboard

Introduction (5 minutes)
Teacher script: "Who's ready for a Conjunction Showdown? Today, we're turning conjunctions into a game! You'll compete to see who can identify conjunctions and combine sentences the fastest and most accurately. Let's get started!"

Activity (15–20 minutes)

1. **Game Rules:**
    - Divide the class into small teams.
    - The teacher displays or reads two sentences aloud.
    - Teams buzz in to answer how to combine the sentences using a conjunction. They must explain what type of conjunction they used.
2. **Example Sentence Prompts:**
    - *I like pizza. I don't like mushrooms.* (Answer: *I like pizza, but I don't like mushrooms.*)
    - *We couldn't go outside. It was raining.* (Answer: *We couldn't go outside because it was raining.*)
    - *She can have ice cream. She can have cake.* (Answer: *She can have either ice cream or cake.*)
3. **Scoring:**
    - Teams earn points for correct answers and explanations.
    - Bonus points are awarded for using more advanced conjunctions or creating compound-complex sentences.

Wrap-Up (5 minutes)
Teacher script: "That was an intense showdown! Remember, conjunctions are key to combining ideas and making your writing more sophisticated. Keep practicing, and you'll be a conjunction master in no time!"

Assessment:
Each team writes a short story using at least five conjunctions (one from each category). They

present their story to the class, and the teacher checks for correct conjunction usage and sentence variety.

Actionable/Observable Assessment Tool: "Conjunctions in Context"

Objective:
Assess students' ability to use conjunctions naturally in conversation and writing.

Instructions:

1. **Conversation Challenge:** Students pair up and hold a 3-minute conversation on a given topic (e.g., their favorite hobby or weekend plans). They must use at least five different conjunctions during the conversation.
2. **Reflection:** After the conversation, each pair shares one sentence they used with a conjunction and explains its purpose.
3. **Scoring:** The teacher observes and gives feedback on conjunction usage and how well students connected ideas.

Chapter 8:

Interjections

The Words that Add Emotion and Energy

Interjections are the bursts of emotion in language—the exclamation points of our everyday speech and writing. They express sudden feelings such as **surprise, excitement, anger, happiness, sadness,** or **frustration.** Unlike other parts of speech that work to connect ideas or describe actions, interjections stand alone, adding personality and emotional tone to our sentences.

Imagine a story without interjections. Instead of *"Wow! That was amazing!"* you would be left with *"That was amazing,"* which sounds flat and emotionless. Interjections bring sentences to life, letting readers hear the excitement, joy, shock, or disappointment in your voice.

Definition and Function of Interjections

An **interjection** is a word or short phrase that expresses a strong emotion or reaction. It is often placed at the beginning of a sentence and separated by punctuation such as an **exclamation mark (!)**, **comma (,)**, or even a **period (.)**, depending on the intensity of the emotion. Interjections can stand alone or be part of a larger sentence, but they don't have a grammatical connection to the rest of the sentence.

Examples:

- **Excitement or Joy:** *Hooray! We won the game!*
- **Surprise:** *Wow! That fireworks display was incredible!*
- **Disappointment or Sadness:** *Oh no! I forgot my homework.*
- **Annoyance or Frustration:** *Ugh, this traffic is terrible!*
- **Pain:** *Ouch! That really hurt!*

Punctuation and Intensity

The punctuation that follows an interjection determines its intensity.

1. **Exclamation Mark (!)** – Used for strong emotions such as excitement, shock, or anger.
   Example: *Yay! We're finally on vacation!*
2. **Comma (,)** – Used for mild or casual emotions.
   Example: *Well, I guess we'll try again tomorrow.*
3. **Period (.)** – Used when the interjection expresses a calmer or reflective tone.
   Example: *Oh. I didn't realize that was the plan.*

Different Expressions of Emotion

Interjections allow us to communicate a wide range of emotions:

- **Happiness:** *Yippee! That's great news.*
- **Disbelief:** *Seriously? You did that all by yourself?*
- **Fear:** *Ahh! There's a spider!*
- **Relief:** *Phew! I thought I lost my phone.*

Why Interjections Matter

Interjections add flavor and authenticity to both speech and writing. They make dialogue more realistic and allow writers to convey emotional nuances quickly and effectively. When used sparingly, they enhance writing by giving it a more personal, expressive tone. However, too many interjections can overwhelm a sentence, so it's important to use them thoughtfully.

In this chapter, we'll explore the many ways interjections can enhance your writing and help you express feelings clearly. Prepare to have fun discovering the most expressive part of speech—**interjections!**

Teacher Training Script: Introduction to Chapter 8 – Interjections

"Today, we're diving into one of the most exciting parts of speech—interjections! If the sentence were a movie, interjections would be the sound effects and the emotional music. They don't just describe; they ***express****! Imagine saying, 'We won the game.' Now add an interjection: Hooray! We won the game! It's instantly more exciting. Interjections bring feelings to life and give personality to our writing."*

"Interjections are like fireworks in language. They can show joy, surprise, anger, frustration, or relief. Think of them as the emotional exclamation marks that make your words burst with energy. Let's explore how these little bursts of emotion can make your writing and speech more colorful and fun!"

List of 10 Examples for Each Type of Interjection

Expressions of Joy	Expressions of Surprise	Expressions of Sadness	Expressions of Frustration/Anger
Yay!	Oh!	Oh no!	Ugh!
Hooray!	Wow!	Alas!	Darn!
Woohoo!	What?!	Sigh...	Grr!
Yippee!	Ah!	Boohoo!	Argh!
Bravo!	Whoa!	Sob!	Shoot!
Whee!	Goodness!	Oh dear!	Rats!
Awesome!	Eek!	Oh well...	Blast!
Sweet!	Oops!	Sniff...	Bah!
Fantastic!	Gasp!	How sad!	For heaven's sake!
Yes!	My goodness!	Poor me...	Humph!

Explanation of Interjections:

- **Expressions of Joy**: Show happiness, excitement, or celebration (e.g., *Yay! We won!*).
- **Expressions of Surprise**: Show amazement, shock, or disbelief (e.g., *Wow! That's incredible!*).
- **Expressions of Sadness**: Convey sorrow or disappointment (e.g., *Oh no! I missed the bus!*).
- **Expressions of Frustration/Anger**: Indicate annoyance, irritation, or anger (e.g., *Ugh! This is so frustrating!*).

"Interjection Expressions"

Interjections shout, they cheer, they cry,
They bring emotion, they amplify!
From Wow! to Oops! and Yay!, you'll see,
They add excitement naturally.

Joyful ones like Yippee!, Hooray!
Can brighten up your writing day.
When shocked or scared, try Ah! or Whoa!,
Interjections help emotions show.

Use them wisely, not too much,
A little burst, a perfect touch.
With Oh no!, Wow!, or Yikes! in play,
Your words will come to life today!

Drama: "Interjection City"

Characters:

- **Narrator**
- **Joyful Interjection**
- **Surprised Interjection**
- **Sad Interjection**
- **Frustrated Interjection**
- **Student 1**
- **Student 2**
- **Teacher**
- **Dialogue Director**
- **Emphasis Editor**

Narrator: *Welcome to Interjection City! Here, words come alive with emotion and energy. Today, we'll learn how interjections bring feelings to sentences. Let's start with Joyful Interjection!*

Joyful Interjection: *Woohoo! I'm all about excitement and happiness! Use me when you want to celebrate—Yay!, Hooray!, Fantastic! I'll make your writing sparkle with joy!*

Surprised Interjection: *Whoa! Did something unexpected happen? That's my specialty! Words like Wow! and Oh! help express surprise. Without me, your writing would be flat!*

Sad Interjection: *(sighs) Sometimes, things go wrong. When they do, I'm here—Oh no!, Aw., Alas. I bring the right tone for disappointment and sadness.*

Frustrated Interjection: *(frowning) Ugh! Frustration is part of life. When you need to vent, use Ugh!, Argh!, or Grr!. I let readers know exactly how you feel.*

Student 1: *I didn't know interjections did so much!*

Student 2: *Me neither! But now I understand how they can add emotion to my writing.*

Teacher: *Interjections are powerful, but remember to use them sparingly. They bring energy, but too many can overwhelm your sentence. Use them when you want to add emotional impact!*

Dialogue Director: *Let's practice adding interjections to dialogue. What sounds more exciting—We won the game or Yay! We won the game!?*

Emphasis Editor: *Exactly! Interjections make writing more engaging. Use them to show joy, surprise, or frustration, and your readers will feel the emotion with you!*

10 Ways to Ask Questions About Interjections Without Using the Word "Interjection"

1. *What word shows sudden emotion in this sentence?*
2. *Which word expresses excitement or joy?*
3. *How does the writer show surprise in this sentence?*
4. *What word is used to show frustration?*
5. *Which word adds emotional emphasis to the sentence?*
6. *How do we know the speaker is happy or excited?*
7. *What word expresses disappointment?*
8. *Which word indicates relief?*
9. *How does the sentence show strong emotion?*
10. *What word stands alone and conveys an immediate reaction?*

Lesson Plan 1: "Emotion Explosion with Interjections" (Whole-Group, Kinesthetic Activity)

Objective:
Students will identify and use interjections to express emotion and understand how they enhance spoken and written language.

Materials:

- Emotion Cards (e.g., Surprise, Happiness, Anger, Disappointment, Excitement)
- Interjection Cards (e.g., Wow!, Oops!, Yay!, Ugh!, Oh no!)
- Chart labeled with different emotions

Introduction (5 minutes)
Teacher script: "Today, we're learning about interjections! Interjections are short words or phrases that express strong emotions like excitement, surprise, or frustration. Imagine watching a soccer game and yelling, 'Yes! We scored!' That's an interjection—it shows your feelings in the moment. Let's explore how interjections make our language more exciting and expressive!"

Activity (15–20 minutes)

1. **Explain Interjections:**
   "Interjections stand alone or are at the beginning of a sentence. They're followed by an exclamation mark (!) for strong emotions or a comma (,) for mild emotions."
   - Example: *Wow! That was amazing.*
   - Example: *Well, I guess it's time to go.*
2. **Emotion Explosion Game:**
   - Draw an Emotion Card (e.g., Surprise).
   - Students brainstorm interjections that match the emotion and act them out.
   - Choose a few Interjection Cards and have students use them in sentences.
3. **Practice:**
   - Ask volunteers to act out a scene using the interjections they brainstormed. For example, pretend to spill water and say, *"Oops! That was clumsy of me!"*

Sample Interjections:

- **Happiness/Excitement:** Yay! Hooray!
- **Surprise:** Wow! Oh!
- **Disappointment:** Oh no! Alas!
- **Frustration:** Ugh! Grr!
- **Pain:** Ouch! Ow!

Wrap-Up (5 minutes)

Teacher script: "Great job expressing emotions with interjections! Remember, interjections help our writing and speech feel real and full of life. Keep using them when you want to show how you feel!"

Assessment:

Students form pairs and create a short skit using at least three different interjections. They perform their skit for the class, and the teacher listens for correct usage and expression.

Lesson Plan 2: "Interjection Charades" (Small-Group, Competitive Game)

Objective:
Students will demonstrate their understanding of interjections by acting them out and identifying the emotions they convey.

Materials:

- Interjection Charades Cards (each card has an interjection, such as Yay!, Ugh!, or Ouch!)
- Timer

Introduction (5 minutes)
Teacher script: "It's time for Interjection Charades! Interjections are powerful because they show how we feel. Today, we'll act out different interjections without speaking, and your classmates will guess which interjection you're using. Get ready to have some fun and show your acting skills!"

Activity (15–20 minutes)

1. **Game Instructions:**
   - Divide the class into small groups.
   - One student from each group draws an Interjection Charades Card and acts out the emotion without speaking.
   - The rest of the group guesses the interjection.
   - Once the interjection is guessed correctly, the group uses it in a sentence.
2. **Scoring:**
   - Teams earn points for correctly guessing the interjection and using it in a sentence.

Sample Charades Cards:

- Yay! (Excitement)
- Ugh! (Frustration)
- Oops! (Accident)
- Wow! (Surprise)
- Ouch! (Pain)

Wrap-Up (5 minutes)
Teacher script: "Fantastic acting! You all did a great job showing how interjections express emotion. Remember, interjections help bring life to your writing and speech. Keep practicing!"

Assessment:
Each student creates and delivers a one-minute story that includes at least five different interjections. The teacher observes for correct usage and emotional expression.

Actionable/Observable Assessment Tool: "Interjection Story Challenge"

Objective:
Assess students' ability to use interjections in context by creating a short story with a range of emotions.

Instructions:

1. **Story Creation:** Students work in small groups to write a short story incorporating at least five interjections.
2. **Performance:** Each group reads their story aloud, emphasizing the interjections.
3. **Reflection:** The class discusses how the interjections added emotion and personality to the story.

Sentences with Interjection Expressions

Expressions of Joy (10 Sentences)

1. *Yay! We finally won the championship!*
2. *Hooray! It's my birthday today!*
3. *Woohoo! Summer vacation starts tomorrow!*
4. *Yippee! I got an A on my math test!*
5. *Bravo! Your performance was amazing!*
6. *Whee! This roller coaster is so much fun!*
7. *Awesome! I just found $20 on the sidewalk!*
8. *Sweet! We're having pizza for dinner!*
9. *Yes! My favorite show is on tonight!*
10. *Fantastic! I got the job I was hoping for!*

Expressions of Surprise (10 Sentences)

11. *Wow! That painting is breathtaking!*
12. *Oh! I didn't see you standing there!*
13. *What?! You already finished the project?*
14. *Ah! You scared me!*
15. *Whoa! That car almost hit the curb!*
16. *Goodness! That was a close call!*
17. *Eek! There's a spider on the wall!*
18. *Oops! I spilled coffee on my notebook!*
19. *Gasp! I forgot my keys at home!*
20. *My goodness! You look so different with short hair!*

Expressions of Sadness (10 Sentences)

21. *Oh no! I missed the last bus!*
22. *Alas! My favorite store is closing down.*
23. *Sigh... It's been such a tough week.*
24. *Boohoo! I lost my lucky charm.*
25. *Oh dear! I failed my driving test.*
26. *Sob! I can't believe we have to say goodbye.*
27. *Oh well... I guess it wasn't meant to be.*
28. *Sniff... I really miss my old neighborhood.*
29. *How sad! They canceled the concert.*
30. *Poor me... I have to stay home while everyone else goes to the party.*

Expressions of Frustration/Anger (10 Sentences)

31. *Ugh! This traffic is unbearable!*
32. *Darn! I forgot to bring my homework!*
33. *Grr! My phone froze again!*
34. *Argh! I can't figure out this math problem!*
35. *Shoot! I spilled coffee on my shirt!*
36. *Rats! I just missed the train by a second!*
37. *Blast! My laptop battery died in the middle of my work!*
38. *Bah! This weather is ruining our plans!*
39. *For heaven's sake! Stop arguing, please!*
40. *Humph! I'm not talking to you right now.*

Chapter 9:

Sentence Construction

Building Strong, Clear, and Complete Thoughts

Sentence construction is one of the most important skills in writing. The way we put words together in a sentence affects the clarity, flow, and meaning of our ideas. Well-constructed sentences help us communicate effectively, while poorly constructed ones can confuse the reader. In this chapter, we'll explore how to build sentences from the ground up, focusing on **subjects and predicates, modifiers like adjectives and adverbs**, and how to write **simple, compound, complex, and compound-complex sentences.** We'll also discuss common sentence errors like **run-on sentences, fragments,** and **comma splices**, and how to avoid them.

The Foundation of a Sentence: Subjects and Predicates

Every sentence must have two essential parts: a **subject** and a **predicate**.

- The **subject** tells who or what the sentence is about.
- The **predicate** tells what the subject is doing or what state it is in. The predicate always contains a verb.

Examples:

- *The cat (subject) sleeps on the couch (predicate).*
- *My brother (subject) loves pizza (predicate).*

Without both a subject and a predicate, a group of words is not a complete sentence—it's a **fragment**.

Using Modifiers Correctly

Modifiers like **adjectives** and **adverbs** enhance writing by adding details and description. However, they must be used carefully to avoid confusion or awkward sentence structure.

- **Adjectives** modify nouns and pronouns, answering questions like *what kind? which one? how many?*
  Example: *The beautiful flower bloomed.* (Adjective *beautiful* modifies *flower*.)
- **Adverbs** modify verbs, adjectives, or other adverbs, answering questions like *how? when? where? to what extent?*
  Example: *She ran quickly.* (Adverb *quickly* modifies *ran*.)

Incorrectly placed modifiers can lead to **misplaced modifiers**, which confuse the meaning of the sentence.
Example: *She only eats fruit.* (Does she eat only fruit, or does she only eat?)

Types of Sentences

1. **Simple Sentences**
   A simple sentence contains one independent clause with a subject and predicate.
   Example: *I love to read.*
2. **Compound Sentences**
   A compound sentence contains two or more independent clauses joined by a **coordinating conjunction** (FANBOYS: for, and, nor, but, or, yet, so).
   Example: *I love to read, and I enjoy writing.*
3. **Complex Sentences**
   A complex sentence contains one independent clause and one or more dependent clauses connected by a **subordinating conjunction** (because, although, since, while, after, if, unless).
   Example: *I stayed home because it was raining.*
4. **Compound-Complex Sentences**
   A compound-complex sentence contains at least two independent clauses and one or more dependent clauses.
   Example: *I stayed home because it was raining, but I still had fun.*

Common Sentence Errors

1. **Fragments**
   A fragment is an incomplete sentence that lacks a subject, a predicate, or both.
   Example: *After the movie.* (This is a fragment. What happened after the movie?)
   Corrected: *After the movie, we went to dinner. (simple)*
2. **Run-On Sentences**
   A run-on sentence occurs when two independent clauses are joined without proper punctuation or conjunctions.
   Example: *I went to the park it was sunny.*
   Corrected: *I went to the park because it was sunny. (complex)*
3. **Comma Splices**
   A comma splice occurs when two independent clauses are joined by only a comma.
   Example: *I love ice cream, it's my favorite dessert.*
   Corrected: *I love ice cream, so it's my favorite dessert. (compound)*

Why Sentence Construction Matters

Mastering sentence construction is essential for effective communication. By learning how to build sentences with correct structure and variety, you can create writing that is both clear and engaging. In this chapter, we'll break down each sentence type, practice identifying and fixing common errors, and learn how to combine ideas smoothly and logically. Get ready to construct powerful sentences that will strengthen your writing!

Phrases and Clauses

Do You Know the Difference?

In every sentence, words work together in groups to convey meaning. These groups of words are either **phrases** or **clauses**, and understanding the difference between them is essential for constructing clear, grammatically correct sentences. The distinction between phrases and clauses lies in whether they contain both a **subject (noun)** and a **predicate (verb).**

A **clause** is a group of words that **contains both a noun and a verb**. It can stand alone as a complete thought or function as part of a longer sentence. In other words, every **complete sentence is a clause**.

Example of a Clause: *The dog barked.* (Contains both a noun *dog* and a verb *barked*)

A **phrase**, on the other hand, is a group of words that works together but **does not contain both a noun and a verb**. Phrases add detail or modify parts of a sentence, but they cannot stand alone as a complete thought.
Example of a Phrase: *on the table* (This phrase contains a noun *table*, but no verb.)

Types of Phrases

1. **Noun Phrases**
   A noun phrase is a group of words that functions as a noun in a sentence. It can include a noun and its modifiers (adjectives or determiners).
   Example: *The large, brown dog barked loudly.*
   (*The large, brown dog* is the noun phrase.)

2. **Verb Phrases**
   A verb phrase consists of a main verb and one or more helping verbs. It shows the action or state of being in the sentence.
   Example: *She has been running for an hour.*
   (*has been running* is the verb phrase.)

3. **Adverbial Phrases**
   An adverbial phrase acts as an adverb, modifying a verb, adjective, or another adverb. It often tells **how, when, where,** or **why** something happens.
   Example: *He spoke with great enthusiasm.*
   (*with great enthusiasm* modifies *spoke* and explains how he spoke.)

4. **Prepositional Phrases**
   A prepositional phrase starts with a preposition and ends with a noun or pronoun (the object of the preposition). These phrases add details about **place, time, cause,** or **manner.**
   Example: *The book is on the table.*
   (*on the table* is a prepositional phrase that tells where the book is.)

The Influence of Prepositional Phrases on Subject-Verb Agreement

Prepositional phrases can sometimes confuse subject-verb agreement because they often appear between the subject and the verb. To avoid mistakes, always focus on the main subject and ignore the noun in the prepositional phrase.

Examples:

- **Correct:** *The group of students is excited.* (The subject *group* is singular, so the verb must be *is*, even though *students* is plural.)
- **Incorrect:** *The group of students are excited.*

By recognizing prepositional phrases, you can ensure that your subject-verb agreement remains accurate and your sentences are grammatically correct.

Why Understanding Phrases and Clauses Matters

Phrases and clauses are the foundation of sentence construction. Knowing how they work will help you build more complex and engaging sentences. It will also prevent common errors like sentence fragments and incorrect subject-verb agreement. In this chapter, we'll explore how to identify different types of phrases and clauses and how to use them effectively in your writing. Get ready to dive deep into the heart of sentence structure!

Teacher Training Script: Introduction to Sentence Construction

"Today, we're learning about sentence construction—the building blocks of communication. Think of a sentence like a house. Every house needs a solid foundation, just like every sentence needs a subject and predicate. The subject is the main character of the sentence, and the predicate tells us what the subject is doing. If the subject is the walls, the predicate is the roof that holds everything together."

"Modifiers like adjectives and adverbs are the decorations—the paint, furniture, and finishing touches that add detail and personality. But just like in decorating, you have to place them carefully, or they can cause confusion. Imagine putting the couch in the middle of the hallway! By learning how to build simple, compound, complex, and compound-complex sentences, you'll create strong, clear writing that communicates exactly what you mean."

"We'll also learn to avoid sentence errors like fragments, run-ons, and comma splices. Think of those as cracks in the walls or missing doors in your sentence house. Fixing them ensures your sentence is complete and ready for readers to understand."

Writers use **complex sentences** for several important reasons. These sentences add depth, variety, and clarity to writing, making it more engaging and sophisticated. Unlike simple or compound sentences, complex sentences combine an independent clause with one or more dependent clauses, allowing writers to express more detailed relationships between ideas.

Reasons Writers Use Complex Sentences:

1. To Show Cause and Effect

Complex sentences help explain why something happens or the consequences of an action. The dependent clause provides the reason or outcome, offering readers a deeper understanding of the event.

- Example: *Because it was raining, the game was postponed.*

2. To Add Details and Elaborate

By using complex sentences, writers can expand on a main idea without starting a new sentence. This keeps the writing concise while adding richness and context.

- Example: *The student who studied all night aced the exam.*

3. To Emphasize Time Relationships

Complex sentences clarify when things happen in relation to each other by using time-related subordinating conjunctions like *after, before, while, since,* and *until.*

- Example: *After the movie ended, we went out for ice cream.*

4. To Show Contrast

Writers use complex sentences to highlight contrasts between ideas. Words like *although* and *even though* help create tension or present opposing ideas in one sentence.

- Example: *Although she was tired, she stayed up to finish her project.*

5. To Create Conditional Statements

Complex sentences allow writers to express conditions, possibilities, or hypothetical situations using conjunctions like *if, unless,* and *as long as.*

- Example: *If you study hard, you will pass the test.*

6. To Improve Sentence Variety

Too many simple sentences can make writing sound choppy and monotonous. Complex sentences add variety and improve the flow of ideas, making the text more interesting to read.

- Example: *The teacher handed out the assignment while the students prepared their materials.*

7. To Clarify Relationships Between Ideas

Complex sentences help connect related ideas in a logical way, making the writing clearer. Dependent clauses often explain or expand on the independent clause, reducing ambiguity.

- Example: *Since I had no other plans, I decided to join them for dinner.*

8. To Reflect Sophistication and Formality

In academic writing or professional contexts, complex sentences convey a more polished, intellectual tone. They show a command of language and help express more abstract or nuanced ideas.

- Example: *While the data supports the hypothesis, further research is needed to confirm the results.*

In summary, writers use complex sentences to enhance their writing by showing relationships between ideas, adding detail, and improving sentence variety. Mastering complex sentence structure helps writers communicate their thoughts more effectively and keeps readers engaged.

"Building Sentences"

A sentence begins with a ***subject*** *so clear,*
Telling who or what is standing here.
Next comes the ***predicate****, the action or state,*
Together they build something strong and great.

Simple *ones are short and sweet,*
One clause complete, nothing to beat.
Compound *adds more with and, but, or so,*
Joining ideas to help them flow.

Complex *sentences tell cause and time,*
Because, while, since—they make it shine!
Compound-complex*? Don't be misled,*
It's just two clauses that have been said!

Avoid the cracks—fragments and splices,
Strong sentences are your best devices!

Drama: "Sentence Builders Unite!"

Characters:

- **Narrator**
- **Simple Sentence**
- **Compound Sentence**
- **Complex Sentence**
- **Compound-Complex Sentence**
- **Subject Sam**
- **Predicate Patty**
- **Modifier Mike**
- **Fragment Frankie**
- **Run-On Randy**
- **Comma Splice Connie**

Narrator: *Welcome to Sentence Builders Unite! Today, we'll learn how sentences are built and how to avoid common errors. Let's start with Subject Sam and Predicate Patty!*

Subject Sam: *I'm the subject! Every sentence starts with me. I'm the who or what the sentence is about—*cat, tree, car, teacher!*

Predicate Patty: *And I'm the predicate! I tell you what the subject is doing. Without me, Sam would just be standing there doing nothing!*

Modifier Mike: *I'm here to add details! I make sentences more interesting by modifying nouns and verbs—blue car, quickly running, or soft pillow. But place me wrong, and I'll confuse everything!*

Simple Sentence: *I'm a simple sentence—just one subject and one predicate. I keep things clear and easy to understand!*

Compound Sentence: *I'm a compound sentence! I join two simple sentences with and, but, or so. Example: I like pizza, and I love pasta. Simple and tasty!*

Complex Sentence: *I'm a complex sentence! I use words like because, since, or although to connect ideas. Example: I stayed home because it was raining. I add depth and explanation.*

Compound-Complex Sentence: *I'm the big boss! I combine everything—a compound sentence and a dependent clause. I can be tricky, but I make writing sophisticated and clear.*

Fragment Frankie: *Oops! I'm a fragment. I'm not a complete sentence because I'm missing something—either a subject, a predicate, or both.*

Run-On Randy: *I'm a run-on sentence! I don't stop when I should, and I confuse readers. You need punctuation or a conjunction to fix me.*

Comma Splice Connie: *I'm a comma splice! I join two independent clauses with just a comma. Don't forget—use a semicolon, conjunction, or period to separate them!*

Student 1: *Wow! I didn't realize how sentences could have so many problems!*

Student 2: *Me neither! But now I know how to build strong ones and fix the weak ones.*

Narrator: *Remember—every sentence needs a subject and a predicate. Use modifiers carefully, build different types of sentences, and avoid errors. You'll be a sentence-building expert in no time!*

---

10 Ways to Ask Questions About Sentence Construction Without Using the Words "Sentence Construction"

1. *How can you combine these two ideas into one thought?*
2. *Which part of this group of words tells us who or what it's about?*
3. *How can we make this phrase into a complete thought?*
4. *What word connects these two independent clauses?*
5. *Is there an action or state described in this group of words?*
6. *What do we need to turn this fragment into a full thought?*
7. *How do we link these clauses to avoid a run-on?*
8. *Which part of this group of words is missing—subject or verb?*
9. *What word shows the relationship between the two ideas here?*
10. *How can we make this sentence clearer by rearranging it?*

Lesson Plan 1: Combining Subjects and Predicates for Subject-Verb Agreement

Grade Level:
4th – 8th Grade

Duration:
60 minutes

Objective:
Students will learn to identify and apply the rules of subject-verb agreement in sentences, ensuring that subjects and verbs agree in number (singular or plural). They will practice recognizing and correcting subject-verb agreement errors in various sentence structures.

Materials:

- Anchor Chart: "Subject-Verb Agreement Rules"
- Sentence Strips with Subject-Verb Agreement Examples (correct and incorrect)
- Whiteboard and markers
- Subject-Verb Agreement Role-Play Cards
- Creative Writing Comic Strip Template for Assessment

Introduction (10–15 minutes)

Teacher Script:
"Today, we're going to learn about subject-verb agreement—making sure that the subject and verb in a sentence match in number. If the subject is singular, the verb must be singular; if the subject is plural, the verb must be plural. Think of it like a dance: the subject and verb must always move together in harmony."

Definition and Explanation:

- **Subject-Verb Agreement:** *"The subject and verb must agree in number (singular or plural) for the sentence to make sense."*
- **Example of Correct Agreement:** *The dog runs fast.* (singular subject, singular verb)
- **Example of Incorrect Agreement:** *The dog run fast.* (singular subject, plural verb)

Anchor Chart:
Common Rules for Subject-Verb Agreement

1. **Singular subjects take singular verbs:** *She plays the piano.*
2. **Plural subjects take plural verbs:** *They play the piano.*
3. **Subjects joined by 'and' are plural:** *Tom and Jerry are friends.*
4. **When subjects are joined by 'or' or 'nor,' the verb agrees with the closest subject:** *Neither the teacher nor the students are ready.*
5. **Indefinite pronouns can be singular or plural:**
   - Singular: *Everyone loves ice cream.*
   - Plural: *Many enjoy sports.*

Activity 1: "Subject-Verb Agreement Detective" (15 minutes)

1. **Set Up:**
   - Write several sentences on the board, mixing correct and incorrect subject-verb agreement.
2. **Instructions:**
   - Students work in pairs to become "Subject-Verb Agreement Detectives."
   - They must identify whether each sentence is correct or incorrect and explain why.

Example Sentences:

1. *The cat chase the mouse.*
2. *The children are playing outside.*
3. *Neither the boy nor his friends was late.*
4. *Each of the apples are fresh.*
5. **Discussion:**
   "Why did you choose that correction? How does changing the verb make the sentence clearer?"

Activity 2: "Subject-Verb Agreement Role-Play" (15 minutes)

1. **Set Up:**
   - Create role-play cards with different sentence scenarios, where students act out subjects and verbs.
2. **Instructions:**

  - One student plays the "subject," and another plays the "verb." They must physically agree by holding hands if their agreement is correct. If not, they must correct the sentence before they can connect.

Example Scenarios:

- *The dog barks.* (The verb barks matches the subject dog, so they hold hands.)
- *The dogs barks.* (Mismatch—they correct the sentence to *The dogs bark.*)

Wrap-Up Discussion (5 minutes)

Teacher Script:
"Great job today! Remember, subject-verb agreement is all about making sure your subjects and verbs match in number. When they agree, your sentences are clear and easy to understand. Keep practicing, and soon this will feel natural!"

Assessment: "Subject-Verb Comic Strip Challenge" (20 minutes)

Objective:
Students will create a comic strip with at least four panels. Each panel must contain a sentence that demonstrates subject-verb agreement.

Instructions:

1. **Creative Writing Prompt:**
   "Create a short comic strip about an adventure or a funny day. Use at least four sentences that demonstrate subject-verb agreement."
2. **Checklist for Success:**
   - Each panel contains a complete sentence with correct subject-verb agreement.
   - At least one sentence includes a compound subject.
   - Use a mix of singular and plural subjects.

Example Comic Strip:

- **Panel 1:** *The dog runs in the park.*
- **Panel 2:** *The cats sleep on the couch.*
- **Panel 3:** *Tom and Jerry are watching TV.*
- **Panel 4:** *Neither the teacher nor the students were late.*

Assessment Rubric:

- **Creativity:** Comic strip is engaging and cohesive (5 points)
- **Subject-Verb Agreement:** Correct use of subject-verb agreement in all sentences (5 points)
- **Sentence Variety:** Includes compound subjects and a mix of singular and plural verbs (5 points)
- **Grammar and Clarity:** Sentences are clear and grammatically correct (5 points)

Total: 20 Points

Extension Activity (Optional): "Subject-Verb Agreement Rap or Song"

Students create a short song or rap about subject-verb agreement rules. Perform it for the class to reinforce their understanding.

Lesson Plan 2: Using Modifiers (Adjectives) Effectively

Grade Level: 4th – 6th Grade
Duration: 45 minutes
Objective:
Students will learn to use adjectives effectively to enhance writing, avoid redundant or misplaced modifiers, and create vivid, engaging descriptions.

Materials:

- Adjective List (printed or projected)
- Sample Sentences (with and without adjectives)
- Chart paper and markers
- Picture Cards (various objects/scenes)
- Adjective Checklist (to guide their writing)
- Creative Writing Prompt for Assessment

Introduction (10 minutes)

Teacher script:
"Imagine a world without color—everything is plain and boring. That's what our sentences would be like without adjectives! Adjectives are the words that bring our writing to life. They help us describe nouns and make our readers see, hear, taste, and feel what we're saying. Today, we'll explore how to use adjectives effectively to create vivid descriptions, and we'll learn how to avoid common mistakes."

Definition and Explanation:
"Adjectives answer questions like what kind, how many, and which one. They describe nouns or pronouns and make our writing more interesting."
Examples:

- *Plain Sentence: I saw a dog.*
- *Enhanced Sentence: I saw a **fluffy, playful** dog with a **golden** coat.*

Activity 1: "Adjective Detective" (10 minutes)

1. **Set Up:** Display sample sentences with missing or misplaced adjectives.
2. **Instructions:**
    - Read the sentence aloud: *"The ____ tree swayed in the wind."*
    - Ask: *"What kind of tree could it be? Tall? Green? Spooky?"*
    - Invite students to fill in the blank with adjectives that enhance the sentence.

Misplaced Modifier Example:

- *Incorrect: She served pizza to the kids on paper plates.*
  (Were the kids on the plates?)
- *Correct: She served pizza on paper plates to the kids.*

Teacher script: "Adjectives must be placed close to the nouns they describe. If they're in the wrong place, the meaning of the sentence can change entirely!"

Activity 2: "Adjective Picture Writing" (15 minutes)

1. **Set Up:** Hand out picture cards with scenes (e.g., a carnival, a park, a spooky forest).
2. **Instructions:**
    - Each student writes a short paragraph describing their scene, using at least five adjectives from the provided list.
    - Encourage them to focus on using adjectives that enhance the picture without repeating or overloading the description.
    - Share a few examples aloud.

Example:

- *"The carnival was loud and colorful. The giant, swirling Ferris wheel lit up the night sky. The smell of sweet, buttery popcorn filled the air."*

Wrap-Up Discussion (5 minutes)

Teacher script:
"Great job, everyone! You used adjectives to bring your scenes to life. Remember, adjectives are like spices in cooking—too little, and your writing is bland; too much, and it's overwhelming. Keep your adjectives purposeful and close to the nouns they describe."

Assessment: "Create a Character" (15 minutes)

Objective:
Students will create a unique character using at least ten adjectives in their description.

Instructions:

1. **Character Profile:**
    - Name your character.
    - Describe their appearance, personality, and actions using adjectives.
    - Example: *"Max is a **curious, adventurous** boy with **shaggy brown hair** and a **mischievous** grin. He loves exploring **dark, hidden** caves and solving **tricky, puzzling** mysteries."*
2. **Illustrate:** Draw the character based on the description.

Assessment Rubric:

- **Creativity:** Character description is original and engaging (5 points)
- **Adjective Usage:** At least ten adjectives are used correctly (5 points)
- **Clarity and Organization:** Sentences are clear and well-structured (5 points)
- **Adjective Placement:** Adjectives are placed appropriately to avoid confusion (5 points)

Total: 20 Points

Extension Activity (Optional): "Adjective Hunt"

Have students go on an adjective scavenger hunt in their favorite books, recording five sentences with strong adjective use. Discuss how the adjectives enhance the descriptions.

Lesson Plan 3: Using Modifiers (Adverbs) Effectively

Activity 1: "Adverb Detectives" (15 minutes)

1. **Set Up:** Display sentences on the board with missing or misplaced adverbs.
2. **Instructions:**
    - Read each sentence aloud: _"She sings ___."
    - Ask: *"How does she sing? Loudly? Softly? Beautifully?"*
    - Invite students to choose an appropriate adverb to complete the sentence.

Example Sentences:

- _We will leave ___. *(Answer: soon, later, tomorrow)*
- _The dog barked ___. *(Answer: loudly, fiercely, continuously)*
- _He finished his homework ___. *(Answer: quickly, carefully, reluctantly)*

Teacher script: "Adverbs must be placed correctly in the sentence to modify the right word. Misplaced adverbs can make the sentence confusing or awkward."

Activity 2: "Adverb Challenge" (20 minutes)

1. **Instructions:**
    - Each student receives a simple sentence card (e.g., *The cat slept.*).
    - Their challenge is to rewrite the sentence by adding two or more adverbs for more detail and clarity.
    - After writing, they read their sentence aloud, emphasizing the adverbs.
2. **Examples:**
    - *The cat slept. → The cat slept **peacefully** on the bed **yesterday**.*
    - *She danced. → She danced **gracefully** under the stars **all night**.*
3. **Adverb Categories for Inspiration:**
    - **Manner:** quickly, softly, clumsily, carefully
    - **Time:** now, later, yesterday, soon
    - **Place:** outside, nearby, there, here
    - **Frequency:** always, never, often, sometimes
    - **Degree:** very, too, almost, extremely

Wrap-Up Discussion (5 minutes)

Teacher script: "Great work today! You used adverbs to add life and precision to your writing. Remember, adverbs are powerful, but use them wisely—too many can clutter your sentences. Focus on choosing the best adverb to enhance your meaning!"

Assessment: "Adverb Story Challenge" (15 minutes)

Objective:
Students will create a short story using at least 10 adverbs from different categories to enhance their writing.

Instructions:

1. **Creative Writing Prompt:** *"Write a story about a mysterious event that happened at school. Use adverbs to describe how, when, where, and to what extent things happened."*
2. **Requirements:**
    - Use at least 10 adverbs (highlight or underline them).
    - Include at least one adverb from each category (manner, time, place, frequency, degree).

Example Story:
*It was a dark and stormy night. The wind howled **fiercely** as I walked **slowly** down the hallway. Suddenly, a door creaked **loudly** behind me. I turned **quickly**, but no one was there. I ran **immediately** to the classroom, my heart beating **wildly**.*

Assessment Rubric:

- **Creativity:** Story is engaging and imaginative (5 points)
- **Adverb Usage:** At least 10 adverbs are used correctly (5 points)
- **Variety:** Adverbs from multiple categories are included (5 points)
- **Sentence Clarity:** Sentences are well-constructed and clear (5 points)

Total: 20 Points

Extension Activity (Optional): "Adverb Relay Game"

Divide the class into two teams. Give each team a sentence and challenge them to add as many appropriate adverbs as possible in 2 minutes. The team with the most logical and well-placed adverbs wins.

Lesson Plan 4: Writing Compound Sentences

Grade Level: 4th – 6th Grade
Duration: 45–50 minutes
Objective:
Students will learn to recognize, construct, and punctuate compound sentences effectively using coordinating conjunctions (FANBOYS).

Materials:

- Anchor Chart: FANBOYS Conjunctions (For, And, Nor, But, Or, Yet, So)
- Sentence Strips (with independent clauses)
- Whiteboard and markers
- FANBOYS Handout
- "Compound Sentence Comic Strip" Template for Assessment

Introduction (10 minutes)

Teacher script:
"Today, we're going to learn about compound sentences. Think of a compound sentence as two strong ideas that are joined together by a bridge—the bridge is called a conjunction. These sentences help us combine related ideas and make our writing more interesting. Instead of writing two short, choppy sentences, we'll use coordinating conjunctions to create smoother, more connected writing."

Definition:
"A compound sentence contains two independent clauses joined by a coordinating conjunction and a comma."

Example:

- Simple Sentences: *I like pizza. I don't like mushrooms.*
- Compound Sentence: *I like pizza, but I don't like mushrooms.*

Teacher script:
"We use coordinating conjunctions—FANBOYS—for different purposes. Each conjunction serves a unique role."

Introduce FANBOYS Chart:

- **F = For** (reason/cause)
- **A = And** (addition)
- **N = Nor** (negative option)
- **B = But** (contrast)
- **O = Or** (choice)
- **Y = Yet** (unexpected outcome)
- **S = So** (result/effect)

Activity 1: "FANBOYS Sentence Match" (15 minutes)

1. **Set Up:**
    - Prepare sentence strips with independent clauses.
    - Create a set of FANBOYS cards.
2. **Instructions:**
    - Each student picks a sentence strip.
    - Another student picks a different strip to create a related idea.
    - Together, they select the best FANBOYS conjunction to join the two clauses.

Example:

- Clause 1: *I wanted to go to the beach.*
- Clause 2: *It started raining.*
- Correct Sentence: *I wanted to go to the beach, but it started raining.*

3. **Discuss:**
    - Ask students why they chose that particular conjunction and how it changes the meaning.

Activity 2: "Build-a-Sentence Relay" (15 minutes)

1. **Set Up:**
   - Divide the class into teams.
   - Place sentence strips with different clauses at one end of the room.
2. **Instructions:**
   - One student from each team races to grab a sentence strip and brings it back to their team.
   - The team selects another strip to pair with it and writes a compound sentence using the correct conjunction.
3. **Winning:**
   - Teams earn points for correctly constructed compound sentences with proper punctuation.

Wrap-Up (5 minutes)

Teacher script:
"Great job combining ideas into compound sentences! Remember, compound sentences help make your writing smoother and more interesting. Keep practicing, and always check that your conjunction fits the relationship between the two clauses."

Assessment: "Compound Sentence Comic Strip" (20 minutes)

Objective:
Students will create a comic strip using compound sentences to tell a short story.

Instructions:

1. **Story Concept:**
   - Each student creates a 4-panel comic strip.
   - Each panel must contain at least one compound sentence using a FANBOYS conjunction.
   - The sentences should connect to create a coherent story.

Example:

- Panel 1: *I woke up early, but I missed the bus.*
- Panel 2: *I walked to school, and I arrived just in time.*
- Panel 3: *I forgot my lunch, so my friend shared his sandwich.*
- Panel 4: *It was a tough day, yet I still had fun.*

Assessment Rubric:

- **Creativity:** Comic strip tells an engaging story (5 points)
- **Compound Sentences:** Correct use of at least four compound sentences (5 points)
- **Punctuation:** Proper use of commas and conjunctions (5 points)
- **Clarity:** Sentences are clear and connected logically (5 points)

Total: 20 Points

Extension Activity (Optional): "Conjunction Song and Movement"

Teach students a catchy FANBOYS song with corresponding hand movements to help them remember the conjunctions.

Lesson Plan 5: Complex Sentences

Grade Level: 4th – 6th Grade
Duration: 45–50 minutes
Objective:
Students will learn to identify, construct, and effectively use complex sentences to enhance their writing by connecting ideas with subordinating conjunctions.

Materials:

- Anchor Chart: Subordinating Conjunctions (with definitions and examples)
- Sentence Strips with independent and dependent clauses
- "Complex Sentence Checklist"
- Creative Writing Assessment Template

Introduction (10 minutes)

Teacher script:
"Today, we're going to learn about complex sentences. These sentences are like two puzzle pieces that fit together to show a complete thought and a related idea. Complex sentences help us explain reasons, conditions, and contrasts in our writing. They connect an independent clause—something that can stand alone—with a dependent clause—something that can't stand alone."

Definition:
"A complex sentence combines an independent clause (a complete sentence) with a dependent clause (an incomplete thought) using a subordinating conjunction."

Examples:

- Independent Clause: *I stayed home.*
- Dependent Clause: *because it was raining.*
- Complex Sentence: *I stayed home because it was raining.*

Anchor Chart: Common Subordinating Conjunctions

Display and explain the most common subordinating conjunctions:

- **Time:** after, before, when, while, since, until
- **Cause and Effect:** because, since, as, so that
- **Condition:** if, unless, though, although
- **Contrast:** even though, although, whereas

Teacher script:
"Subordinating conjunctions are the glue that connects your independent and dependent clauses. Without them, your sentence doesn't make sense!"

Activity 1: "Clause Matching Game" (15 minutes)

1. **Set Up:** Prepare sentence strips with independent clauses on one color and dependent clauses on another.
2. **Instructions:**
    - Students walk around and find a matching clause to create a complex sentence.
    - Once they form a sentence, they choose a subordinating conjunction and read it aloud to the class.

Example:

- Independent Clause: *I went to the park.*
- Dependent Clause: *even though it was raining.*
- Complex Sentence: *I went to the park even though it was raining.*

3. **Teacher Discussion:**
    - Ask why they chose that conjunction and how it changes the sentence's meaning.

Activity 2: "Complex Sentence Scavenger Hunt" (15 minutes)

1. **Set Up:** Write examples of both simple and complex sentences around the classroom.
2. **Instructions:**
    - Students work in pairs to hunt for complex sentences.
    - They must underline the dependent clause and circle the subordinating conjunction in each sentence.

Example Sentences for the Hunt:

1. *I didn't go swimming because the water was too cold.*
2. *While I was eating dinner, my dog stole my shoe.*
3. *You can go outside after you finish your homework.*

Discussion:
Teacher script: "Notice how the dependent clause adds detail or explanation to the main idea. Without it, the sentence wouldn't be as interesting!"

Wrap-Up Discussion (5 minutes)

Teacher script:
"Great job, everyone! Complex sentences are powerful tools for connecting ideas and adding depth to your writing. Remember, the dependent clause can go at the beginning, middle, or end of a sentence, but always watch for that subordinating conjunction to know it's a complex sentence!"

Assessment: "Complex Sentence Story Challenge" (20 minutes)

Objective:
Students will write a short story using at least five complex sentences to explain a series of events or a personal experience.

Instructions:

1. **Creative Writing Prompt:** *"Write about a time you had an exciting adventure or an unexpected surprise. Use at least five complex sentences to add detail and explain why or how things happened."*
2. **Checklist for Success:**
   - Use at least five different subordinating conjunctions.
   - Underline the dependent clauses in your story.
   - Highlight the subordinating conjunctions.

Example Story:
While I was hiking in the mountains, I heard a strange noise. Because I was curious, I decided to follow it. After walking for a few minutes, I discovered a hidden waterfall. Although it was cold, I jumped into the water. It was the best adventure I've ever had.

Assessment Rubric:

- **Creativity:** Story is engaging and coherent (5 points)
- **Complex Sentence Usage:** At least five complex sentences are used correctly (5 points)
- **Subordinating Conjunctions:** Conjunctions are varied and appropriate (5 points)
- **Clarity and Structure:** Sentences are clear, with correct punctuation (5 points)

Total: 20 Points

Extension Activity (Optional): "Complex Sentence Comics"

Students create a 3-panel comic strip where each panel contains a complex sentence describing the story.

Lesson Plan 6: "Mastering Compound-Complex Sentences"

Grade Level:

5th – 8th Grade
Duration: 60 minutes
Objective:
Students will learn to recognize, construct, and effectively use compound-complex sentences to create more sophisticated and dynamic writing.

Materials:

- Anchor Chart: Definitions and Examples of Compound-Complex Sentences
- FANBOYS & Subordinating Conjunctions Chart
- Sentence Building Cards (independent and dependent clauses)
- Whiteboard and markers
- Creative Writing Comic Template for Assessment

Introduction (10–15 minutes)

Teacher Script:
"Today, we're taking your writing to the next level! You've already mastered simple, compound, and complex sentences. Now, we're going to combine those skills to create the ultimate sentence structure: the compound-complex sentence. These sentences allow you to connect multiple ideas and show relationships between them all in one powerful sentence."

Definition and Explanation:

- **Compound-Complex Sentence:**
  "A compound-complex sentence contains at least two independent clauses and one or more dependent clauses."
  "Think of it as combining a compound sentence and a complex sentence together."

Examples:

1. *Although I was tired, I stayed up late, and I finished my homework.*
   - Dependent Clause: *Although I was tired*
   - Independent Clauses: *I stayed up late / I finished my homework*
2. *She loves to read because it's relaxing, and she often loses track of time.*

  - Dependent Clause: *because it's relaxing*
  - Independent Clauses: *She loves to read / she often loses track of time*

Anchor Chart: Recognizing Compound-Complex Sentences

1. **Independent Clause:** A complete thought that can stand alone.
   Example: *I like pizza.*
2. **Dependent Clause:** Cannot stand alone. It starts with a subordinating conjunction like *because, although, when, if, while.*
   Example: *Although I like pizza*
3. **Coordinating Conjunctions (FANBOYS):** *For, And, Nor, But, Or, Yet, So* – Used to connect independent clauses.

Activity 1: "Clause Building Challenge" (15–20 minutes)

1. **Set Up:** Prepare cards with independent and dependent clauses.
2. **Instructions:**
   - Students work in pairs to draw two independent clause cards and one dependent clause card.
   - Their challenge is to combine all three into a compound-complex sentence using a coordinating conjunction and subordinating conjunction.

Examples:

- Independent Clauses: *I went to the park. / It started to rain.*
- Dependent Clause: *Because I forgot my umbrella*
- Correct Sentence: *I went to the park, but it started to rain because I forgot my umbrella.*

3. **Discussion:**
   - Share sentences aloud and explain the conjunction choices.

Activity 2: "Sentence Relay Race" (15 minutes)

1. **Set Up:** Divide the class into teams.
2. **Instructions:**
   - Teams take turns building compound-complex sentences on the board.
   - Each student writes one clause and hands the marker to the next teammate.
   - Teams earn points for correctly punctuated and structured sentences.

Wrap-Up Discussion (5 minutes)

Teacher Script:
"Compound-complex sentences are like the Swiss Army knife of writing—they help us express complex ideas clearly and efficiently. Use them to make your writing more engaging and to show relationships between multiple ideas in one sentence!"

Assessment: "My Day as a Compound-Complex Sentence" (20 minutes)

Objective:
Students will create a short narrative using at least five compound-complex sentences to describe a sequence of events.

Instructions:

1. **Creative Writing Prompt:**
   "Write about a day in your life using at least five compound-complex sentences. Describe what happened, how you felt, and what the results were."
2. **Checklist for Success:**
   - Use at least five compound-complex sentences.
   - Highlight each independent clause in blue and each dependent clause in green.
   - Underline the conjunctions (both coordinating and subordinating).

Example Narrative:
Although I woke up late, I still managed to eat breakfast, and I made it to school on time. My teacher gave us a surprise quiz, but since I had studied the night before, I did well. During lunch, it started raining, so we stayed inside while we played games. I had a great day, even though it didn't start off perfectly.

Assessment Rubric:

- **Creativity:** Story is engaging and coherent (5 points)
- **Sentence Structure:** At least five correctly constructed compound-complex sentences (5 points)
- **Conjunction Use:** Varied and appropriate conjunctions (5 points)
- **Clarity and Grammar:** Sentences are clear, with correct punctuation (5 points)

Total: 20 Points

Extension Activity (Optional): "Compound-Complex Comics"

Students create a 3-panel comic strip where each panel contains a compound-complex sentence that advances the story.

Lesson Plan 7: "Correcting Comma Splices"

Grade Level:
5th – 8th Grade
Duration:
45–50 minutes

Objective:
Students will learn to identify and correct comma splices using three primary strategies: adding a coordinating conjunction, using a semicolon, or separating the sentence into two sentences.

Materials:

- Anchor Chart: "Comma Splice Fix-It Strategies"
- Sentence Strips with Comma Splice Examples
- Whiteboard and markers
- "Fix the Sentence" Creative Writing Template
- Peer Review Checklist for Assessment

Introduction (10 minutes)

Teacher Script:
"Today, we're going to tackle one of the trickiest sentence errors—comma splices. A comma splice happens when we join two complete sentences with only a comma. It's like using glue when you need a stronger tool. But don't worry! We'll learn how to spot comma splices and fix them with different strategies."

Definition and Explanation:

- *"A comma splice is when two independent clauses (complete sentences) are incorrectly joined by just a comma."*
- Example: *I love pizza, it is my favorite food.*

Teacher Script:
"Notice how both parts of the sentence could stand alone, but they're joined by just a comma. That's what makes this a comma splice. Let's explore three ways to fix it."

Anchor Chart: Three Ways to Fix a Comma Splice

1. **Add a Coordinating Conjunction (FANBOYS)**
   I love pizza, and it is my favorite food.
2. **Use a Semicolon**
   I love pizza; it is my favorite food.
3. **Separate into Two Sentences**
   I love pizza. It is my favorite food.

Teacher Script:
"Each method has a slightly different effect on your writing, but all three are correct. Let's practice identifying and fixing comma splices."

Activity 1: "Comma Splice Detective" (15 minutes)

1. **Set Up:** Display a series of sentences on the board, some with comma splices and others without.
2. **Instructions:**
   - Students work in pairs to identify which sentences are comma splices.
   - Once identified, they choose the best method to correct each one.
   - Example Sentences:
     1. *We went to the park, it was a sunny day.*
     2. *I studied hard, so I did well on the test.*
     3. *She loves reading, her favorite books are mysteries.*

Teacher Discussion:
"Why did you choose that method to fix the comma splice? How does it change the sentence's tone or flow?"

Activity 2: "Fix-It Relay" (15 minutes)

1. **Set Up:** Divide the class into teams and give each team a stack of comma splice sentence strips.
2. **Instructions:**
   - Each student races to the board, selects a sentence strip, and corrects the comma splice using one of the three methods.
   - Teams earn points for each correctly corrected sentence.
   - The team with the most points wins!

Wrap-Up Discussion (5 minutes)

Teacher Script:
"Great job, everyone! Remember, fixing comma splices makes your writing clearer and easier to read. Whether you use a coordinating conjunction, a semicolon, or break the sentence into two, you're making your writing more professional and polished!"

Assessment: "Comma Splice Story Challenge" (20 minutes)

Objective:
Students will write a short story using at least five examples of comma splices intentionally and then correct them using the strategies they've learned.

Instructions:

1. **Creative Writing Prompt:**
   "Write a short story about a funny or exciting day. Include at least five comma splices on purpose, then fix each one using a different method."
2. **Correction Process:**
   - Highlight the comma splices in the original story.
   - Rewrite the story with corrected sentences using the three methods.

Example Story:
It was a beautiful day, I decided to go hiking. I packed my bag, it was full of snacks and water. The trail was long, it took hours to reach the top. When I got there, the view was amazing.

Correction:

- *It was a beautiful day, so I decided to go hiking.*
- *I packed my bag; it was full of snacks and water.*
- *The trail was long. It took hours to reach the top.*

Assessment Rubric:

- **Creativity:** Story is engaging and coherent (5 points)
- **Comma Splice Identification:** Correctly identifies five comma splices (5 points)
- **Correction Variety:** Uses at least one of each method to correct comma splices (5 points)
- **Clarity and Grammar:** Sentences are clear, with correct punctuation (5 points)

Total: 20 Points

Extension Activity (Optional): "Comma Splice Rap"

Students create a short rap or rhyme about how to fix comma splices, incorporating the three methods. Perform it in groups for a fun and memorable review.

Lesson Plan 8: "Run-On Sentence Relay"

Grade Level: 5th – 8th Grade

Duration: 45–50 minutes

Objective:
Students will learn to identify and correct run-on sentences using three primary strategies: adding punctuation, using coordinating conjunctions, and restructuring the sentence.

Materials:

- Anchor Chart: "How to Fix Run-On Sentences"
- Sentence Strips with Examples of Run-On Sentences
- Whiteboard and markers
- Peer Review Checklist
- Creative Writing Storyboard Template for Assessment

Introduction (10–15 minutes)

Teacher Script:
"Imagine trying to read a sentence that never ends! That's what a run-on sentence feels like. Today, we're going to learn how to spot and fix run-on sentences so your writing is clear and easy to understand."

Definition:

- *"A run-on sentence occurs when two or more independent clauses (complete sentences) are joined without proper punctuation or connecting words."*
- Example of a Run-On Sentence: *I went to the park it was a sunny day I saw my friends.*

Anchor Chart: How to Fix Run-On Sentences

Three Ways to Correct a Run-On Sentence:

1. **Add a Period (Separate into Two Sentences)**
    - *I went to the park. It was a sunny day.*

2. **Use a Comma and a Coordinating Conjunction (FANBOYS)**
   - *I went to the park, and it was a sunny day.*
3. **Use a Semicolon**
   - *I went to the park; it was a sunny day.*

Activity 1: "Run-On Sentence Detective" (15 minutes)

1. **Set Up:** Prepare a series of sentence strips with a mix of run-on sentences and properly constructed sentences.
2. **Instructions:**
   - Students work in pairs to read each sentence and decide if it is a run-on sentence or a correct sentence.
   - If they identify a run-on, they must decide the best method to fix it.
   - Example Sentences:
     1. *I love reading it helps me relax.*
     2. *We went to the store, and we bought some snacks.*
     3. *The dog barked the mailman ran away.*
3. **Discussion:**
   - Ask pairs to share how they corrected one sentence and why they chose that method.

Teacher Script:
*"Every run-on sentence has multiple ways to fix it. The method you choose depends on how you want the sentence to flow."_

Activity 2: "Fix-It Relay Race" (15 minutes)

1. **Set Up:** Divide the class into teams and give each team a stack of run-on sentence strips.
2. **Instructions:**
   - One student from each team runs to the board, selects a sentence strip, and corrects the sentence using one of the three methods.
   - Teams earn points for each correctly fixed sentence.
   - The team with the most points wins!

Wrap-Up Discussion (5 minutes)

Teacher Script:
"Great job, everyone! Remember, run-on sentences can confuse your reader and make your writing harder to understand. Fixing them will make your writing clearer, stronger, and more enjoyable to read."

Assessment: "Run-On Sentence Comic Strip Challenge" (20 minutes)

Objective:
Students will create a comic strip using at least five corrected run-on sentences to tell a story.

Instructions:

1. **Creative Writing Prompt:**
   "Create a 4-panel comic strip about a fun day at the park, school, or home. Use at least five sentences that were originally run-ons and show how you corrected them."
2. **Checklist for Success:**
   - Use at least five sentences that were run-ons and corrected.
   - Label each correction method used (period, comma + conjunction, or semicolon).
   - Ensure the comic strip tells a cohesive story.

Example Comic:

- Panel 1: *I woke up late it was a busy morning.* → Corrected: *I woke up late. It was a busy morning.*
- Panel 2: *I ran downstairs grabbed my backpack.* → Corrected: *I ran downstairs, and I grabbed my backpack.*

Assessment Rubric:

- **Creativity:** Story is engaging and coherent (5 points)
- **Run-On Sentence Identification:** At least five run-on sentences are identified and corrected (5 points)
- **Variety of Correction Methods:** Uses all three correction methods at least once (5 points)
- **Clarity and Grammar:** Sentences are clear and properly punctuated (5 points)

Total: 20 Points

Extension Activity (Optional): "Run-On Sentence Song or Rap"

Students work in groups to create a song or rap about how to fix run-on sentences, incorporating the three methods. They can perform it for the class as a fun and memorable review.

Lesson Plan 9: "Spot the Sentence Fragment"

Grade Level:
4th – 8th Grade
Duration:
45–50 minutes

Objective:
Students will learn to recognize and correct sentence fragments by identifying missing subjects, predicates, or complete thoughts. They will practice rewriting fragments into complete sentences using various strategies.

Materials:

- Anchor Chart: "What is a Sentence Fragment?"
- Sentence Strip Examples (fragments and complete sentences)
- "Fragment Fixers" Creative Writing Template
- Peer Review Checklist for Assessment
- Whiteboard and markers

Introduction (10–15 minutes)

Teacher Script:
"Imagine trying to tell a story with only half your sentences finished—it would sound confusing, right? That's what happens when we use sentence fragments in our writing. Today, we're going to learn how to spot these fragments and turn them into strong, complete sentences that clearly express your ideas."

Definition:

"A sentence fragment is a group of words that looks like a sentence but isn't complete. It might be missing a subject, a predicate, or a complete thought."

Examples of Sentence Fragments:

1. *Running through the park.* (Missing subject and verb)
2. *When the rain started.* (Dependent clause without an independent clause)
3. *The girl with the blue hat.* (Missing predicate)

Teacher Script:
"Every sentence needs a subject (who or what) and a predicate (what they are doing or what state they are in). If one of these is missing—or if the sentence doesn't express a complete thought—it's a fragment."

Anchor Chart: "How to Fix Sentence Fragments"

Three Ways to Fix a Fragment:

1. **Add the Missing Subject or Predicate**
   - Fragment: *Running through the park.*
   - Fixed: *The dog was running through the park.*
2. **Attach the Fragment to a Nearby Sentence**
   - Fragment: *When the rain started.*
   - Fixed: *We ran inside when the rain started.*
3. **Rewrite the Sentence as a Complete Thought**
   - Fragment: *The girl with the blue hat.*
   - Fixed: *The girl with the blue hat smiled at me.*

Activity 1: "Fragment or Complete Sentence?" (15 minutes)

1. **Set Up:**
   - Write a mix of sentence fragments and complete sentences on the board or distribute sentence strips to groups.
2. **Instructions:**
   - Students work in pairs to decide if each sentence is a fragment or a complete sentence.
   - If it's a fragment, they must fix it using one of the strategies from the anchor chart.

Example Sentences:

1. *During the big storm.*
2. *We had a great time at the park.*
3. *Because I was tired.*
4. *The cat under the table.*
5. **Discussion:**
   "What strategy did you use to fix the fragment? Did it change the meaning or clarify the sentence?"

Activity 2: "Fragment Fix Relay" (15 minutes)

1. **Set Up:**
   - Divide the class into teams.
   - Give each team a set of sentence fragment strips.
2. **Instructions:**
   - Each student races to the board, selects a fragment, and writes a corrected version.
   - Teams earn points for each correctly corrected fragment.

Example Fragments for the Relay:

1. *After the show.*
2. *Without saying a word.*
3. *Jumping on the trampoline.*

Wrap-Up Discussion (5 minutes)

Teacher Script:
"Great job identifying and fixing sentence fragments! Remember, complete sentences help your reader understand your ideas clearly. Keep an eye out for fragments when you revise your writing. Fixing them will make your work stronger and easier to read!"

Assessment: "Fragment-Free Story Challenge" (20 minutes)

Objective:
Students will write a short story with at least 8 sentences. Half of the sentences will intentionally start as fragments, and students will correct them to make the story complete and cohesive.

Instructions:

1. **Creative Writing Prompt:**
   "Write a story about a surprising or funny moment. Include at least four sentence fragments and correct each one to form a complete sentence."
2. **Checklist for Success:**
   - Write a story with at least 8 sentences.
   - Correct all sentence fragments using one of the strategies from the lesson.
   - Underline each corrected sentence.

Example Story:
Fragment: After the party. Corrected: We went to the park after the party.
Fragment: Because the dog was barking. Corrected: We couldn't sleep because the dog was barking.

Assessment Rubric:

- **Creativity:** Story is engaging and cohesive (5 points)
- **Fragment Identification:** At least four sentence fragments are correctly identified (5 points)
- **Correction Variety:** Uses multiple strategies to correct fragments (5 points)
- **Clarity and Grammar:** Sentences are clear and grammatically correct (5 points)

Total: 20 Points

Extension Activity (Optional): "Fragment-Free Song or Rhyme"

Students create a short song or rhyme about how to spot and fix sentence fragments. They can perform it for the class to reinforce their understanding.

Lesson Plan 10: "Phrases vs. Clauses—What's the Difference?"

Objective:
Students will learn to distinguish between phrases and clauses, understanding their structure and function in sentences.

Materials:

- Sentence Strips (examples of phrases and clauses)
- Anchor Chart: Definitions and examples of phrases and clauses
- Phrases & Clauses Sorting Cards
- Whiteboard and markers

Introduction (5–10 minutes)

Teacher script: "Today, we're learning about two essential parts of sentence structure—phrases and clauses. They might seem similar, but they are very different in how they help us build sentences. Imagine a phrase as a small piece of a puzzle and a clause as a complete section of the puzzle. Both are important, but they serve different purposes. Let's break it down!"

Definitions and Examples:

- **Phrase:** A group of words that act together but don't contain both a subject and a verb. Example: *under the table, before the storm, running fast*
- **Clause:** A group of words that contain both a subject and a verb. Clauses can be independent (complete sentences) or dependent (incomplete thoughts). Example: *She ran home. (independent) / Because it was raining. (dependent)*

Teacher script: "A clause has a subject and a verb, but a phrase doesn't. Phrases add extra detail, while clauses give us complete or almost-complete thoughts."

Activity 1: Sorting Phrases and Clauses (15 minutes)

1. **Set Up:**
   - Place Sentence Strips around the room with examples of phrases and clauses.
   - Create two labeled sections: *Phrases* and *Clauses*.
2. **Instructions:**
   - Students walk around and collect one sentence strip.
   - They read the sentence strip and decide if it is a phrase or a clause.
   - They place it in the correct section.

3. **Discussion:**
   - Go over each sentence together.
   - Ask: *"Why is this a clause? Why is this a phrase?"*

Example Sentences for Sorting:

- Phrase: *after the game, by the river, running fast*
- Clause: *I went home, because she was late, when the bell rang*

Activity 2: Phrase vs. Clause Relay Race (10 minutes)

1. **Set Up:** Create two relay lines with stacks of cards—one stack with phrases and one with clauses.
2. **Instructions:**
   - Students take turns running to the stack, grabbing a card, and bringing it back to their team.
   - The team decides if it's a phrase or a clause and places it in the correct column on the board.
3. **Winning:** The first team to sort all cards correctly wins!

Wrap-Up (5 minutes)

Teacher script: "Great work today! Remember, a phrase gives extra detail, but it doesn't have a subject and verb together. A clause has both a subject and verb and can sometimes be a full sentence. Knowing the difference helps us write more powerful sentences!"

Assessment: "Build-a-Sentence Challenge"

Objective:
Students will create their own sentences using both phrases and clauses to show understanding.

Instructions:

1. **Sentence Creation:** Each student writes a sentence that contains at least one phrase and one clause.
   - Example: *Before the game, we practiced on the field.*
2. **Share:** Students read their sentences aloud, identifying the phrase and the clause.

Chapter 10:

Sentence Weather

The Technique that Teaches Parts of Speech

The Science Behind Sentence Weather: How Multisensory Learning Boosts Retention

Teaching grammar concepts like parts of speech can be a daunting task for students, especially when those concepts seem abstract or disconnected from real life. However, using a **multisensory approach** such as **Sentence Weather Symbols**, where each part of speech is represented by a visual symbol and paired with a physical movement, has a profound impact on how the brain processes and stores information. This approach taps into the **visual, auditory, and kinesthetic learning styles**, creating stronger memory connections and improving comprehension for all types of learners.

The Brain's Multisensory Learning Process

Research in **cognitive science** shows that the brain is more likely to retain new information when it is presented in multiple ways. According to **Fleming's VARK model**, the most effective learning occurs when all learning styles—**Visual, Auditory, Reading/Writing, and Kinesthetic**—are engaged. Sentence Weather accomplishes this by combining **visual symbols (sun, star, cloud, etc.)**, **auditory repetition (chants and songs)**, and **kinesthetic movements (acting out each part of speech)**.

- **Visual Learning**: Seeing a symbol like a ○ for nouns or for adjectives gives students a **tangible representation** of these abstract concepts, making it easier to recall.
- **Auditory Learning**: Reciting chants such as *"Who, What, What, When, Where"* reinforces sentence structure through rhythm and sound, improving **auditory memory**.
- **Kinesthetic Learning**: Physical movement, like using your arms to mimic a **rainbow for conjunctions** or a **raindrop for verbs**, activates the **motor cortex**, anchoring the concept in the brain through muscle memory.

These multiple entry points to learning don't just create **redundant pathways** for information; they also **open new areas of the brain** where the concepts can be stored and retrieved more easily. This makes Sentence Weather highly effective for **long-term retention**.

Effective for All Types of Learners

1. **The Regular Learner**: For students who naturally excel in language arts, Sentence Weather adds depth and novelty, making an already strong foundation even stronger. They connect parts of speech with symbols, making their learning faster and richer.
2. **The New Learner**: For students just beginning to explore grammar, this multisensory approach simplifies complex ideas. The **layered structure**—starting with basic nouns and verbs and adding adjectives, adverbs, and prepositions—offers a gradual, engaging introduction to grammar.
3. **The Academically Challenged Learner**: For students with learning difficulties, abstract concepts can seem impossible to grasp. Sentence Weather transforms abstract ideas into **concrete, relatable experiences**, helping struggling learners access grammar in new, memorable ways. This approach is also beneficial for **English language learners (ELLs)**, giving them a **visual and physical scaffold** for understanding sentence structure.

Creating Neural Pathways for Advanced Grammar

As students become familiar with parts of speech and sentence construction through Sentence Weather, they build the **cognitive framework** necessary for advanced grammar concepts, such as **diagramming sentences** in upper grades.

- **Diagramming sentences** requires students to identify and categorize parts of speech, recognizing how words relate to one another in a sentence.
- Sentence Weather symbols make this transition seamless by reinforcing the roles of nouns, verbs, adjectives, and conjunctions early on.
- When students move into diagramming, they already have a **multisensory reference** for each part of speech, making it easier to break down complex sentences.

Supporting Research

Numerous studies underscore the importance of multisensory learning in improving comprehension and memory:

- **Marzano's research** on vocabulary acquisition found that using visuals with verbal explanations can increase retention by up to 55%.
- **Kinesthetic learning**, according to a study in the *Journal of Educational Psychology*, improves recall and engagement by activating motor neurons that connect directly to memory pathways.
- **Howard Gardner's theory of Multiple Intelligences** highlights the necessity of engaging visual-spatial, linguistic, and bodily-kinesthetic intelligences to reach a diverse group of learners.

Conclusion

Sentence Weather isn't just an engaging way to teach parts of speech—it's a **brain-friendly approach** that helps students make lasting connections. By addressing multiple learning styles, it provides all students—whether they are excelling, struggling, or just beginning—with a toolset for understanding and mastering grammar. As students progress, Sentence Weather becomes the perfect bridge to more advanced language concepts, preparing them for sentence diagramming and more sophisticated writing tasks.

By making grammar fun, interactive, and unforgettable, Sentence Weather turns language into an adventure that students are excited to explore.

Sentence Weather: Learning Parts of Speech through Symbols and Movement

Understanding the parts of speech can be challenging for students, but **Sentence Weather Symbols** transform this complex concept into something visual, physical, and fun. By associating each part of speech with a unique weather-related symbol, students engage multiple senses—visual, kinesthetic, and auditory—helping them absorb and retain the information more effectively. Adding body language and movement to represent these symbols makes the learning process active and memorable.

Here's how **Sentence Weather Symbols** work:

The Symbols and Their Meaning

1. **Nouns – The Sun**
   Nouns represent people, places, things, or ideas. Just like the sun shines on everything, nouns are everywhere in a sentence.
   Body Motion: Hold your arms in a big circle over your head to represent the sun.
   Example: *dog, park, happiness*
2. **Proper Nouns – The Sun with a Smile**
   Proper nouns are specific names. Adding a smiley face to the sun helps distinguish them.
   Body Motion: Smile while making the sun motion.
   Example: *New York, Sarah, Mount Everest*
3. **Pronouns – The Moon**
   Pronouns substitute for nouns, just like the moon reflects the sun. They step in to keep sentences from becoming repetitive.
   Body Motion: Make a crescent shape with your hand to symbolize the moon.
   Example: *he, she, it, they*
4. **Articles – A Tiny Dot •**
   Articles are small but essential words that introduce nouns. Like a tiny dot, they are subtle but important.
   Body Motion: Tap your finger in the air to represent a small dot.
   Example: *a, an, the*
5. **Verbs – The Raindrop**
   Verbs bring action or state of being to sentences, just like rain brings life and movement to nature.
   Body Motion: Drop your hand down in a quick motion to represent falling rain.
   Example: *run, think, is, was*
6. **Adverbs – Two Raindrops**
   Adverbs modify verbs, adjectives, or other adverbs, adding detail about **how, when, where,** or **to what extent**. They are like extra raindrops that bring more information.
   Body Motion: Drop both hands twice in a rhythmic motion to represent two raindrops.
   Example: *quickly, yesterday, very*

7. **Prepositions – The Cloud**
   Prepositions show relationships of time, place, or direction—just like clouds in the sky provide context for weather.
   Body Motion: Spread your hands wide to form a cloud shape.
   Example: *on, under, during, with*
8. **Conjunctions – The Rainbow**
   Conjunctions connect words and ideas, just as rainbows bridge rain and sunlight.
   Body Motion: Make an arching motion with your arms to represent a rainbow.
   Example: *and, but, or, because*
9. **Interjections – The Lightning Bolt**
   Interjections express sudden emotion, just like a flash of lightning breaks through a storm.
   Body Motion: Strike down sharply with your hand to represent a lightning bolt.
   Example: *Wow! Oops! Hey!*

Why Symbols and Body Language Work

1. **Engages Multiple Learning Styles:**
   - **Visual learners** benefit from seeing symbols.
   - **Kinesthetic learners** retain concepts through movement and body language.
   - **Auditory learners** reinforce their knowledge by saying the symbol names aloud.
2. **Makes Abstract Concepts Concrete:**
   Parts of speech can be abstract and difficult to grasp. By associating them with concrete symbols and physical movements, students gain a tangible connection to these ideas.
3. **Enhances Retention and Recall:**
   The combination of symbols, motion, and verbal repetition creates strong memory hooks. When students encounter parts of speech in their writing, they can recall the weather symbols and body language, making identification easier.

Classroom Activity: Acting Out Sentence Weather

1. **Step 1:** Write a simple sentence on the board (e.g., *The happy dog runs quickly across the park.*).
2. **Step 2:** Ask students to identify each word's part of speech and its corresponding weather symbol.
3. **Step 3:** As students identify each part of speech, they perform the appropriate body motion.
4. **Step 4:** For reinforcement, have small groups create their own sentences and act them out using the weather symbols.

Why Sentence Weather Symbols Matter

Learning grammar can be overwhelming, but **Sentence Weather Symbols** turn the process into a fun, interactive experience. When students visualize nouns as the sun or verbs as raindrops, they develop a deeper understanding of how words work together in sentences. This method not only improves grammar knowledge but also makes learning active, memorable, and enjoyable! ☀️ 💧 ⚡ 🌈

Sentence Weather Examples

1. Simple Sentence – Fully Labeled (☀️, 💧, ☁️, •)

Sentence: *The dog runs across the yard.*

Labeled Sentence with Weather Symbols:

- *The* (• Article)
- *dog* (☀️ Noun – Subject)
- *runs* (💧 Verb)
- *across* (☁️ Preposition)
- *the* (• Article)
- *yard* (☀️ Noun – Object of the Preposition)

---

2. Compound Sentence – Fully Labeled (☀️, 💧, ☁️, •, 🌈)

Sentence: *The cat sleeps on the chair, and the dog runs outside.*

Labeled Sentence with Weather Symbols:

- *The* (• Article)
- *cat* (☀️ Noun – Subject)
- *sleeps* (💧 Verb)
- *on* (☁️ Preposition)
- *the* (• Article)
- *chair* (☀️ Noun – Object of the Preposition)
- *,* (Comma)
- *and* (🌈 Coordinating Conjunction)
- *the* (• Article)
- *dog* (☀️ Noun – Subject)
- *runs* (💧 Verb)
- *outside* (☁️ Adverb of Place)

3. Complex Sentence – Fully Labeled (, , , •,)

Sentence: *The child smiled because she saw the rainbow.*

Labeled Sentence with Weather Symbols:

- *The* (• Article)
- *child* (Noun – Subject)
- *smiled* (Verb)
- *because* (Subordinating Conjunction)
- *she* (Pronoun – Subject of Dependent Clause)
- *saw* (Verb)
- *the* (• Article)
- *rainbow* (Noun – Object of the Verb)

Why This Method Works

By labeling every word with **Sentence Weather Symbols**, students get a visual and physical understanding of how each word functions. It helps them identify **articles, nouns, verbs, prepositions, conjunctions,** and **pronouns** with ease, turning grammar analysis into an engaging and memorable learning experience.

The Expanding Pyramid

Pyramid Sentence

Sentence: *The dog runs.*

Now, here's how we'll build the pyramid sentence by adding more words in layers.

1. **The dog runs.**
2. **The big dog runs fast.**
3. **The big dog runs fast across the yard.**
4. **The big brown dog runs very fast across the large yard.**
5. **The big brown dog happily runs very fast across the large green yard.**

Fully Expanded Pyramid Sentence with Symbols for Every Word

Sentence: *The big brown dog happily runs very fast across the large green yard.*

Word-by-Word Labeling with Sentence Weather Symbols

1. **The** (• Article)
2. **big** (Adjective – Modifying *dog*)
3. **brown** (Adjective – Modifying *dog*)
4. **dog** (Noun – Subject)
5. **happily** (Adverb – Modifying *runs*)
6. **runs** (Verb)
7. **very** (Adverb – Modifying *fast*)
8. **fast** (Adverb – Modifying *runs*)
9. **across** (Preposition)
10. **the** (• Article)
11. **large** (Adjective – Modifying *yard*)
12. **green** (Adjective – Modifying *yard*)
13. **yard** (Noun – Object of the Preposition)

Visual Summary with Weather Symbols

• •

Explanation:

This sentence incorporates a rich mix of **nouns, adjectives, verbs, adverbs, prepositions,** and **articles**, each represented by a specific weather symbol. By associating each part of speech with a symbol, students can better visualize and understand how these elements work together to form clear, engaging sentences.

5. Science Concept Pyramid Sentence

Sentence: *The bright yellow sun slowly warms the cold wet ground in the early morning.*

Word-by-Word Labeling with Sentence Weather Symbols:

1. **The** (• Article)
2. **bright** (Adjective – Modifying *sun*)
3. **yellow** (Adjective – Modifying *sun*)
4. **sun** (Noun – Subject)
5. **slowly** (Adverb – Modifying *warms*)
6. **warms** (Verb)
7. **the** (• Article)
8. **cold** (Adjective – Modifying *ground*)
9. **wet** (Adjective – Modifying *ground*)
10. **ground** (Noun – Object)
11. **in** (Preposition)
12. **the** (• Article)
13. **early** (Adjective – Modifying *morning*)
14. **morning** (Noun – Object of Preposition)

6. Social Studies Concept Pyramid Sentence

Sentence: *The brave explorers carefully mapped the uncharted land during their long expedition.*

Word-by-Word Labeling with Sentence Weather Symbols:

1. **The** (• Article)
2. **brave** (Adjective – Modifying *explorers*)
3. **explorers** (Noun – Subject)
4. **carefully** (Adverb – Modifying *mapped*)
5. **mapped** (Verb)
6. **the** (• Article)
7. **uncharted** (Adjective – Modifying *land*)
8. **land** (Noun – Object)
9. **during** (Preposition)
10. **their** (Pronoun – Possessive)
11. **long** (Adjective – Modifying *expedition*)
12. **expedition** (Noun – Object of Preposition)

7. Fine Arts Concept Pyramid Sentence

Sentence: *The talented young artist quickly painted a beautiful landscape with bright blue skies.*

Word-by-Word Labeling with Sentence Weather Symbols:

1. **The** (• Article)
2. **talented** (Adjective – Modifying *artist*)
3. **young** (Adjective – Modifying *artist*)
4. **artist** (Noun – Subject)
5. **quickly** (Adverb – Modifying *painted*)
6. **painted** (Verb)
7. **a** (• Article)
8. **beautiful** (Adjective – Modifying *landscape*)
9. **landscape** (Noun – Object)
10. **with** (Preposition)
11. **bright** (Adjective – Modifying *skies*)
12. **blue** (Adjective – Modifying *skies*)
13. **skies** (Noun – Object of Preposition)

8. Physical Education Concept Pyramid Sentence (Sport)

Sentence: *The determined soccer players ran tirelessly across the muddy field during practice.*

Word-by-Word Labeling with Sentence Weather Symbols:

1. **The** (• Article)
2. **determined** (Adjective – Modifying *players*)
3. **soccer** (Adjective – Modifying *players*)
4. **players** (Noun – Subject)
5. **ran** (Verb)
6. **tirelessly** (Adverb – Modifying *ran*)
7. **across** (Preposition)
8. **the** (• Article)
9. **muddy** (Adjective – Modifying *field*)
10. **field** (Noun – Object of Preposition)
11. **during** (Preposition)
12. **practice** (Noun – Object of Preposition)

Visual Summary of Weather Symbols in Pyramid Sentences

- **Noun**
- **Verb**
- **Adverb**
- **Preposition**
- **• Article**
- **Pronoun**
- **Adjective**

Using **Sentence Weather Symbols**, students will grasp the roles of each word within a sentence, gaining a deeper understanding of grammar and sentence construction. This method offers a visual and interactive way to reinforce learning! Would you like these formatted into a **printable classroom worksheet with symbols and visuals?**

Parts of Speech Chart with Symbols, Examples, and Motions

Part of Speech	Symbol	Example	Motion
Noun	Sun	*dog, house, freedom*	Arms overhead in a circle to represent the sun.
Adjective	Star	*big, happy, red*	Point upward with both hands like shining stars.
Pronoun	Moon	*he, she, they*	Curve your hand into a "C" shape to mimic the crescent moon.
Article	• Dot	*the, a, an*	Tap your index finger in the air like placing a small dot.
Verb	Raindrop	*run, is, think*	Drop your hand downward quickly to represent falling rain.
Adverb	Two Raindrops	*quickly, yesterday, very*	Drop both hands twice in rhythm to show multiple raindrops.
Preposition	Cloud	*on, under, with*	Spread your hands outward to create a cloud shape.
Conjunction	Rainbow	*and, but, or*	Arch both arms overhead to form a rainbow shape.
Interjection	Lightning Bolt	*Wow! Hey! Ouch!*	Strike your hand downward like a lightning bolt.

"The Parts of Speech Poem"

Nouns name people, places, or things,
Dog, *teacher*, *mountain*, or *rings*.
They're the **sun** that shines so bright,
Naming everything in sight.

Adjectives tell *what kind*, *which one*, *how many*,
Big, *blue*, *happy*, or *any*.
They add color, spice, and flair,
Like shining stars that fill the air.

Pronouns step in, that's what they do,
He, *she*, *it*, *we*, *they*, *you*.
They replace nouns, short and sweet,
The **moon** that keeps your words neat.

• **Articles** are tiny but grand—
The, *a*, *an* help nouns stand.
Like **dots** they show what's near or far,
Pointing out just who you are.

Verbs show action or just how things be,
Jump, *run*, *think*, or *is*, you'll see.
Raindrops falling, full of might,
They bring your sentences to life!

Adverbs tell *how*, *when*, *where*, *how much*,
Quickly, *soon*, *very*, and such.
Two raindrops falling, swift and strong,
They help your verbs and move along.

Prepositions lead the way,
On, under, before today.
They form **clouds** to help you know
Where things happen or where to go.

Conjunctions link words and ideas with cheer,
And, but, or, they keep thoughts near.
Like a **rainbow**, bright and wide,
They connect and help things glide.

Interjections shout with glee—
Wow! Hey! Oops! Oh no! Whee!
They're **lightning bolts**, quick and loud,
Adding voice that makes you proud.

Remember this poem, and soon you'll see,
The parts of speech in harmony.
Each one plays a special role,
Helping words come together, whole!

Parts of Speech Song

(To the tune of "Twinkle, Twinkle, Little Star")

♫ Verse 1

Nouns will name a person, place,
Dog or school, a friendly face.
Adjectives will help describe,
Big and blue, or tall and wide.
Verbs show action, fast or slow,
Jump or think, or start to grow.

♫ Verse 2

Pronouns step in, short and neat,
He, she, they, to make words sweet.
Adverbs tell us *how* or *when*,
Quickly now, or late again.
Prepositions show the way,
On the chair, or *near* the bay.

♫ Verse 3

Conjunctions link and help combine,
And, *but*, *or*, they all align.
Interjections shout with glee,
Wow! Oh no! Just look at me!
Parts of speech will guide your song,
Learn them well, you'll write so strong.

Parts of Speech Song with Hand Motions

(To the tune of "Twinkle, Twinkle, Little Star")

Verse 1 (Nouns, Adjectives, Verbs)

🎵 **Nouns will name a person, place,**
👉 **Hand Motion:** Point to yourself (*person*), around the room (*place*), and then at an object (*thing*).

🎵 **Dog or school, a friendly face.**
👉 **Hand Motion:** Pretend to pet a dog, then draw a house shape with your fingers for *school*, and smile big for *friendly face*.

🎵 **Adjectives will help describe,**
👉 **Hand Motion:** Hold up both hands like a frame around your face, pretending to "describe" with your fingers.

🎵 **Big and blue, or tall and wide.**
👉 **Hand Motion:** Stretch your arms out wide for *big*, point up high for *tall*, and stretch your arms out sideways for *wide*.

🎵 **Verbs show action, fast or slow,**
👉 **Hand Motion:** Run in place quickly for *fast*, then pretend to walk in slow motion for *slow*.

🎵 **Jump or think, or start to grow.**
👉 **Hand Motion:** Jump in place, tap your chin for *think*, and stretch upward like you're growing.

Verse 2 (Pronouns, Adverbs, Prepositions)

🎵 **Pronouns step in, short and neat,**
👉 **Hand Motion:** Use your fingers to make a small gesture, showing *short and neat*.

🎵 **He, she, they, to make words sweet.**
👉 **Hand Motion:** Point outward for *he*, then toward yourself for *she*, and spread both arms for *they*.

🎵 **Adverbs tell us *how* or *when*,**
👉 **Hand Motion:** Move your hand in a small circle to show *how*, and then point to your wrist like you're tapping a watch for *when*.

🎵 **Quickly now, or late again.**
👉 **Hand Motion:** Run in place fast for *quickly*, then pretend to look disappointed for *late again*.

🎵 **Prepositions show the way,**
👉 **Hand Motion:** Move your hand like a path, showing direction.

🎵 ***On* the chair, or *near* the bay.**
👉 **Hand Motion:** Tap a chair for *on*, and point into the distance for *near*.

Verse 3 (Conjunctions, Interjections)

🎵 **Conjunctions link and help combine,**
👉 **Hand Motion:** Clasp your hands together to show connection.

🎵 ***And*, *but*, *or*, they all align.**
👉 **Hand Motion:** Count on your fingers as you say *and, but, or.*

🎵 **Interjections shout with glee,**
👉 **Hand Motion:** Pretend to yell joyfully and raise your arms up high.

🎵 **Wow! Oh no! Just look at me!**
👉 **Hand Motion:** Throw your hands up for *wow*, act shocked for *oh no*, and point to yourself for *me*.

🎵 **Parts of speech will guide your song,**
👉 **Hand Motion:** Move your hand in a sweeping motion like leading the group.

🎵 **Learn them well, you'll write so strong!**
👉 **Hand Motion:** Flex your muscles on *write so strong*!

Why Hand Motions Help

- **Kinesthetic learners** connect movement with learning, which reinforces memory.
- **Visual learners** associate motions with each part of speech.
- **Auditory learners** remember the words through singing and repetition.

The Sentence Weather Forecast

A Readers Theater for Learning Parts of Speech

Characters:

- **Narrator**
- **News Anchor Kelly** – The news broadcaster back at the station
- **Sunny Noun** – The main weather forecaster (Represents nouns)
- **Verb Vortex** – A storm chaser (Represents verbs)
- **Adjective Breeze** – A calm, cheerful reporter (Represents adjectives)
- **Raindrop Adverb** – A serious weather analyst (Represents adverbs)
- **Preposition Cloud** – A cloud specialist (Represents prepositions)
- **Conjunction Rainbow** – A connecting expert (Represents conjunctions)
- **Lightning Bolt Interjection** – An energetic field reporter (Represents interjections)
- **Student 1** – Watching the weather at home
- **Student 2** – Watching the weather at home
- **Student 3** – Random passerby

Scene: A TV Studio and Living Room
[The stage is divided into two sections. One side is the "TV Studio" where the weather forecast is broadcast, and the other side is a living room with three students watching TV.]

Narrator:
Welcome to the Sentence Weather Forecast, where we predict not the weather in the sky but the sentence weather of writing! Our team of reporters will explain how nouns, verbs, adjectives, and more create the perfect sentence climate. Let's go live to the station with News Anchor Kelly!

News Anchor Kelly:
Thank you, Narrator! I'm Kelly, and today's forecast is looking lively for anyone writing sentences. We've got expert weathercaster Sunny Noun at the map. Sunny, what's the outlook?

Sunny Noun: (Pointing to a weather map filled with symbols)
Good morning! I'm Sunny Noun, and it's going to be a sunny day for ***nouns****! Nouns name people, places, and things—everything from dog to freedom! If you don't have nouns, you can't build a sentence. Now let's check in with Verb Vortex, who's tracking action in the field.*

Verb Vortex: (Standing in front of a stormy backdrop)
Thanks, Sunny! I'm out here with fast-moving ***verbs****! They're bringing action into sentences—words like run, jump, and think. Watch out for irregular verbs, though! They're unpredictable and can change form without warning.*

Sunny Noun:
Sounds like a lot of action, Verb Vortex! Stay safe out there and watch for any tense changes. Back to the station!

News Anchor Kelly:
Thanks, Sunny and Verb Vortex! Let's hear from Adjective Breeze, who's bringing us a little flair for sentence descriptions.

Adjective Breeze: (Calm and cheerful, holding a microphone)
Hello, everyone! I'm Adjective Breeze, bringing color and detail to your sentences with ***adjectives****! Adjectives help describe nouns, making your writing more vivid. Instead of dog, try big brown dog! Adding adjectives makes your writing more interesting and fun!*

Sunny Noun:
Thanks, Adjective Breeze! But be careful—too many adjectives can make your sentence cloudy and cluttered. Now over to Raindrop Adverb for a look at how verbs are getting extra detail today.

Raindrop Adverb: (Serious, pointing to a radar map)
Thanks, Sunny. I'm Raindrop Adverb, and I'm here to modify verbs and adjectives with words like quickly, very, and yesterday. Just a sprinkle of adverbs can make your writing clearer, but don't flood your sentences with too many, or they'll slow everything down.

News Anchor Kelly:
Great advice, Raindrop Adverb! Now, Preposition Cloud is floating into the studio to explain how prepositions help connect ideas.

Preposition Cloud: (Floating onto the stage with a cloud cutout)
Hi, everyone! I'm Preposition Cloud. I create ***prepositional phrases*** *like on the table or under the bed. Prepositions help show where and when things happen, giving your sentences structure. Without prepositions, your sentence would feel lost!*

Sunny Noun:
Excellent, Preposition Cloud! Now let's brighten things up with Conjunction Rainbow!

Conjunction Rainbow: (Wearing a rainbow scarf, smiling brightly)
Hi, I'm Conjunction Rainbow! I link words and ideas with ***conjunctions*** *like and, but, and or. Think of me as the rainbow that makes your sentences flow smoothly.*

Lightning Bolt Interjection: (Energetically jumping in)
BOOM! I'm Lightning Bolt Interjection! I add emotion with words like Wow! Hey! Oops! Use me to express feelings and excitement. Just remember, too many interjections can turn your writing into a storm!

[Scene shifts to the living room, where three students are watching the broadcast on TV.]

Student 1: (Pointing at the TV)
Whoa! This is the best grammar lesson ever! I didn't know nouns were like the sun!

Student 2:
And verbs are storms? That totally makes sense! Without verbs, nothing happens.

Student 3: (Walking in)
What's going on?

Student 1:
It's the Sentence Weather Forecast! They're explaining parts of speech with weather symbols.

Student 2:
And it's actually fun! I finally understand the difference between adjectives and adverbs.

Student 3: (Thinking)
Adjectives describe nouns, and adverbs describe verbs, right?

Student 2:
Exactly! And prepositions tell us where and when things happen, like in the park or during lunch.

Student 1:
Don't forget conjunctions—they connect everything! Without them, your sentences would be choppy.

Student 3: (Laughing)
I'd definitely be Lightning Bolt Interjection. I love adding excitement!

Narrator:
And that wraps up today's Sentence Weather Forecast! Remember, nouns are the sun, verbs bring the action, and adjectives and adverbs add the perfect touch. Stay creative and keep your sentence skies clear!

Various Ways Sentence Weather helps students during assessments:

1. **Builds Confidence** – Familiar tools reduce uncertainty, making students feel more prepared and capable of tackling the task.
2. **Improves Focus and Organization** – The structured approach guides students to focus on one part of the sentence at a time, preventing them from getting lost in lengthy or complex sentences.
3. **Encourages Self-Monitoring** – With a visual, step-by-step process, students can check their work systematically, improving accuracy.
4. **Supports Memory and Retention** – Symbols act as cues, helping students recall strategies for identifying sentence parts (subject, verb, punctuation, etc.) even under pressure.
5. **Enhances Time Management** – Chunking content into manageable pieces helps students pace themselves and avoid rushing through the assessment.
6. **Develops Independence** – By internalizing the steps, students rely less on external support and more on their own problem-solving skills.
7. **Engages Multiple Learning Styles** – Visual learners benefit from symbols, while kinesthetic learners can draw or physically interact with the symbols, strengthening understanding.
8. **Reduces Test Anxiety** – Familiar routines offer comfort and predictability, making the testing experience less intimidating.
9. **Promotes Strategic Thinking** – It encourages students to pause, plan, and approach the question thoughtfully rather than reactively.
10. **Increases Overall Comprehension** – Breaking sentences into smaller parts enhances their ability to identify key information, leading to better answers.

Section 2

CAPITALIZATION

Capitalization Case Scenarios

Sentence Starters
First word of every sentence

Proper Nouns
Names of people, places, organizations, and specific items

Titles
Titles of books, articles, and works

Days, Months, and Holidays
Rules for dates and celebrations

Pronoun "I"
Always capitalized regardless of placement

Acronyms and Initialisms
NASA, FBI, CIA

Quotations
First word of a direct quote

Headings and Subheadings
Title case and sentence case rules

Geography
Names of continents, countries, states, cities, bodies of water, and landmarks

Historical Documents
Declaration of Independence, U.S. Constitution

Abbreviations
Proper capitalization of standard and formal abbreviations

Capitalization: Why It's Essential for Reading and Writing Fluency

Capitalization is a powerful tool in reading and writing, giving structure, emphasis, and clarity to language. It acts as a guidepost for readers, signaling the beginning of a sentence, highlighting proper nouns, and providing visual cues that improve comprehension. Without capitalization, writing can quickly become confusing and difficult to read. Imagine trying to identify names, places, or the start of new sentences without these crucial markers—your reading pace would slow, and your understanding would suffer. For young readers, consistent use of capitalization helps build fluency, making it easier to recognize sentence patterns and essential words.

The historical roots of capitalization can be traced back to ancient Rome. The earliest Roman inscriptions were written entirely in uppercase letters, known as **majuscule script**. This style remained dominant for centuries. However, during the Middle Ages, scribes in monasteries began to develop **minuscule script** (lowercase letters), which allowed for faster writing and easier reading. This innovation marked the beginning of distinguishing between uppercase and lowercase letters.

The modern use of capitalization—distinguishing sentence beginnings, proper nouns, and key words—took shape around the 15th century with the invention of the printing press. Early printers such as William Caxton began standardizing capitalization rules to improve readability. By the 18th century, English grammar guides established more formal rules for capitalization, closely resembling those we use today.

In today's writing, capitalization is crucial for reading fluency and comprehension. It allows writers to highlight important information and makes texts easier to navigate. Capitalization helps avoid ambiguity and confusion, ensuring that written communication is not only accurate but also clear and engaging. For readers, it provides essential visual cues that guide the flow of a sentence, making reading an intuitive and enjoyable process.

Why Do Students Struggle with Capitalization?

Capitalization may seem like a simple rule, but for many students, remembering all the situations in which it applies can be a significant challenge. This difficulty arises because capitalization rules are diverse and vary based on context. Unlike basic punctuation, which follows more predictable patterns, capitalization involves memorizing multiple categories such as sentence beginnings, proper nouns, titles, geographical locations, and specific names of holidays and historical documents. These categories often don't appear in a logical sequence, making it harder for students to internalize them.

One reason students struggle is that **capitalization rules aren't always consistent across different languages**. For example, while English capitalizes days of the week, languages like Spanish do not. This can confuse bilingual learners or students learning English as a second language. Additionally, some rules feel intuitive (capitalizing names), while others, like capitalizing headings or acronyms, feel more arbitrary and require intentional memorization.

Another reason is **exposure to informal writing**, such as texting and social media, where capitalization is often ignored. In these informal settings, students don't consistently see correct capitalization in use, making it harder for them to apply the rules in formal writing. This lack of reinforcement blurs the line between what is necessary in casual versus academic writing.

Capitalization also demands students to multitask while writing—**focusing on sentence structure, spelling, grammar, and content**—which makes it easy to overlook capitalization errors. When students are more concerned with expressing their ideas, they may not notice missing capital letters.

Helping students overcome these challenges requires **consistent practice, visual reminders, and engaging activities** that make the rules stick. Acronyms like **SPOTLIGHT**, charts, and games can help reinforce capitalization rules in fun, memorable ways. Providing clear, real-world examples and making corrections part of daily writing routines will gradually help students master the art of capitalization.

The most frequent types of capitalization errors fall into several categories:

1. Start of Sentences (S in SPOTLIGHT)

Common Error: Forgetting to capitalize the first word of a sentence.
Why It Happens:

- Students focus on getting their ideas out quickly and overlook basic sentence structure.
- Inconsistent exposure to properly written text.
  Example: *"the dog ran fast."* → *"The dog ran fast."*

2. Proper Nouns (P in SPOTLIGHT)

Common Error: Failure to capitalize names of people, places, or specific titles.
Why It Happens:

- Students struggle to distinguish between common and proper nouns.
- Limited understanding of what qualifies as a proper noun.
  Example: *"we visited new york."* → *"We visited New York."*

3. Days, Months, and Holidays (H in SPOTLIGHT)

Common Error: Forgetting to capitalize days of the week, months, and holiday names.
Why It Happens:

- Students may remember capitalization for the names of people but forget the same rule applies to calendar-related terms.
  Example: *"i love christmas."* → *"I love Christmas."*

4. Titles of Books, Articles, and Songs (T in SPOTLIGHT)

Common Error: Failing to capitalize important words in titles or capitalizing every word.
Why It Happens:

- Confusion over which words in a title should be capitalized.
  Example: *"the great gatsby"* → *"The Great Gatsby"*

5. Acronyms and Abbreviations (I in SPOTLIGHT)

Common Error: Forgetting to capitalize letters in commonly used acronyms or abbreviations.
Why It Happens:

- Students often treat acronyms as regular words in casual writing.
  Example: *"nasa is amazing."* → *"NASA is amazing."*

Why These Errors Are Common

- **Focus on Content Over Mechanics:** Students prioritize getting their ideas on paper over checking for capitalization.
- **Informal Writing Habits:** Frequent use of texting, social media, and other informal writing influences how students approach capitalization.
- **Incomplete Mastery of Capitalization Rules:** Students may understand some capitalization rules but forget others, especially in longer pieces of writing.

Solution: Frequent practice and visual reminders like the **SPOTLIGHT acronym** can help students internalize capitalization rules and apply them consistently!

Creative Strategies to Help Kids Slow Down and Apply Capitalization Rules

Teaching students to slow down when they write is essential for encouraging them to apply the rules they already know—especially capitalization. Since many mistakes happen due to rushing or focusing only on ideas, here are some creative, engaging ways to help students develop intentional, careful writing habits.

---

1. STOP Strategy (Self-Check Acronym)

Use a simple acronym like **STOP (Slow, Think, Observe, Proofread)** to remind students to pause and check for capitalization before moving on.

Teacher Script:
"Before you finish writing, STOP! Look at each sentence and ask yourself: Did I capitalize the start of my sentence? Proper nouns? Titles? If not, fix it before moving on!"

Activity: Create STOP posters for the classroom and incorporate a "STOP Check" at the end of every writing assignment.

---

2. Capitalization Detective

Make students "Capitalization Detectives" and give them a short writing passage with intentional capitalization mistakes. Their task is to circle the mistakes and correct them.

Extension: Have students exchange papers after their own writing and play detective on a peer's work.

---

3. Highlighter Revision Game

Give students highlighters and have them go back over their writing to highlight every capital letter. If they find a sentence or word that should be capitalized but isn't, they mark it and correct it.

Why It Works: Highlighting slows students down and makes them visually focus on capitalization.

4. Capitalization Rap or Chant

Use a catchy chant or rap to remind students of the key capitalization rules. Practice it before every writing session. For example:

"Start each sentence with a big letter, names and places—make them better! Titles, months, and holidays, capitalize them all the way!"

Add body movements (like pointing up for a capital letter) to engage kinesthetic learners.

---

5. Sentence Detective Partner Game

Students write a short paragraph, then trade papers with a partner who becomes a "sentence detective." Their job is to search for missing capitals and underline them. Afterward, they discuss and correct the errors together.

---

6. Visual Symbols for Capitalization

Use visual cues or symbols to reinforce capitalization rules. For example:

- **Sun symbol** for the start of a sentence
- **Crown symbol** for proper nouns
- **Flag symbol** for titles

Students can create their own visual symbols and draw them in the margins as reminders.

---

7. Writing Reflection Time

Build "Reflection Time" into every writing session. After finishing their first draft, give students 5 minutes to reflect on their writing with a checklist:

- Did I capitalize the first word in each sentence?
- Did I capitalize names and places?
- Did I capitalize titles and important words?

8. Capitalization Corners

Set up four corners in the classroom labeled: **Start of Sentence**, **Proper Nouns**, **Titles**, and **Holidays/Months/Days**. Read a sentence aloud and ask students to walk to the corner representing the capitalization rule they hear.

Example: *"We are going to Disney World next summer."* (Students walk to the Proper Nouns corner.)

Why Slowing Down Matters

When students slow down and focus on capitalization, their writing becomes clearer and more polished. These strategies turn what might seem like a tedious task into a fun and thoughtful part of the writing process. With practice and reinforcement, students will internalize these habits and apply them naturally.

SPOTLIGHT Acronym for Capitalization

This acronym highlights when to capitalize and serves as a reminder that capitalization brings focus or "spotlight" to important words.

- **S – Start of Sentences**
  Example: The dog ran to the park.
- **P – Proper Nouns and Pronouns (I)**
  Example: Sarah went to Paris. I love pizza.
- **O – Official Titles and Headings**
  Example: President of the United States, The Great Gatsby
- **T – Titles (Books, Articles, Songs)**
  Example: Harry Potter and the Sorcerer's Stone
- **L – Landmarks and Locations (Geography)**
  Example: Mount Everest, Pacific Ocean, Eiffel Tower
- **I – Initials, Acronyms, and Abbreviations**
  Example: NASA, Mr., Dr. Seuss
- **G – Geographical Features and Historical Documents**
  Example: Declaration of Independence, Rocky Mountains
- **H – Holidays, Days, and Months**
  Example: Christmas, Monday, October
- **T – Text in Quotations (When starting a new sentence)**
  Example: He said, "Let's go to the park!"

Why SPOTLIGHT Works

By remembering this acronym, students can cover all major capitalization rules. Each letter ties to a specific category, making it easy to recall when writing or editing. **SPOTLIGHT** is also a fun metaphor—just as spotlights bring attention to something, capitalization highlights what's important in writing.

Reference Chart based on the SPOTLIGHT acronym for capitalization

Letter	What It Stands For	Examples
S	Start of Sentences	The dog barked loudly.
P	Proper Nouns and Pronouns (I)	Sarah, London, I love reading.
O	Official Titles and Headings	President, The Great Gatsby
T	Titles of Books, Articles, Songs	Harry Potter and the Sorcerer's Stone
L	Landmarks and Locations (Geography)	Mount Everest, Pacific Ocean, Eiffel Tower
I	Initials, Acronyms, and Abbreviations	NASA, Mr., Dr. Seuss
G	Geographical Features and Historical Documents	Rocky Mountains, Declaration of Independence
H	Holidays, Days, and Months	Christmas, Monday, October
T	Text in Quotations (Starting with a new sentence)	He said, "Let's go to the park!"

Rainbow Revision: A Colorful Way to Master Capitalization and Punctuation

The **Rainbow Revision Technique** is a fun, visual strategy that helps students improve their capitalization and punctuation skills by turning their revision process into a colorful and interactive activity. By using colored pencils, markers, or crayons, students can identify and correct errors in their writing with ease and confidence. This technique builds both grammar awareness and mathematical reasoning while fostering a careful, reflective approach to writing.

How It Works

1. **Step 1: Green for Capital Letters**
   Students begin by **circling every capital letter** at the start of each sentence with a **green** marker, crayon, or colored pencil. This ensures that they are checking the beginning of every sentence for proper capitalization.

   Teacher Script:
   "Use your green marker to find and circle every capital letter at the beginning of a sentence. This will help you see if you've missed any."

   Example:

   - Correct: *Green circles on sentences like:* ***The dog barked.***
   - Missing: No green circle? Check that you've capitalized the first letter!
2. **Step 2: Red for Ending Punctuation**
   Next, students **circle every punctuation mark** at the end of each sentence in **red**. This helps them ensure that every sentence is properly closed with a period, question mark, or exclamation mark.

   Teacher Script:
   "Now grab your red marker and circle all the ending punctuation marks. Make sure each sentence has one!"

   Example:

   - Correct: *Red circles on punctuation like:* ***The cat is sleeping.***
   - Missing: No red circle? Double-check for missing periods, question marks, or exclamation marks.

3. **Step 3: Math Meets Writing**
   After circling both capital letters and punctuation marks, students **count** how many green and red circles they have. **The numbers should match!** If they don't, this is a clue that something is missing.

   Green Circles ≠ Red Circles:

   - **Fewer Green Circles?** Check for missing capital letters at the beginning of sentences.
   - **Fewer Red Circles?** You may have forgotten to add ending punctuation.

   Teacher Script:
   "Compare your green and red circles. The numbers should match. If they don't, go back and find what's missing!"

Why Rainbow Revision Works

- **Visual Reinforcement:** Students can **see their progress** as they mark their writing with colorful circles.
- **Immediate Feedback:** Missing circles reveal errors that might otherwise go unnoticed.
- **Cross-Curricular Practice:** Counting and comparing green and red circles integrates math concepts like one-to-one correspondence and equal sets into language arts.
- **Slows Down the Writing Process:** Encourages students to pause and reflect, reducing careless errors.

Extension Activities

- **Graph Your Results:** After counting the green and red circles, students can create a simple bar graph to track their progress over multiple writing pieces.
- **Peer Review Challenge:** Students swap papers and check each other's work using the Rainbow Revision technique.

Final Thought

The **Rainbow Revision Technique** transforms the sometimes dull task of editing into a hands-on, engaging experience that reinforces grammar skills while making learning fun. By adding a splash of color and a touch of math, students develop stronger writing habits and learn to pay close attention to every capital letter and punctuation mark!

Mentor Paragraph: The Creation of Presidents' Day

Presidents' day, celebrated on the third monday of february, honors the legacy of America's leaders. Originally established in 1885 to recognize george Washington's birthday, the holiday later expanded to honor abraham lincoln and all U.S. Presidents. The celebration was officially moved in 1971 as part of the uniform monday holiday act to provide more long weekends for workers. Across the country, schools, businesses, and even large Landmarks like the statue of liberty mark the occasion with educational events and festivities. The day serves as a reminder of the importance of leadership, unity, and public service.

Creative Method: SPOTLIGHT Capitalization Detective Hunt

Transform the process of identifying capitalization errors into an interactive **"Capitalization Detective Hunt"** using the **SPOTLIGHT acronym**.

1. **Detective Preparation:**
   Give each student a detective badge and a copy of the paragraph. Explain that they are now **Capitalization Detectives** on a mission to find capitalization mistakes using the **SPOTLIGHT Rulebook**.
2. **Color-Coded Annotation:**
   Assign each type of capitalization from the SPOTLIGHT acronym a color:
   - **Start of Sentences:** Green Circle
   - **Proper Nouns and Pronouns:** Blue Underline
   - **Official Titles and Headings:** Yellow Highlight
   - **Titles (Books, Songs, Holidays):** Pink Highlight
   - **Landmarks and Locations:** Red Star
   - **Initials, Acronyms, Abbreviations:** Purple Box
   - **Holidays, Days, and Months:** Orange Underline
3. **Hunt and Annotate:**
   Students read the paragraph and annotate errors with the assigned colors.

   Example:

   - Green circle around "Presidents' day" (should be "Presidents' Day")
   - Yellow highlight for "uniform monday holiday act" (should be "Uniform Monday Holiday Act")
   - Red star for "statue of liberty" (should be "Statue of Liberty")
4. **Create a SPOTLIGHT Error Count:**
   After the hunt, students count how many errors they found in each category and compare their results with a partner.
5. **Reflection Discussion:**
   "Why do you think these errors are common? How can we remember to capitalize these words in our own writing?"

SPOTLIGHT Capitalization Symbol & Color Chart

Letter	Capitalization Rule	Annotation	Example
S	Start of Sentences	**Green Circle**	*presidents' day* → **Presidents' Day**
P	Proper Nouns and Pronouns (I)	**Blue Underline**	*george Washington* → **George Washington**
O	Official Titles and Headings	**Yellow Highlight**	*uniform monday holiday act* → **Uniform Monday Holiday Act**
T	Titles (Books, Songs, Holidays)	**Pink Highlight**	*third monday of february* → **Third Monday of February**
L	Landmarks and Locations	**Red Star**	*statue of liberty* → **Statue of Liberty**
I	Initials, Acronyms, Abbreviations	**Purple Box**	*U.S. Presidents* → **U.S. Presidents**
G	Geographical Features and Historical Documents	**Gray Squiggly Line**	*america* → **America**, *constitution* → **Constitution**
H	Holidays, Days, and Months	**Orange Underline**	*february* → **February**, *monday* → **Monday**

SPOTLIGHT Capitalization Station Rotation with five engaging and interactive stations to reinforce capitalization skills. Each station focuses on a different aspect of the **SPOTLIGHT** acronym and encourages hands-on practice.

Station 1: "S — Start of Sentences"

Activity Name: "Sentence Fix-It Factory"
Objective: Identify and correct missing capitalization at the beginning of sentences.
Materials:

- Sentence strips with lowercase sentence beginnings
- Green highlighters
- Fix-It Checklist

Instructions:

1. Each student selects a sentence strip.
2. Identify the first word and highlight it with a **green highlighter** if it starts with a capital letter.
3. If it's incorrect, rewrite the sentence with the correct capitalization.
4. Compare answers with a partner.

Example Sentences:

- "the cat jumped on the table."
- "yesterday, we went to the park."

Station 2: "P — Proper Nouns"

Activity Name: "Name It Right!"
Objective: Differentiate between proper and common nouns and capitalize proper nouns.
Materials:

- Sorting cards labeled with common and proper nouns
- Chart with two columns: **Common Nouns** and **Proper Nouns**
- Blue markers

Instructions:

1. Sort the noun cards into the correct columns.
2. Write proper nouns with a **blue marker** and capitalize them correctly.
3. Share with the group and discuss why proper nouns are capitalized.

Example Cards:

- *dog (common) → Fido (proper)*
- *city (common) → Paris (proper)*

Station 3: "H — Holidays, Days, and Months"

Activity Name: "Calendar Challenge"
Objective: Practice identifying and capitalizing days, months, and holidays.
Materials:

- Calendar worksheets with missing capitalization
- Orange crayons

Instructions:

1. Circle all incorrectly written days, months, and holidays with an **orange crayon**.
2. Rewrite them with correct capitalization.
3. Create a mini holiday sentence using at least three correctly capitalized words.

Example Sentences:

- "I love christmas in december." → "I love Christmas in December."

Station 4: "T — Titles and Headlines"

Activity Name: "Title Tamer"
Objective: Identify correct capitalization in titles of books, articles, and songs.
Materials:

- Title cards with capitalization errors
- Title Rule Poster
- Pink highlighters

Instructions:

1. Read each title card carefully.
2. Highlight words that need capitalization with a **pink highlighter**.
3. Rewrite the title correctly on your worksheet.

Example Titles:

- "the great gatsby" → "The Great Gatsby"
- "harry potter and the chamber of secrets" → "Harry Potter and the Chamber of Secrets"

Station 5: "I — Initials, Acronyms, and Abbreviations"

Activity Name: "Acronym Explorer"
Objective: Identify and correctly capitalize commonly used initials, acronyms, and abbreviations.
Materials:

- Acronym cards (NASA, FBI, Dr., Mr., etc.)
- Purple markers
- "Acronym Explorer" worksheet

Instructions:

1. Choose an acronym card and read it aloud.
2. Use a **purple marker** to write the acronym in all caps on your worksheet.
3. Create a sentence using the acronym and share it with your group.

Example Acronyms:

*NASA: "NASA launched a new satellite." *FBI: "The FBI is investigating the case."

Wrap-Up Reflection

After completing all stations:

- Have students share one new thing they learned at each station.
- Use a **SPOTLIGHT Challenge** quiz to assess understanding, reinforcing how capitalization affects writing clarity and comprehension.

Major project ideas that teachers can assign to help students reinforce and master the **SPOTLIGHT capitalization acronym** in fun and meaningful ways:

1. Create a Capitalization Poster Series

Project Objective: Design posters that represent each letter of the **SPOTLIGHT** acronym with definitions, rules, and examples.
Details:

- Assign each group of students a letter from **SPOTLIGHT** (S, P, O, T, etc.).
- Each group will create a visually engaging poster with examples of correct capitalization and illustrations.
- Hang the posters around the classroom for future reference.
Skills Reinforced: Visual learning, collaboration, presentation

---

2. Write a Children's Book

Project Objective: Write and illustrate a short children's book explaining capitalization rules through a story.
Details:

- Students can create a story that features characters like **Captain Capital** or **Punctuation Pal**, teaching capitalization rules as part of the plot.
- Include examples of each **SPOTLIGHT** category in the text.
- Share the completed books with younger students.
Skills Reinforced: Writing, creativity, peer teaching

3. Capitalization Escape Room

Project Objective: Create an interactive escape room activity where students solve capitalization-related puzzles to "escape" the room.
Details:

- Set up different stations with puzzles based on each **SPOTLIGHT** rule.
- Students must identify errors, rewrite sentences, or complete challenges to unlock the next clue.
- Reward teams with certificates or prizes for escaping.
  Skills Reinforced: Critical thinking, teamwork, problem-solving

---

4. Capitalization Documentary or Video Project

Project Objective: Create a short video explaining the importance of capitalization in writing and communication.
Details:

- Divide students into production teams (writers, actors, directors).
- Each team focuses on one **SPOTLIGHT** rule and explains it through examples and scenarios.
- Edit the video and present it to the class or publish it on the school's website.
  Skills Reinforced: Media literacy, collaboration, public speaking

---

5. Create a Capitalization Board Game

Project Objective: Design a board game where players test their capitalization knowledge.
Details:

- Use each **SPOTLIGHT** rule as a category for game cards.
- Players must answer capitalization questions correctly to move forward.
- Include bonus spaces for mastering tricky rules.
  Skills Reinforced: Game design, strategic thinking, rule application

6. Capitalization Newspaper Project

Project Objective: Create a classroom newspaper featuring articles, advertisements, and editorials that emphasize capitalization rules.
Details:

- Assign roles (editor, reporter, graphic designer).
- Students write articles and ensure all capitalization is correct, especially in headlines and proper nouns.
- Publish and distribute the newspaper.
  Skills Reinforced: Writing, editing, team collaboration

---

7. Capitalization Songwriting and Performance

Project Objective: Write and perform a song or rap about capitalization rules.
Details:

- Use the **SPOTLIGHT** acronym to build verses for the song.
- Perform the song live or record it as a music video.
  Skills Reinforced: Music, rhythm, verbal memory

---

8. Capitalization Scrapbook

Project Objective: Create a personal scrapbook featuring photos, illustrations, and writing with correctly applied capitalization rules.
Details:

- Each scrapbook page focuses on a different **SPOTLIGHT** rule.
- Students label and describe photos or images using proper capitalization.
  Skills Reinforced: Personal expression, organization, writing clarity

9. Interactive Capitalization Museum

Project Objective: Create a "Capitalization Museum" where each **SPOTLIGHT** rule is a themed exhibit.
Details:

- Students build interactive displays for each rule (like a model, game, or infographic).
- Host a "museum walk" where other classes can visit and learn.
  Skills Reinforced: Research, creativity, presentation

---

10. Capitalization Comic Strip

Project Objective: Write and illustrate a comic strip that explains each **SPOTLIGHT** rule.
Details:

- Characters encounter capitalization challenges and solve them with creative solutions.
- The comic should be humorous but informative.
  Skills Reinforced: Storytelling, drawing, conceptual thinking

Capitalization Escape Room: The Ultimate SPOTLIGHT Challenge

Objective:
Students will work in small teams to solve capitalization-related puzzles, each based on a rule from the **SPOTLIGHT** acronym. Successfully solving each challenge will lead them to the next clue until they escape the room! This interactive experience builds teamwork, reinforces capitalization rules, and engages students in critical thinking and problem-solving.

Setting the Stage: Room Decorations & Ambience

Transform your classroom into an exciting escape room atmosphere!

Decorations:

- **Dim the lights** and use desk lamps for a mysterious effect.
- Create a **"SPOTLIGHT Command Center"** table where students begin the challenge.
- Hang **SPOTLIGHT banners** or posters with symbols for each capitalization rule.
- Use caution tape or paper chains to "lock" certain areas or clues.
- Place **fake locks** on boxes or folders containing puzzles.
- Use **spy gadgets** (magnifying glasses, flashlights) for added fun.

Materials Needed:

1. **Station Signs** (labeled with each SPOTLIGHT rule)
2. **Puzzle Envelopes** (containing task cards, worksheets, and sentence strips)
3. **Answer Sheets** for students to record their answers
4. **Clue Cards** to guide students to the next station once they solve the puzzle
5. **Certificates of Escape** for each team
6. **Props and Decor:** Flashlights, magnifying glasses, fake keys, printable locks

Instructions for Setup:

1. **Divide the Classroom into Stations** – Each station corresponds to a rule in the **SPOTLIGHT** acronym:
    - **Station 1: Start of Sentences**
    - **Station 2: Proper Nouns**
    - **Station 3: Official Titles and Headlines**
    - **Station 4: Titles of Books, Articles, and Songs**
    - **Station 5: Landmarks and Locations**
    - **Station 6: Initials, Acronyms, and Abbreviations**
    - **Station 7: Holidays, Days, and Months**
2. **Create a Clue Path** – Students will move to the next station once they solve the challenge at the current one.
3. **Prepare Puzzle Tasks** – Each station will contain a unique capitalization-related puzzle. Once students complete the puzzle, they'll receive a clue directing them to the next station.

Station Activities and Clues

Station 1: Start of Sentences (S)

Activity:
Students are given a short paragraph with lowercase letters at the beginning of each sentence. They must rewrite it with the correct capitalization.

Puzzle Example:
the dog barked loudly. it started raining. my friends and I ran inside.
Task: Correct the sentences to:
The dog barked loudly. It started raining. My friends and I ran inside.

Clue to Next Station:
"Look for names and places in the next challenge!"

Station 2: Proper Nouns (P)

Activity:
Students are given a list of common nouns and must rewrite them as proper nouns.

Puzzle Example:

- city → **New York**
- teacher → **Mrs. Johnson**
- holiday → **Thanksgiving**

Clue to Next Station:
"Now find the room with headlines and important titles!"

Station 3: Official Titles and Headlines (O)

Activity:
Students are shown sample headlines and titles with incorrect capitalization and must fix them.

Puzzle Example:
the great gatsby → **The Great Gatsby**
declaration of independence → **Declaration of Independence**

Clue to Next Station:
"Head to the station with books and songs!"

Station 4: Titles of Books, Articles, and Songs (T)

Activity:
Students will sort titles into correctly and incorrectly capitalized categories.

Puzzle Example:

- Correct: *Charlotte's Web, The Hunger Games*
- Incorrect: *harry potter and the sorcerer's stone*

Clue to Next Station:
"You're halfway there! Now visit famous places and landmarks."

Station 5: Landmarks and Locations (L)

Activity:
Students must circle correctly capitalized landmarks and fix incorrect ones.

Puzzle Example:

- Correct: *Statue of Liberty*
- Incorrect: *grand canyon* → *Grand Canyon*

Clue to Next Station:
"Almost there! Go to the station with initials and acronyms!"

Station 6: Initials, Acronyms, and Abbreviations (I)

Activity:
Students match common acronyms with their correct meanings and ensure they are properly capitalized.

Puzzle Example:

- **NASA** → National Aeronautics and Space Administration
- **FBI** → Federal Bureau of Investigation

Clue to Next Station:
"Your final challenge is all about days, months, and holidays!"

Station 7: Holidays, Days, and Months (H)

Activity:
Students complete a word search with incorrectly capitalized days, months, and holidays and rewrite them correctly.

Puzzle Example:

- *december* → *December*
- *halloween* → *Halloween*

Final Clue:
"Congratulations! You've unlocked the key to proper capitalization. Return to the command center to claim your prize!"

Assessment and Reflection

1. **Observation:** Monitor student engagement and teamwork.
2. **Reflection Discussion:**
   "Which capitalization rule did you find the most challenging? How can you remember it in your writing?"
3. **Certificates of Escape:** Reward each team with a **Certificate of Escape** and celebrate their success!

Optional Extensions:

- **Create Your Own Clue:** Students can design their own escape room challenges for other classmates to solve.
- **SPOTLIGHT Hall of Fame:** Post the names of students who successfully escaped on a classroom wall.

Task Cards and **Clue Cards** for each station in the **SPOTLIGHT Capitalization Escape Room** project:

Station 1: Start of Sentences (S)

Task Cards:

Card 1:
Rewrite the paragraph below, making sure to capitalize the first word of every sentence.

yesterday, we went to the park. we played soccer and ate lunch. it was so much fun! later, we went to the movies.

Card 2:
Fix the following sentences by capitalizing the first word in each sentence.

1. the cat is sleeping.
2. she loves ice cream.
3. my friends and i are going swimming.

Card 3:
Identify and correct the capitalization errors in these sentences.

- today, i will bake cookies.
- it's raining outside.
- my brother plays basketball every saturday.

Clue Card:

"Great job! Now, head to the station where you'll need to capitalize names and places!"

Station 2: Proper Nouns (P)

Task Cards:

Card 1:
Rewrite these sentences, changing the common nouns to proper nouns.

1. I live in a city. → **I live in New York City.**
2. My teacher is nice. → **Mrs. Carter is nice.**
3. We had dinner at a restaurant. → **We had dinner at Olive Garden.**

Card 2:
Identify and capitalize the proper nouns in these sentences.

- we went to the beach in california.
- my friend jack loves to play chess.
- our school mascot is a lion.

Card 3:
Match the common noun to its proper noun equivalent.

1. country → **United States**
2. holiday → **Thanksgiving**
3. river → **Mississippi River**

Clue Card:

"Excellent! Now, head to the station with official titles and headlines!"

Station 3: Official Titles and Headlines (O)

Task Cards:

Card 1:
Correct the capitalization errors in the following titles and headlines.

1. the great gatsby → **The Great Gatsby**
2. declaration of independence → **Declaration of Independence**
3. to kill a mockingbird → **To Kill a Mockingbird**

Card 2:
Which of these headlines is correctly capitalized? Circle the correct answer.

1. "Summer vacation begins in june!"
2. "The Science Fair is on Friday!"
3. "read all about it: School wins Championship"

Clue Card:

"Well done! Now, move to the station with book and song titles!"

Station 4: Titles of Books, Articles, and Songs (T)

Task Cards:

Card 1:
Sort these titles into correct and incorrect capitalization columns.

1. *charlotte's web*
2. *The Lion, the Witch, and the Wardrobe*
3. *the cat in the hat*

Card 2:
Fix the capitalization errors in these sentences with titles.

1. We read *harry potter and the chamber of secrets.*
2. My favorite song is *let it go* from Frozen.

Clue Card:

"Great work! Now, head to the station with famous landmarks and locations!"

Station 5: Landmarks and Locations (L)

Task Cards:

Card 1:
Correct the capitalization errors in these famous landmarks.

1. statue of liberty → **Statue of Liberty**
2. eiffel tower → **Eiffel Tower**
3. grand canyon → **Grand Canyon**

Card 2:
Write a sentence using the correctly capitalized name of a landmark.
Example: "I visited the **Statue of Liberty** last summer."

Clue Card:

"Keep going! Now, find the station with acronyms and abbreviations!"

Station 6: Initials, Acronyms, and Abbreviations (I)

Task Cards:

Card 1:
Identify and correct the capitalization for these acronyms.

1. nasa → **NASA**
2. fbi → **FBI**
3. nba → **NBA**

Card 2:
Write a sentence using each acronym correctly.

1. **NASA** launched a new satellite.
2. The **FBI** is investigating the case.

Clue Card:

"Almost there! Now, head to the station with holidays, days, and months!"

Station 7: Holidays, Days, and Months (H)

Task Cards:

Card 1:

Circle the correctly capitalized words in the sentences below.

1. I love christmas in december.
2. My birthday is on friday.
3. We celebrate halloween every october.

Card 2:

Rewrite these sentences with correct capitalization for holidays, days, and months.

1. We will visit family on thanksgiving.
2. My favorite holiday is valentine's day.
3. School starts in august.

Clue Card:

"Congratulations! You've completed the SPOTLIGHT Escape Room! Return to the Command Center to claim your prize!"

Bonus Task Cards for Extra Challenge

- **Write a short paragraph using one example from each SPOTLIGHT category.**
- **Create your own sentence with three capitalization errors and swap with a partner for correction.**

Section 3

PUNCTUATION

The Power of Punctuation: Why It Matters in Reading and Writing Fluency

Punctuation is the essential road map of language. It provides structure, clarity, and rhythm to both written and spoken communication. Without punctuation, sentences lose their meaning and flow, making it difficult for readers to understand the writer's intended message. For example, compare these two sentences: *Let's eat, Grandma!* and *Let's eat Grandma!*—a simple comma makes all the difference! Proper punctuation ensures smooth reading and supports writing fluency by guiding the reader through pauses, stops, and shifts in tone or emphasis. It allows writers to convey ideas with precision and creativity.

Historically, punctuation has played a crucial role in written language, evolving over centuries. The earliest forms of punctuation date back to ancient Greece, where playwrights used simple marks to indicate when actors should pause during performances. However, punctuation as we know it today began to take shape with the efforts of Aristophanes of Byzantium in the 3rd century BCE. He introduced a system of dots—placed high, middle, or low—to indicate different lengths of pauses.

In English, the development of modern punctuation became more standardized during the late medieval period with the rise of the printing press in the 15th century. Early printers, such as William Caxton, helped establish consistent use of punctuation marks like the period, comma, colon, and question mark to clarify meaning. By the 18th century, punctuation had become more formalized, resembling the rules we follow today.

Understanding punctuation is crucial for readers and writers of all levels. It supports reading fluency by creating predictable patterns in text, while also helping writers organize and express ideas effectively. By mastering punctuation, students can transform their writing from a confusing collection of words into clear, engaging communication that truly connects with the reader.

Types of Punctuation

Ending Punctuation
Periods, question marks, exclamation points

Commas
Listing items in a series, separating clauses, separating introductory elements, adding appositives, using nonrestrictive modifiers, separating adjectives, using dates, addresses, titles, and direct address

Quotation Marks
Denotes dialogue, direct quotes, and titles of short works

Apostrophes
Demonstrates possession and contractions

Colons
Introduces lists, explanations, and quotations

Semicolons
Connects independent clauses and separating complex list items

Parentheses
Adds additional information or asides

Dashes
Incorporates dashes for emphasis, dividing words at end of lines and for ranges

Hyphens
Creates compound words, prefixes, and suffixes

Ellipses
Indicates omissions or pauses

Brackets
Adds clarifications or editorial notes

Slash
Shows alternatives or fractions

Teacher scripts to Introduce Punctuation Marks

1. Question Mark (?)

Elementary Script:
"When we ask something, we're curious, right? So instead of ending with a period, we use a question mark. It's like a little hook that shows we're waiting for an answer—like in 'Do you want to play?'"

High School Script:
"The question mark signals a direct question. It tells the reader, 'This sentence is looking for a response.' Use it when your sentence is genuinely seeking an answer, not when you're making a statement."

---

2. Exclamation Point (!)

Elementary Script:
"This little mark means you're excited or surprised! It's like your sentence is yelling or jumping up and down. 'I won the game!' See how that feels different from just a period?"

High School Script:
"Use exclamation points to show strong emotion—surprise, excitement, even anger. But use them wisely. Too many and you lose your effect. 'I can't believe it!' should pack a punch."

---

3. Comma (,)

Elementary Script:
"Commas are like little pauses in our sentences. We use them when we list things—like, 'I like pizza, burgers, and ice cream.' Or when we take a breath after an introduction—'After lunch, we played outside.'"

High School Script:
"Commas organize your thoughts. They separate items, clauses, and make your writing easier to follow. Think of them as traffic signals—not too many, not too few. Misplacing a comma can totally change your meaning."

4. Quotation Marks (" ")

Elementary Script:
"Quotation marks show when someone is talking. They hug the words that are being said. For example: 'I love recess!' said Sarah. The quotes go around what Sarah said."

High School Script:
"Use quotation marks to enclose direct dialogue or cited text. They tell your reader, 'These aren't my words—they belong to someone else.' And yes, punctuation usually goes inside the quotes."

---

5. Apostrophe (')

Elementary Script:
"Apostrophes are tiny but mighty! They show that something belongs to someone—like 'Sam's book.' Or they stand in for missing letters—'can't' means 'cannot.'"

High School Script:
"Use apostrophes to form contractions or to show possession. Remember: 'it's' means 'it is,' and 'its' shows ownership without the apostrophe. It's one of the most common mix-ups, so double-check!"

---

6. Colon (:)

Elementary Script:
"A colon is like a drumroll! It says, 'Get ready—something is coming!' Like in: 'I need three things: paper, pencils, and crayons.'"

High School Script:
"A colon introduces a list, explanation, or quote. It tells the reader: what's next expands on what came before. Just make sure what comes before the colon is a full sentence."

7. Semicolon (;)

Elementary Script:
"This one's a little tricky. A semicolon is stronger than a comma but not quite a period. It connects two complete thoughts that go together—like twins holding hands: 'I like cake; it's my favorite dessert.'"

High School Script:
"Semicolons link independent clauses that are closely related. Use them when two sentences feel too connected to split. Also useful in complex lists: 'We visited Dallas, Texas; Atlanta, Georgia; and Denver, Colorado.'"

---

8. Parentheses ( )

Elementary Script:
"Parentheses are like whispering in your writing. They add extra information or a fun side note. Like: 'I played soccer today (and scored two goals!).'"

High School Script:
"Parentheses insert extra information without interrupting the main sentence. It's background or clarification—but not crucial to the core meaning. Don't overuse them—they're for optional asides."

---

9. Dash (—)

Elementary Script:
"A dash adds drama or surprise. It's like a sudden change in your sentence: 'I opened the box—and screamed!' It helps your reader feel the excitement or shock."

High School Script:
"An em dash is used for emphasis, interruption, or to insert a thought mid-sentence. It creates a strong pause—almost like the writer is speaking directly to you. Use it for dramatic effect or informal tone."

10. Hyphen (-)

Elementary Script:
"Hyphens stick words together. Like when we say 'well-known author' or 'twenty-one.' It helps the words become one idea."

High School Script:
"Hyphens connect words into compound terms or divide syllables at line breaks. They clarify meaning: 'small-business owner' is different from 'small business owner.'"

---

11. Ellipsis (...)

Elementary Script:
"Ellipses show when someone trails off or something is missing. It's like your sentence is whispering... fading away... or skipping part of something."

High School Script:
"Use ellipses to show omitted text or a trailing thought. In formal writing, they condense quotes. In creative writing, they can show hesitation or an unfinished idea."

---

12. Brackets [ ]

Elementary Script:
"Brackets are like little editors in your sentence. They fix or explain things inside a quote. Like: 'He [the teacher] said we could go.'"

High School Script:
"Brackets allow you to clarify or adjust words inside a quotation. Use them to insert your own words into someone else's quote—especially when adding context."

C.A.P.E.S. Acronym to Help Recall the Most Common Punctuation Marks

This acronym stands for the **most commonly used punctuation marks** and emphasizes their importance in writing. Think of **C.A.P.E.S.** as the "superhero" of punctuation—saving your sentences from confusion!

- **C** – **Commas** (Separating items in a list, clauses, dates, and more)
- **A** – **Apostrophes** (Showing possession and contractions)
- **P** – **Periods** (Ending statements, abbreviations)
- **E** – **Endings** (Including question marks and exclamation points)
- **S** – **Semicolons** (Connecting related independent clauses or separating complex list items)

C.A.P.E.S. Punctuation Chart

Letter	Punctuation Type	Explanation	Example
C	Commas	Separate items in a list, clauses, or introductory elements.	I bought apples, oranges, and bananas.
A	Apostrophes	Show possession or form contractions.	It's a beautiful day. (contraction)
P	Periods	End declarative sentences or abbreviations.	The meeting is at 3 p.m.
E	Endings (?!.)	Mark the end of a sentence: period (.), question mark (?), exclamation point (!)	Are you coming? Wow, that's amazing!
S	Semicolons	Connect related independent clauses or separate items in a complex list.	I have a big day tomorrow; I need to sleep early.

Activity: Punctuation Superheroes – CAPES Squad

Objective:

Students will become superhero protectors of writing by mastering punctuation marks in the **C.A.P.E.S.** acronym: Commas, Apostrophes, Periods, Endings, and Semicolons. They will design their superhero persona and practice saving sentences from punctuation problems.

Materials Needed:

- Printable cape templates or fabric capes
- Markers, crayons, and stickers for cape decoration
- Sentence cards with punctuation errors
- Superhero masks or headbands (optional)

Step-by-Step Instructions:

Step 1: Introduction to CAPES Superheroes

Explain each letter in **C.A.P.E.S.** and its punctuation mark:

1. **C – Commas:** "Comma Commander" – Keeps lists, clauses, and dates organized.
2. **A – Apostrophes:** "Apostrophe Ace" – Guards contractions and shows possession.
3. **P – Periods:** "Period Power" – Brings sentences to a full stop.
4. **E – Endings:** "Exclamation Extraordinaire" – Makes sure every sentence ends correctly with question marks or exclamation points.
5. **S – Semicolon Savvy:** "Semicolon Sage" – Connects related ideas and keeps complex lists clean.

Step 2: Design Your Superhero Cape

- Each student designs a superhero cape with their favorite punctuation symbol from the CAPES acronym.
- Encourage creativity: Draw symbols, add colors, and choose a superhero name (e.g., **"Comma Kid"**, **"Period Power"**).

Step 3: Punctuation Mission – Sentence Rescue. Set up **Punctuation Rescue Stations**:

- Each station has sentence cards with missing or incorrect punctuation.
- Students must identify the correct punctuation and place it in the sentence to "rescue" it.
- Example:
  - **Incorrect:** The cat sat on the mat it was very cute
  - **Correct:** The cat sat on the mat; it was very cute.

Be a Comma S.A.N.D.C.A.T.

- **S – Series** (Items in a list)
- **A – Appositives** (Extra noun phrases that rename or explain a noun)
- **N – Nonrestrictive Modifiers** (Information that can be removed without changing the sentence's main meaning)
- **D – Dates** (Use commas to separate the parts of a full date)
- **C – Clauses** (Commas in compound and complex sentences)
- **A – Addresses** (Commas between city, state, and zip code)
- **T – Titles** (Commas around degrees or titles following names)

Why S.A.N.D.C.A.T.?

SANDCAT is a memorable word, and it can remind students that commas act as little "pawprints" that organize and clarify writing. Just like a sandcat leaves tracks in the sand, commas leave important marks in our writing to help sentences make sense.

Lesson Plan: Mastering Commas in a Series

Grade Level: 4th–6th Grade
Duration: 60 minutes
Objective:
Students will learn how to correctly use commas in a series to separate three or more items in a sentence. They will practice identifying and writing sentences with commas in a series through interactive activities and apply their learning in an authentic assessment task.

Standards:

- Demonstrate command of the conventions of standard English grammar and usage when writing or speaking.
- Use commas in a series to separate elements in a list.

Materials Needed:

- Whiteboard and markers
- Example sentence strips
- "Comma Detective" activity sheets
- Chart paper for group activity
- Colored markers/highlighters
- Authentic assessment checklist

Introduction (10 minutes)

Teacher Script (Italicized):
"Today, we're going to learn about how commas help organize lists in sentences. Imagine trying to read a long list without commas—it could be confusing! For example, if I say, 'I bought apples bananas oranges'—you might wonder if I bought three things or just one weird thing called 'apples bananas oranges.' But if I say, 'I bought apples, bananas, and oranges,' it's clear that I bought three things. The comma makes all the difference!"

"We use commas in a series to separate items in a list of three or more. You might list your favorite foods, describe what you did over the weekend, or share what you packed for a trip. Let's practice identifying these commas and using them correctly."

Direct Instruction (15 minutes)

Explain the Rule:

1. **Use a comma to separate three or more items in a series.**
   Example: *I like pizza, burgers, and ice cream.*
2. **Place the comma after each item except the last one.**
   Example: *We visited New York, Boston, and Philadelphia.*
3. **The last comma before "and" is called the Oxford comma. It's optional but often used for clarity.**
   Example: *She packed pencils, notebooks, and erasers.*

Teacher Script (Italicized):
"Notice that the commas act like little separators between each item, helping us read the sentence smoothly and clearly. Without commas, the sentence would run together and get confusing. Let's try a few examples together on the board."

Guided Practice (15 minutes)

Activity: Comma Detective

1. Hand out a "Comma Detective" worksheet with sentences containing lists.
2. Students will work in pairs to read each sentence, identify where commas are missing, and insert them correctly.
3. Sentences will range from simple lists to more complex ones with adjectives and items.

Sample Sentences for Activity:

1. I need eggs milk bread and cheese from the store.
2. My favorite colors are red blue green and yellow.
3. We saw lions tigers and bears at the zoo.

Teacher Script (Italicized):
"Now you'll become Comma Detectives! Your job is to spot where the commas are missing in these sentences and add them in the correct places. Work with your partner to solve each case. Remember, the commas separate each item in the list!"

Independent Practice (10 minutes)

Activity: Create Your Own List Sentences

1. Ask students to write five original sentences using commas in a series.
2. Encourage creativity—students can write about their favorite foods, hobbies, or things they see on a nature walk.

Example:

- My favorite fruits are strawberries, blueberries, and raspberries.
- I packed a hat, sunscreen, and a towel for the beach.

Assessment: Authentic Task (10 minutes)

Activity: Classroom Recipe Book

1. Each student will create a short recipe that lists at least three ingredients using commas in a series.
2. Compile all recipes into a "Classroom Recipe Book" and share it with the class.

Instructions:

- Title your recipe.
- Write a short sentence describing what you're making.
- List the ingredients, using commas in a series.

Example Recipe:
Title: The Best Sandwich Ever
Description: This is how I make my favorite sandwich.
Ingredients: Bread, peanut butter, jelly, and bananas.

Assessment Checklist:

- The sentence contains three or more items.
- Commas are correctly placed between each item in the list.
- The sentence is clear and easy to read.

Closure (5 minutes)

Teacher Script (Italicized):
"You did an amazing job learning how to use commas in a series! Remember, commas help make your writing clear and organized. Next time you write a list, check to see if you've used commas in the right places. Great work, everyone!"

Extensions:

- **Comma Challenge:** Give students a long sentence with a list of items and have them rewrite it with commas.
- **Class Comma Game:** Have students race to correct a list of sentences on the board.

Lesson Plan: Mastering Appositives Separated by Commas

Grade Level: 5th–8th Grade
Duration: 60 minutes
Objective:
Students will understand and apply the use of **appositives** and **appositive phrases** separated by commas. They will learn how to identify and correctly place appositives in sentences to add detail and clarity.

Standards:

- Demonstrate command of standard English grammar and punctuation when writing or speaking.
- Use commas to set off appositives and appositive phrases for clarity and precision in writing.

Materials Needed:

- Whiteboard and markers
- Example sentence strips
- "Appositive Challenge" task cards
- Chart paper for group activity
- Exit ticket cards
- Authentic assessment rubric

Introduction (10 minutes)

Teacher Script (Italicized):
"Today, we're going to learn about appositives. An appositive is a noun or noun phrase that renames or gives more information about another noun in the sentence. It's like giving a nickname or extra detail about the noun. For example, in the sentence 'My brother, a talented musician, plays the guitar,' the phrase 'a talented musician' is an appositive because it gives us more information about 'my brother.'"

"We separate appositives with commas to show that they are extra information—not essential to the main meaning of the sentence. Imagine writing without appositives—it would be like watching a movie without any background details!"

Direct Instruction (15 minutes)

1. Explain the Rule:

- **Appositives add extra detail but can be removed without changing the main idea.** Example: *My dog, a golden retriever, loves to swim.* (The appositive is "a golden retriever.")
- **Use commas to set off appositives from the rest of the sentence.** Example: *Sara, my best friend, lives next door.*
- **Appositives can appear at the beginning, middle, or end of a sentence.** Example:
    - Beginning: *A brilliant artist, Carlos painted the mural.*
    - Middle: *My teacher, Mrs. Smith, loves reading mysteries.*
    - End: *I visited Paris, the city of lights.*

Teacher Script (Italicized):
"Notice how the appositive adds extra information. Without it, the sentence would still make sense, but the appositive helps paint a clearer picture. Also, pay attention to the commas around the appositive—they help separate it from the main sentence."

Guided Practice (15 minutes)

Activity: Appositive Detective

1. Distribute **Appositive Challenge** task cards with sentences that contain appositives (some correctly punctuated, others missing commas).
2. Students will work in small groups to identify the appositives and determine if commas are used correctly.
3. Groups will rewrite incorrect sentences with proper comma placement.

Sample Task Card Sentences:

1. The car a red convertible sped down the highway.
2. My cat Whiskers loves to sleep in the sun.
3. Mrs. Jones my math teacher gave us extra homework.

Teacher Script (Italicized):
"Now it's your turn to become Appositive Detectives! Each group will look at these sentences

and decide where the commas should go. Discuss with your team and be ready to share your answers!"

Independent Practice (10 minutes)

Activity: Create Your Own Appositive Sentences

1. Ask students to write five original sentences using appositives.
2. Encourage them to be creative—write about family, pets, hobbies, or favorite places.

Example Sentences:

- My dog, **Max**, loves to chase balls.
- We visited San Francisco, **a beautiful city in California**.
- Julia, **my cousin**, plays the violin.

Assessment: Authentic Task (10 minutes)

Activity: Class Biography Wall

1. Each student will create a **"Who Am I?" biography poster** using appositives to describe themselves.
2. They must include at least three sentences that use appositives to add detail.
3. Display the posters on a "Biography Wall" in the classroom.

Instructions:

- Write your name and three descriptive sentences about yourself using appositives.
- Example:
  I am Alex, a soccer player and artist.
  My favorite pet, a golden retriever named Buddy, keeps me company.
  I live in Chicago, the Windy City.

Assessment Rubric:

- Sentences include correctly punctuated appositives.
- Sentences are creative and descriptive.
- The poster is neat and organized.

Closure (5 minutes)

Teacher Script (Italicized):
"Appositives are a powerful tool to make your writing more descriptive and interesting. They help give extra details without making your sentences too long or confusing. Great job today! Next time you write, think about how you can use appositives to add color and detail to your sentences!"

Extensions:

- **Appositive Scavenger Hunt:** Have students find appositives in books or articles and share them with the class.
- **Peer Review:** Pair students to review each other's writing for appositive usage.

Lesson Plan: Mastering Nonrestrictive Modifiers with Commas

Grade Level: 6th–8th Grade
Duration: 60 minutes
Objective:
Students will learn how to identify and use **nonrestrictive modifiers** correctly with commas in writing. They will differentiate between restrictive and nonrestrictive elements and apply commas to set off nonessential information in sentences.

Standards:

- Demonstrate command of the conventions of standard English grammar and punctuation when writing or speaking.
- Use commas to set off nonrestrictive/parenthetical elements.

Materials Needed:

- Whiteboard and markers
- Example sentence strips
- "Nonrestrictive Modifier Detective" worksheets
- Chart paper for group work
- Exit ticket cards
- Assessment checklist

Introduction (10 minutes)

Teacher Script (Italicized):
"Today, we're going to learn about nonrestrictive modifiers. Think of nonrestrictive modifiers as extra information in a sentence—details that are nice to have but not necessary for the sentence to make sense. Imagine telling your friend about your dog. You might say, 'My dog, who loves to chase balls, is very playful.' The phrase 'who loves to chase balls' is a nonrestrictive modifier because it gives us more detail about your dog, but if we removed it, the sentence would still make sense: 'My dog is very playful.'"

"We use commas to set off these nonrestrictive modifiers. It's like wrapping extra details in commas to signal that they're not essential to the main point. Without commas, your sentence might confuse readers. Let's practice identifying these modifiers and using commas to clarify our writing."

Direct Instruction (15 minutes)

Explain the Rule:

1. **Nonrestrictive modifiers add extra information that isn't essential to the meaning of the sentence.**
   Example: *My brother, who lives in New York, is visiting us next week.*
   (The phrase "who lives in New York" is extra information.)
2. **Use commas to set off nonrestrictive modifiers from the rest of the sentence.**
   Example: *The car, which is red, belongs to my neighbor.*
3. **Restrictive modifiers are essential to the sentence's meaning and do not use commas.**
   Example: *The students who studied hard passed the test.* (Here, the modifier "who studied hard" is essential—it tells us which students passed.)

Teacher Script (Italicized):
"Notice how the commas create a pause and separate the extra information. Without them, it's harder to tell what information is essential. Remember, restrictive modifiers are necessary to the meaning of the sentence, while nonrestrictive ones are just extra details."

Guided Practice (15 minutes)

Activity: Nonrestrictive Modifier Detective

1. Distribute the **Nonrestrictive Modifier Detective** worksheet with sentences that contain both restrictive and nonrestrictive modifiers.
2. Students will work in pairs to read each sentence, identify whether the modifier is restrictive or nonrestrictive, and insert commas where needed.
3. Sentences will range from simple to more complex structures.

Sample Sentences for Activity:

1. The house that is painted blue belongs to my aunt.
2. My teacher Mrs. Thompson loves to read mystery novels.
3. The dog which has a red collar barked loudly.

Teacher Script (Italicized):
"You're now Nonrestrictive Modifier Detectives! Work with your partner to decide if each modifier is essential or extra. Add commas to set off the nonrestrictive modifiers and share your reasoning."

Independent Practice (10 minutes)

Activity: Create Your Own Sentences

1. Ask students to write five original sentences using both restrictive and nonrestrictive modifiers.
2. Encourage them to be creative—write about family, hobbies, or favorite activities.
3. Students will underline nonrestrictive modifiers and circle the commas they added.

Example Sentences:

- *My cat, who loves to sleep in the sun, is very lazy.*
- *The book that I borrowed from the library is due tomorrow.*
- *Our principal, Mr. Harris, announced a new school policy.*

Assessment: Authentic Task (15 minutes)

Activity: Class Newspaper Project

1. Each student will write a short news article (5–6 sentences) about a real or fictional event, incorporating at least three nonrestrictive modifiers.
2. Compile the articles into a class newspaper.

Instructions:

- Choose an event to write about (school news, a sports game, or a fun weekend activity).
- Include at least three nonrestrictive modifiers, properly set off by commas.
- Example: *Our school's basketball team, which won the championship last year, will play in the finals again this week.*

Assessment Checklist:

- Sentences include correctly punctuated nonrestrictive modifiers.
- Nonrestrictive modifiers are used effectively to add detail.
- The writing is clear and well-organized.

Closure (5 minutes)

Teacher Script (Italicized):
"Great work today! Nonrestrictive modifiers are a fantastic way to add detail and make your writing more descriptive. Remember to use commas to set off these extra details. Next time you write, try to include a few nonrestrictive modifiers to give your sentences some extra flair!"

Extensions:

- **Modifier Hunt:** Have students find nonrestrictive modifiers in books or articles and share them with the class.
- **Peer Review:** Pair students to review each other's writing for nonrestrictive modifier usage.

Lesson Plan: Mastering Commas in Dates

Grade Level: 4th–6th Grade
Duration: 60 minutes
Objective:
Students will learn how to correctly use commas when writing dates in sentences and lists. They will practice identifying and writing dates using proper punctuation rules and apply their knowledge in an interactive activity and assessment task.

Standards:

- Demonstrate command of the conventions of standard English grammar and punctuation when writing or speaking.
- Use commas to separate elements in dates correctly.

Materials Needed:

- Whiteboard and markers
- Sample sentence strips
- "Commas in Dates" task cards
- Student journals or paper
- Chart paper for group work
- Calendar handouts
- Authentic assessment rubric

Introduction (10 minutes)

Teacher Script (Italicized):
"Today, we're going to focus on a punctuation rule that you see every day—commas in dates! Imagine you're writing a sentence about your birthday or an important holiday. Without commas, your writing might look confusing or rushed. For example, 'I was born on August 15 2011 in New York.' Hmm, something is missing! Adding commas makes this sentence clearer: 'I was born on August 15, 2011, in New York.' Those commas help separate the parts of the date and make the sentence easier to read."

"Let's explore how to use commas correctly in dates and why they matter."

Direct Instruction (15 minutes)

Explain the Rules for Using Commas in Dates:

1. **When a date includes the month, day, and year, place a comma after the day and after the year (if the sentence continues).**
   Example: *On December 25, 2021, we celebrated Christmas.*
2. **If the sentence ends with the year, no comma is needed after the year.**
   Example: *We moved to the city on May 20, 2020.*
3. **When a date includes only the month and year, no commas are needed.**
   Example: *We visited Paris in July 2019.*

Teacher Script (Italicized):
"Notice how the commas separate the day from the year and the year from the rest of the sentence. Without those commas, it's harder to tell where the date ends and the next part begins. Let's practice together!"

Guided Practice (15 minutes)

Activity: Fix the Dates

1. Display several sentences with incorrectly punctuated dates on the board.
2. Ask students to work in pairs to correct the punctuation.
3. Discuss the corrections as a class and explain the reasoning.

Sample Sentences for Practice:

1. We went to the zoo on June 14 2018 and had a great time.
2. My sister was born on February 2 2005 in Texas.
3. Our last day of school will be on May 25 2023.

Teacher Script (Italicized):
"Now you'll work in pairs to correct these sentences. Remember to place a comma after the day and after the year if the sentence continues."

Independent Practice (10 minutes)

Activity: Write and Share

1. Ask students to write five sentences about important events in their lives, using dates with commas.
2. Encourage them to include family birthdays, vacations, or historical events they've learned about.
3. Students will share one of their sentences with the class.

Example Sentences:

- I went to Disney World on April 10, 2019, with my family.
- My dog was born on August 5, 2021.
- The first day of school was September 7, 2022.

Assessment: Authentic Task (15 minutes)

Activity: Class Time Capsule Letter

1. Each student will write a letter to their future self, describing a memorable event from this school year.
2. They must include at least two correctly punctuated dates in their letter.
3. Collect the letters and store them in a class time capsule to be opened at the end of the year.

Instructions:

- Write a short letter about something special from this school year.
- Include at least two dates, using commas correctly.
- Example: *On October 1, 2023, we had our first field trip. I can't wait to see what happens on May 25, 2024, the last day of school!*

Assessment Checklist:

- Sentences include correctly punctuated dates.
- Dates are meaningful and connected to the letter's content.
- Writing is clear and organized.

Closure (5 minutes)

Teacher Script (Italicized):
"Great job today! Now you're experts at using commas in dates. Remember, commas help keep your writing organized and clear. Next time you write about a special event, use commas to separate the parts of the date. Keep practicing—you're doing awesome!"

Extensions:

- **Historical Timeline Activity:** Create a timeline of historical events, practicing commas in dates.
- **Peer Review:** Pair students to review each other's writing for comma usage in dates.

Lesson Plan: Using Commas Before Coordinating Conjunctions in Compound Sentences

Grade Level: 5th–8th Grade
Duration: 60 minutes
Objective:
Students will learn to correctly place commas before coordinating conjunctions in compound sentences. They will practice identifying and writing compound sentences, using commas to separate independent clauses for clarity and fluency in writing.

Standards:

- Demonstrate command of the conventions of standard English grammar and punctuation when writing or speaking.
- Use commas before coordinating conjunctions (FANBOYS) to join independent clauses in compound sentences.

Materials Needed:

- Whiteboard and markers
- Sentence strips with coordinating conjunctions (FANBOYS)
- "Comma Connector" task cards
- Student journals or writing paper
- Exit tickets
- Assessment rubric

Introduction (10 minutes)

Teacher Script (Italicized):
"Today, we're going to learn how commas can help us combine ideas and avoid confusion when we write compound sentences. Compound sentences are made up of two independent clauses—two complete thoughts—joined by a coordinating conjunction like 'and,' 'but,' or 'so.' These coordinating conjunctions help connect the ideas smoothly, but we need a comma before the conjunction to separate the clauses and make the sentence clear."

"For example, look at this sentence: 'I wanted to go to the park but it started to rain.' This sentence needs a comma before 'but' because we're connecting two complete thoughts: 'I wanted to go to the park' and 'it started to rain.' The comma helps the reader know where one thought ends and the next begins."

Direct Instruction (15 minutes)

Explain the Rule:

1. **A compound sentence consists of two independent clauses joined by a coordinating conjunction.**
   - Independent clause: A group of words with a subject and a verb that can stand alone as a complete sentence.
     Example: *I love pizza.*
     Example: *I hate mushrooms.*
2. **Coordinating conjunctions (FANBOYS) connect the clauses:**
   - For, And, Nor, But, Or, Yet, So
3. **Place a comma before the coordinating conjunction to separate the two clauses.**
   Example: *I love pizza, but I hate mushrooms.*

Teacher Script (Italicized):
"The comma works like a traffic signal. It tells the reader to pause before moving on to the second idea. Without it, the sentence could be confusing or read too quickly. Remember: You only use a comma when both parts of the sentence are complete thoughts."

Guided Practice (15 minutes)

Activity: Comma Connector Game

1. Display sentence strips with incomplete sentences and coordinating conjunctions.
2. Students will work in pairs to combine two independent clauses using a coordinating conjunction and a comma.
3. Each pair will share their sentence with the class, explaining why the comma is necessary.

Example Sentence Strips:

- *I wanted to play outside / it started to rain.*
- *We can go to the movies / we can stay home.*
- *She likes chocolate / she doesn't like vanilla.*

Teacher Script (Italicized):
"You'll work with a partner to connect these clauses using a comma and a coordinating conjunction. Be sure to explain why the comma belongs there!"

Independent Practice (10 minutes)

Activity: Sentence Building Challenge

1. Students will write five original compound sentences using commas and coordinating conjunctions.
2. Encourage creativity—students can write about hobbies, school experiences, or favorite activities.

Example Sentences:

- *I love swimming, and I also enjoy running.*
- *She studied hard, so she passed the test.*
- *The dog barked loudly, but the cat stayed calm.*

Assessment: Authentic Task (15 minutes)

Activity: Create a Story with Compound Sentences

1. Each student will write a short story (6–8 sentences) about a personal experience or fictional event.
2. The story must include at least three compound sentences with commas before coordinating conjunctions.
3. Students will underline their compound sentences and explain why they used commas.

Instructions:

- Write a short story about something exciting or funny that happened to you.
- Include at least three compound sentences using commas and coordinating conjunctions.
- Underline your compound sentences and check for proper comma placement.

Assessment Checklist:

- Story includes at least three compound sentences.
- Commas are correctly placed before coordinating conjunctions.
- Writing is clear, creative, and well-organized.

Closure (5 minutes)

Teacher Script (Italicized):
"Great work today! Remember, commas are essential in compound sentences to keep your writing clear and organized. Next time you write, check your sentences to see if you have two complete thoughts joined by a coordinating conjunction. If you do, add a comma! You're becoming experts in punctuation!"

Extensions:

- **Comma Challenge:** Have students race to correct sentences with missing commas on the board.
- **Peer Review:** Pair students to review each other's stories for correct comma usage.

Lesson Plan: Using Commas Before Subordinating Conjunctions in Complex Sentences

Grade Level: 6th–8th Grade
Duration: 60 minutes

Objective:
Students will understand and apply the correct use of commas in complex sentences with **subordinating conjunctions**. They will practice identifying dependent and independent clauses and learn how to punctuate complex sentences correctly.

Standards:

- Demonstrate command of the conventions of standard English grammar and punctuation when writing or speaking.
- Use commas to separate dependent clauses from independent clauses when the dependent clause comes first in a sentence.

Materials Needed:

- Whiteboard and markers
- Sentence strips with subordinating conjunctions
- "Comma Complex" task cards
- Graphic organizers for clause identification
- Student journals or writing paper
- Rubric for authentic assessment

Introduction (10 minutes)

Teacher Script (Italicized):
"Today, we're diving into complex sentences! Complex sentences are special because they help us combine ideas in interesting ways. They have an independent clause, which is a complete thought, and a dependent clause, which is an incomplete thought that depends on the rest of the sentence to make sense.

For example, if I say, 'Because it was raining,' you'd be left wondering what happened. But if I complete the sentence, 'Because it was raining, we stayed inside,' it makes sense! Notice the comma after the dependent clause? That comma is crucial when the dependent clause comes first in the sentence."

Direct Instruction (15 minutes)

Explain the Rule:

1. **Complex sentences consist of an independent clause and a dependent clause.**
   - Independent clause: A complete thought that can stand alone as a sentence. Example: *I went to the store.*
   - Dependent clause: An incomplete thought that cannot stand alone. Example: *Because it was raining.*
2. **Subordinating conjunctions introduce dependent clauses.**
   Common subordinating conjunctions: because, although, since, while, if, after, unless, before, when, even though
3. **When the dependent clause comes first, use a comma to separate it from the independent clause.**
   Example: *Although I was tired, I finished my homework.*
4. **No comma is needed when the independent clause comes first.**
   Example: *I finished my homework although I was tired.*

Teacher Script (Italicized):
"The comma is like a bridge between the dependent and independent clauses. It tells the reader to pause before continuing to the main idea. This rule only applies when the dependent clause comes first. Let's practice identifying clauses and using commas in the right places."

Guided Practice (15 minutes)

Activity: Clause Sort Game

1. Provide students with sentence strips containing independent clauses, dependent clauses, and subordinating conjunctions.
2. In small groups, students will combine the clauses to form complex sentences.
3. Groups must decide whether to add a comma and explain why.

Example Sentence Strips:

- Dependent Clause: *Because it was late*
- Independent Clause: *we decided to leave the party.*
- Subordinating Conjunction: *Although*

Teacher Script (Italicized):
"Your job is to combine these clauses into a complete sentence. Pay attention to the order. If the dependent clause comes first, don't forget to add a comma!"

Independent Practice (10 minutes)

Activity: Complex Sentence Creation

1. Ask students to write five original complex sentences, ensuring that at least three begin with a dependent clause.
2. Students will underline the dependent clause and circle the comma if applicable.

Example Sentences:

- *Since I missed the bus, I walked to school.*
- *Although it was cold, we played outside.*
- *We stayed home because it was snowing.*

Assessment: Authentic Task (15 minutes)

Activity: Personal Narrative with Complex Sentences

1. Each student will write a short personal narrative (8–10 sentences) about a memorable day.
2. The narrative must include at least three complex sentences, with at least two starting with a dependent clause.
3. Students will underline their dependent clauses and highlight their commas.

Instructions:

- Write a personal story about a day you'll never forget.
- Include at least three complex sentences.
- Underline the dependent clauses and highlight the commas where needed.

Assessment Rubric:

- Writing includes at least three complex sentences.
- Commas are correctly placed before independent clauses when necessary.
- Writing is clear, organized, and creative.

Closure (5 minutes)

Teacher Script (Italicized):
"Great work today! Complex sentences are a powerful tool to connect ideas and add depth to your writing. Remember, when the dependent clause comes first, always add that comma. Keep practicing, and soon it will become second nature!"

Extensions:

- **Clause Hunt:** Have students find complex sentences in books or articles and identify the dependent and independent clauses.
- **Peer Review:** Pair students to review each other's writing for complex sentence usage and comma placement.

Lesson Plan: Using Commas in Addresses

Grade Level: 4th–6th Grade
Duration: 60 minutes

Objective:
Students will learn how to correctly use commas in addresses within sentences. They will identify the placement of commas in multi-part addresses, practice writing addresses, and apply their knowledge in a creative and engaging activity.

Standards:

- Demonstrate command of the conventions of standard English grammar and punctuation when writing or speaking.
- Use commas to separate parts of an address in sentences.

Materials Needed:

- Whiteboard and markers
- Sentence strips with addresses
- "Comma Detective" worksheets
- Student journals or writing paper
- Authentic assessment rubric
- Envelopes and index cards

Introduction (10 minutes)

Teacher Script (Italicized):
"Today, we're going to learn about commas in addresses. Imagine sending a letter to your friend without using commas in the address. How would the postal worker know where to deliver it? Commas are like signposts in an address, helping us separate the parts so that they're easy to read and understand. If we don't use commas, it can look messy and confusing."

"For example, look at this sentence: 'My address is 123 Main Street Houston Texas 77002.' That's hard to read, right? But with commas, it's much clearer: 'My address is 123 Main Street, Houston, Texas 77002.' See how the commas break it into parts? Let's explore how to use commas in addresses properly."

Direct Instruction (15 minutes)

Explain the Rule:

1. **Use commas to separate each part of an address except between the state and the zip code.**
   Example: *I live at 456 Elm Street, Austin, Texas 78704.*
2. **When writing an address within a sentence, place a comma after the city and after the state if the sentence continues.**
   Example: *We moved to 789 Oak Drive, Dallas, Texas, last summer.*
3. **No comma is needed when only the city and state are mentioned.**
   Example: *I'm traveling to Denver, Colorado, next week.*

Teacher Script (Italicized):
"Think of commas in an address as little breaks that guide the reader. After the street name, use a comma. After the city, use another comma. But remember, no comma between the state and zip code!"

Guided Practice (15 minutes)

Activity: Comma Detective

1. Distribute "Comma Detective" worksheets with sentences containing addresses.
2. Students will work in pairs to correct the punctuation errors by adding commas where needed.
3. Review the corrected sentences together.

Sample Sentences for Practice:

1. I live at 101 Pine Avenue Miami Florida 33101.
2. The meeting is at 300 Maple Street Dallas Texas 75201 on Monday.
3. Our new house is at 987 Cedar Road Austin Texas 78704.

Teacher Script (Italicized):
"You are now comma detectives! Your mission is to find the missing commas in these addresses and add them to make the sentences clear. Work with your partner to solve each one!"

Independent Practice (10 minutes)

Activity: Create Your Own Address Sentences

1. Ask students to write five sentences about different places they've visited or would like to visit. Each sentence must contain a full address with commas.
2. Encourage creativity—students can write about fictional places or real locations.

Example Sentences:

- *I visited 456 Ocean Boulevard, Miami, Florida 33139, last summer.*
- *The party is at 123 Magnolia Lane, Orlando, Florida, on Saturday.*
- *Our family reunion is at 789 Sunset Drive, Denver, Colorado, next month.*

Assessment: Authentic Task (15 minutes)

Activity: Design a Postcard and Address It Correctly

1. Each student will design a postcard from a real or imaginary destination.
2. On the back of the postcard, they will write a short message and address it correctly, using commas in the address.
3. Display the postcards in the classroom or create a "Postcard Wall."

Instructions:

- Design a postcard for a fun destination.
- Write a short message to a friend or family member.
- Include an address on the back, using commas in the correct places.

Assessment Rubric:

- Address includes commas in the correct places.
- Writing is neat and clear.
- Postcard design is creative and relevant.

Closure (5 minutes)

Teacher Script (Italicized):
"Great work today! Now you know how commas help organize addresses so they're clear and easy to read. Next time you write an address, remember to use commas as your guideposts. Keep practicing, and soon it will become second nature!"

Extensions:

- **Map It Out:** Have students find real addresses on a map and write them correctly with commas.
- **Address Hunt:** Challenge students to find examples of addresses in books or on the internet and check for correct comma usage.

Apostrophes and their Various Jobs

1. To Show Possession

Singular nouns

- Add **'s** even if the word ends in *s*:
  - *the dog's leash*
  - *Jess's book*

Plural nouns that end in "s"

- Add only the **apostrophe**:
  - *the teachers' lounge*
  - *the Joneses' house*

Plural nouns that don't end in "s"

- Add **'s**:
  - *the children's toys*
  - *the men's restroom*

---

2. To Show Contractions (Missing Letters)

Apostrophes take the place of **omitted letters**:

- *can't* = cannot
- *it's* = it is or it has
- *don't* = do not
- *they're* = they are

3. To Show Time or Quantity Possession (a form of possessive use)

Even when there's no person involved, apostrophes show possession:

- *a day's work*
- *two weeks' notice*
- *a dollar's worth*

4. To Avoid Confusion (Rare but Real)

Sometimes apostrophes are used to **clarify meaning**, especially with awkward plurals:

- *Dot your i's and cross your t's* (without apostrophes, it looks like "is" and "ts")
- *Mind your p's and q's*

---

5. NEVER for Plurals of Regular Words

This is the most common mistake.

- No apostrophe needed:
  - **Correct**: bananas, 1980s, CDs
  - **Incorrect**: banana's, 1980's, CD's (unless showing possession!)

Quick Troubleshoot: "Its" vs. "It's"

- *It's* = it is or it has
- *Its* = possessive form of "it" (like "his" or "her")
  - *It's raining today.*
  - *The cat chased its tail.*

Lesson Title:

The Power of the Apostrophe!

Grade Level:

Upper Elementary to Middle School (4th–8th grade)

Objective:

Students will identify and correctly use apostrophes in five different contexts:

1. Singular Possession
2. Plural Possession
3. Contractions
4. Time/Quantity Possession
5. Clarifying Meaning (awkward plurals)

T-Shirt Slogan (for class shirts, posters, or visual cues):

"Little Mark, Big Meaning!" (written in stylish italics on shirts/posters)

Materials Needed:

- Butcher paper or chart paper (5 large pieces—one for each rule)
- Arts and crafts supplies: markers, glue sticks, scissors, construction paper, stickers
- Pre-cut sentence strips with apostrophe errors and correct examples
- Sentence sorting envelopes
- Index cards
- T-shirts or cardstock shirt cutouts for slogans
- Folders or construction paper for foldables
- Anchor chart printables or templates
- Printed apostrophe mini-posters for small group work

Introduction (10 minutes):

Hook Activity: "Who Wore It Better?"

- Project 2 nearly identical sentences with just apostrophe differences.
  Example:
- *Its raining outside.*
- *It's raining outside.*
  Ask students: "Who wore it better? Which sentence looks 'right' and why?"

Have students briefly turn and talk, then gather ideas to guide into the 5 apostrophe rules.

Mini-Lesson & Chart Activity (20–25 minutes):

Break the class into 5 small groups. Each group gets a piece of butcher paper and an apostrophe "rule card."

Each group will:

1. Read their rule aloud.
2. Create a **mini-anchor chart** on their paper:
   - Rule name
   - Examples
   - A drawing or doodle that represents the rule
   - 1 sentence showing the wrong way (in red)
   - 2 correct sentences (in green)
   - Bonus phrase using the T-shirt slogan *"Little Mark, Big Meaning!"*

After 15 minutes, each group presents and hangs their chart.

Interactive Foldable (15 minutes):

Students create a **"Pop-Up Apostrophe Foldable"**:

Inside, they'll create 5 labeled flaps:

1. Singular Possession
2. Plural Possession
3. Contractions

4. Time/Quantity
5. Clarifying Meaning

Under each flap:

- Write the rule in their own words
- Create 2 examples
- Add a mini doodle or sticker for memory hook

Practice Game (10–15 minutes):

"Apostrophe Alley" Sorting Relay

- Spread sentence strips around the room (or in hallway "alley")
- Students work in pairs to grab a strip, decide the type of apostrophe use, and tape it under the correct poster/rule zone
- Fast-paced, collaborative, visual, and physical

Assessment (Exit Ticket):

Each student completes a short 5-question apostrophe quiz using the 5 rule types.

- Write one original sentence for each apostrophe rule.
- Bonus: Write a "T-shirt slogan" sentence using *"Little Mark, Big Meaning!"*

Intervention:

Apostrophe Detective Binder

- Provide struggling students with guided mini-lessons using color-coded apostrophe rules
- Highlight key parts of sentences and use scaffolded fill-in-the-blank examples
- Use manipulatives like apostrophe tokens to insert into laminated sentence cards

Enrichment:

"Author's Apostrophe Challenge"

- Have students write a short comic strip, skit, or paragraph that uses all 5 apostrophe types
- Add illustrations or speech bubbles
- Present to the class or post on a hallway bulletin board titled *"Little Mark, Big Meaning!"*

10 examples for each apostrophe rule:

1. Singular Possession

(Showing ownership by one person or thing – use **'s**)

1. The cat's toy
2. Sarah's backpack
3. The teacher's desk
4. The child's crayon
5. The car's engine
6. The president's speech
7. The artist's brush
8. The tree's leaves
9. The phone's battery
10. The dog's collar

---

2. Plural Possession

(Showing ownership by more than one person or thing – usually **s'**, but irregular plurals still use **'s**)

1. The students' lockers
2. The teachers' lounge
3. The dogs' leashes
4. The parents' meeting
5. The houses' roofs
6. The babies' bottles
7. The girls' soccer team
8. The men's restroom *(irregular plural)*
9. The women's jackets *(irregular plural)*
10. The children's books *(irregular plural)*

3. Contractions

(Apostrophe replaces **missing letters**)

1. Can't = cannot
2. Don't = do not
3. It's = it is / it has
4. You're = you are
5. I'm = I am
6. They're = they are
7. Won't = will not
8. She's = she is / she has
9. We've = we have
10. Who's = who is / who has

---

4. Time/Quantity Possession

(Apostrophe shows relationship to time or amount)

1. A day's pay
2. Two weeks' notice
3. A year's worth
4. An hour's delay
5. Five minutes' break
6. A month's rent
7. Three years' experience
8. One night's sleep
9. Ten dollars' value
10. A second's pause

5. Clarifying Meaning (Awkward Plurals)

(Apostrophe used to prevent confusion—not for possession)

1. Mind your p's and q's
2. Dot your i's and cross your t's
3. Find all the a's in the sentence
4. He got straight A's on his report card
5. The sign had too many &'s
6. She uses too many but's in her writing
7. Always capitalize your I's
8. He wrote several 7's backward
9. Avoid using too many do's and don't's *(stylized for clarity)*
10. There are two s's in "possessive"

Lesson plan focused specifically on helping students discern between singular and plural possessive apostrophes

Lesson Title:

"One Owner or Many? Apostrophes in Possession"

Grade Level:

Upper Elementary to Middle School (4th–8th grade)

Objective:

Students will be able to **identify**, **differentiate**, and **accurately use** apostrophes to show **singular vs. plural possession** in written sentences.

T-Shirt Slogan:

"One's Got It. Many Share It."

Materials Needed:

- Butcher paper (2 large sheets: one labeled "Singular Possession," one labeled "Plural Possession")
- Color-coded sentence strips (red = incorrect, green = correct)
- Sticky notes
- Markers, glue, scissors, construction paper
- Chart paper for anchor chart
- "Apostrophe Detective" sorting cards
- Foldable template or construction paper for a 2-tab comparison
- Printable handout with practice sentences
- Apostrophe punctuation stickers or cutouts

Introduction (10 minutes):

Hook Activity: "Whose Lunch?"

Project or write these two sentences:

- *The student's lunch was missing.*
- *The students' lunch was missing.*

Ask:
"Are these sentences the same? If not, who's missing their lunch—one kid or a whole group?"

Use this moment to introduce **why apostrophe placement matters** and that today's mission is to **spot the difference** between singular and plural ownership.

Mini-Lesson & Anchor Chart (15 minutes):

Create a two-column anchor chart labeled:

- **Singular Possessive = 's**
- **Plural Possessive = s'** (or 's for irregular plurals)

Add example sentences under each:

- *The dog's bone was buried.*
- *The dogs' owner was calling them.*
- *The children's toys were everywhere. (Irregular plural)*

Use a marker color code:

- **Blue** for subject
- **Green** for ownership
- **Red** underline for apostrophe

Foldable Activity (15–20 minutes):

Students create a **"Possession Split Flap"** foldable:

Outside flaps:

- Tab 1: *Singular Possession = 's*
- Tab 2: *Plural Possession = s' or irregular + 's*

Inside flaps:

- Rule definition
- 3 original examples per rule
- A doodle of "one owner" vs "many owners"
- A warning: *"Don't just look for an 's'—think about who owns what!"*

Interactive Group Activity (15–20 minutes):

"Apostrophe Street Sort"

- Set up 2 butcher-paper "houses" on opposite ends of the room:
    - *House 1: One Owner*
    - *House 2: Many Owners*
- Pass out **ownership cards** like:
    - *The girl shoes*
    - *The boys backpacks*
    - *The teacher desk*
- In teams, students rewrite each phrase with the correct apostrophe and race to deliver it to the correct "house."

Assessment (Exit Ticket):

Each student completes a short form:

1. Choose SINGULAR or PLURAL for 5 possessive phrases
2. Rewrite 3 incorrect possessive phrases correctly
3. Write 1 sentence of their own for each type (singular/plural)

Intervention Activity:

"Apostrophe Clinic"

- Use mini-whiteboards and guided examples.
- Provide manipulatives: sentence strips with velcro apostrophes they can move around.
- Use this prompt: *"Is there one or many? Who owns what?"*
- Scaffold with color-coded noun/owner cards.

Enrichment Activity:

"Possession Detective Comic Strip"

- Students create a short comic strip or cartoon story that includes at least 2 examples of singular and 2 examples of plural possession.
- They must underline the apostrophe in each and explain the ownership in a caption.
- Optional: add a tagline with *"One's Got It. Many Share It."* for display.

Passage with Apostrophe Errors

1. In the 1830's, settlers from the United States began moving into Texas, which was part of Mexico at the time. 2. Tensions grew between the Mexican government and the settlers, especially over law's and religion. 3. One of the most famous battle's in Texas history occurred at the Alamo, where the Texan's made their stand. 4. Although the Mexican army won that fight, the Texan's spirit's remained strong. 5. A few weeks later, Sam Houston's troop's defeated General Santa Anna's army at the Battle of San Jacinto.

Editing Questions:

1) What change should be made in sentence 1?

A. Change 1830's to 1830s
B. Change settlers' to settler's
C. Change United States to united states
D. Change began to begun

2) What change should be made in sentence 2?

A. Change religion to religion's
B. Change grew to growed
C. Change law's to laws
D. Change Mexican to mexican

3) What change should be made in sentence 5?

A. Change Houston's to Houstons
B. Change troop's to troops
C. Change later to latter
D. Change army to armi

Answer Analysis

Original Sentence 1:
In the 1830's, settlers from the United States began moving into Texas, which was part of Mexico at the time.

Question 1: What change should be made in sentence 1?

A. Change 1830's to 1830s
B. Change settlers' to settler's
C. Change United States to united states
D. Change began to begun

Correct Answer: A. Change 1830's to 1830s

Explanation:
A. Correct: 1830's should be changed to 1830s. The apostrophe is incorrect here because we are not showing possession—just referring to a decade.
B. Incorrect: Changing settlers to settler's still results in an incorrect form. The correct form should be settlers (plural, no apostrophe), not possessive.
C. Incorrect: "United States" is a proper noun and must remain capitalized. Changing it to lowercase is grammatically incorrect.
D. Incorrect: "Began" is the correct past-tense verb. "Begun" is the past participle and would require a helping verb (e.g., has begun).

Original Sentence 2:
Tensions grew between the Mexican government and the settlers, especially over law's and religion.

Question 2: What change should be made in sentence 2?

A. Change religion to religion's
B. Change grew to growed
C. Change law's to laws
D. Change Mexican to mexican

Correct Answer: A. Change law's to laws

Explanation:
A. Incorrect: Religion is correctly used here as a general noun. Adding an apostrophe would make it possessive, which does not fit the sentence.
B. Incorrect: "Growed" is not a word. The past tense of "grow" is "grew," which is already correct.
C. Correct: Law's is incorrect because we are using the word as a plural, not to show possession. It should be laws.
D. Incorrect: "Mexican" is correctly capitalized because it's a proper adjective. Changing it to lowercase would be grammatically.

Original Sentence 5:
A few weeks later, Sam Houston's troop's defeated General Santa Anna's army at the Battle of San Jacinto.

Question 3: What change should be made in sentence 5?

A. Change Houston's to Houstons
B. Change troop's to troops
C. Change later to latter
D. Change army to armies

Correct Answer: A. Change troop's to troops

Explanation:
A. Incorrect: "Houston's" correctly shows possession (Sam Houston's troops). Removing the apostrophe would make it incorrect.
B. Correct: Troop's is written as a possessive, but in this sentence, we need the plural form: troops.
C. Incorrect: "Later" is correct in this context. "Latter" is a comparative word used when referring to the second of two items.
D. Incorrect: "Army" is correctly singular here, referring to Santa Anna's army. Changing it to "armies" would alter the meaning unnecessarily.

Part 4

EDITING

Editing vs. Revising: Understanding the Difference

Editing and **revising** are both essential steps in the writing process, but they serve different purposes. **Revising** focuses on improving the overall content of the writing, while **editing** deals with correcting grammar, punctuation, spelling, and sentence structure. Knowing when to revise and when to edit helps produce polished and effective writing.

What is Editing?

Editing involves correcting **surface-level errors** to improve the clarity and correctness of a passage. It is often the final step in the writing process, ensuring the writing is grammatically sound, free of typos, and easy to read. Common editing tasks include:

- **Correcting grammar errors** (subject-verb agreement, verb tense consistency)
- **Fixing punctuation mistakes** (commas, apostrophes, periods)
- **Checking spelling and capitalization**
- **Improving sentence structure for clarity and correctness**
- **Ensuring proper word usage** (e.g., distinguishing between *there* and *their*)

Editing requires a keen eye for detail because even small mistakes can affect how professional and polished the writing appears. For example, a sentence like *Their going too the store after school* would need multiple edits to become *They're going to the store after school.* Editing ensures that such mistakes are caught and corrected.

What is Revising?

Revising is a broader process that focuses on improving **content and organization**. When revising, writers rethink the overall structure, word choice, sentence variety, and how well ideas are connected. This may involve rearranging sentences, adding key details, deleting irrelevant information, or exchanging weaker words for stronger ones. Revising helps make the writing more engaging, clear, and logical.

For instance, if a paragraph lacks a strong opening sentence, revising might involve writing a new one that introduces the main idea clearly. Revising is about making the writing stronger and more meaningful, not just technically correct.

Editing vs. Revising: The Key Difference

While revising improves the content and flow, editing polishes the writing by fixing technical errors. A good way to remember this is:

- **Revising = Content** (What you say and how you say it)
- **Editing = Corrections** (How your writing follows grammar rules and conventions)

Both are critical for effective writing. Revising makes your ideas clear and organized, while editing makes sure your reader can understand your polished, error-free text. Combining both ensures your writing is powerful, precise, and professional.

SCRiPTS acronym with **Capitalization replacing Clarity** and **Spelling standing alone**:

"SCRiPTS"

(Like a script for writing—perfect for editing!)

- **S – Spelling** (Correcting misspellings)
- **C – Capitalization** (Correct capitalization in names, places, and titles)
- **R – Replacement of Words** (Choosing correct word usage, correcting homophones, avoiding redundancy)
- **i** *(used as a filler for pronunciation in acronyms)*
- **P – Punctuation** (Correcting commas, apostrophes, quotation marks, colons, and semicolons)
- **T – Tense & Agreement** (Ensuring correct verb tense, subject-verb agreement, and pronoun-antecedent agreement)
- **S – Sentence Structure** (Correcting run-ons, fragments, misplaced modifiers, and improving clarity)

Why "SCRiPTS"?

Easy to remember – A **script** is used to refine writing, just like editing!
Relates directly to editing – Helps students remember key grammar and writing skills

Mnemonic to Help Students Remember SCRiPTS:

"Strong Writers Follow Their SCRiPTS!"
(Just like actors follow scripts to perform well, students follow their **SCRiPTS** to edit their writing!)

- **S – Spelling** → "Check your spelling so your writing isn't confusing!"
- **C – Capitalization** → "Names, places, and titles need capital letters!"
- **R – Replacement of Words** → "Choose the best words—avoid awkward or repeated ones!"
- **P – Punctuation** → "Use commas, periods, and apostrophes correctly!"
- **T – Tense & Agreement** → "Make sure verbs and subjects match in time and number!"
- **S – Sentence Structure** → "Fix fragments and run-ons for smooth writing!"

Visual Aid Idea: SCRiPTS Star ⭐

A **star-shaped anchor chart** can be drawn with each letter of SCRiPTS on a point of the star, reminding students to follow **all editing steps** before submitting their work!

Center of the Star: "Strong Writers Follow Their SCRiPTS!"

Points of the Star: Each letter from **SCRiPTS** with an example (e.g., "C – Capitalization: 'george washington' → 'George Washington'")

Bottom of the Poster: A reminder: **"Before you turn in your writing, check your SCRiPTS!"**

How to Interweave SCRiPTS into General Editing Questions

1. **Spelling Correction Example:**
   What change should be made in sentence 3?
   - A. Change **recieve** to **receive**
   - B. Change **there** to **their**
   - C. Change **its** to **it's**
   - D. No change needed
2. **Capitalization Correction Example:**
   What change should be made in sentence 5?
   - A. Change **the white house** to **the White House**
   - B. Change **president Washington** to **President Washington**
   - C. Change **main street** to **Main Street**
   - D. No change needed
3. **Word Replacement Example:**
   What is the best replacement for the word "good" in sentence 7?
   - A. Great
   - B. Strong
   - C. Excellent
   - D. No change needed
4. **Punctuation Correction Example:**
   What change should be made in sentence 9?
   - A. Add a comma after "however"
   - B. Remove the apostrophe in "student's"
   - C. Add quotation marks around "The teacher said that it was time to go."
   - D. No change needed
5. **Tense & Agreement Correction Example:**
   What change should be made in sentence 4?
   - A. Change **was** to **were**
   - B. Change **run** to **ran**
   - C. Change **have went** to **have gone**
   - D. No change needed
6. **Sentence Structure Example:**
   What change should be made in sentence 10?
   - A. Fix the run-on sentence by adding a period
   - B. Turn the sentence fragment into a complete thought
   - C. Rearrange the misplaced modifier for clarity
   - D. No change needed

Final Teaching Tip

Use the **SCRiPT method** to remind students of what to check when editing! Have them ask:

S – Are all the words spelled correctly?
C – Are names and titles capitalized?
R – Do the words make sense and fit the sentence?
P – Are commas, periods, and quotation marks correct?
T – Do the verbs match the subject?
S – Are sentences complete and clear?

Abraham Lincoln's Greatest Accomplishments

(1) **abraham lincoln** was one of the most important leaders in American history. (2) He was born in 1809 and became the 16th president of the United States in 1861. (3) Lincoln was known for his leadership during the **civil war** and his efforts to end slavery. (4) He gave many powerful speeches, including the **gettysburg address** which is one of the most famous speeches in history.

(5) One of **Lincolns** greatest accomplishments was signing the Emancipation Proclamation in 1863. (6) This document declared that enslaved people in Confederate states were free. (7) It was an important step towards ending slavery in the United States. (8) Lincoln **believe** that all men should be free and have rights.

(9) Lincoln also worked hard to bring the country back together after the war. (10) He said, "with malice toward none, with charity for all," meaning that he wanted Americans to forgive each other and rebuild the nation.

(11) **Unfortunatly**, Lincoln's leadership was cut short. (12) On April 14, 1865, he was **assasinated** while watching a play at **Fords Theatre**. (13) His death was a great loss, but his ideas and leadership continued to shape the nation.

(14) **Lincolns** legacy remains strong today. (15) His work to end slavery and keep the United States together made him one of the most respected presidents in history. (16) Many historians consider him one of the greatest leaders of all time.

Editing Questions

(1) What change, if any, should be made to sentence (1)?

A. Change abraham lincoln to Abraham Lincoln
B. Change leaders to leader's
C. Change was to were
D. No change needed

(2) What change, if any, should be made to sentence (4)?

A. Change gettysburg address to Gettysburg Address
B. Add a comma after history
C. Change which to who
D. No change needed

(3) What change, if any, should be made to sentence (8)?

A. Change believe to believed
B. Change should to shall
C. Change men to man
D. No change needed

(4) What change, if any, should be made to sentence (12)?

A. Change assasinated to assassinated
B. Change watching to watched
C. Change Fords Theatre to Ford's Theatre
D. No change needed

(5) What change, if any, should be made to sentence (14)?

A. Change Lincolns to Lincoln's
B. Change remains to remained
C. Change today to yesterday
D. No change needed

Editing Questions with SCRiPTS Labels

(1) What change, if any, should be made to sentence (1)?

A. Change **abraham lincoln** to **Abraham Lincoln** *(C - Capitalization)*
B. Change **leaders** to **leader's** *(P - Punctuation)*
C. Change **was** to **were** *(T - Tense & Agreement)*
D. No change needed

---

(2) What change, if any, should be made to sentence (4)?

A. Change **gettysburg address** to **Gettysburg Address** *(C - Capitalization)*
B. Add a comma after **history** *(P - Punctuation)*
C. Change **which** to **who** *(R - Replacement of Words)*
D. No change needed

---

(3) What change, if any, should be made to sentence (8)?

A. Change **believe** to **believed** *(T - Tense & Agreement)*
B. Change **should** to **shall** *(R - Replacement of Words)*
C. Change **men** to **man** *(T - Tense & Agreement)*
D. No change needed

---

(4) What change, if any, should be made to sentence (12)?

A. Change **assasinated** to **assassinated** *(S - Spelling)*
B. Change **watching** to **watched** *(T - Tense & Agreement)*
C. Change **Fords Theatre** to **Ford's Theatre** *(P - Punctuation)*
D. No change needed

(5) What change, if any, should be made to sentence (14)?

A. Change **Lincolns** to **Lincoln's** *(P - Punctuation)*
B. Change **remains** to **remained** *(T - Tense & Agreement)*
C. Change **today** to **yesterday** *(R - Replacement of Words)*
D. No change needed

Purpose of Mixed-Concept Answer Choices in an Editing Assessment

The inclusion of **mixed-concept answer choices** on an editing assessment serves an essential role in preparing students for real-world writing and reading challenges. These questions assess not only students' knowledge of individual grammar and writing rules but also their ability to **think critically, apply multiple skills simultaneously, and make decisions based on context**. Here are the key reasons for using mixed-concept answer choices:

---

1. Encourages Higher-Order Thinking

Mixed-concept questions require students to go beyond identifying a single type of error (such as capitalization or punctuation) and instead analyze the sentence holistically. They must evaluate:

- What kind of error exists (if any).
- Which type of correction improves the sentence most effectively.

This process mimics real-life editing, where errors often involve **multiple layers** of writing conventions. It forces students to think critically about **sentence clarity, accuracy, and structure**.

---

2. Builds Decision-Making Skills

When faced with answer choices from different angles—such as **capitalization, punctuation, verb tense, and sentence structure**—students must decide which correction is the most relevant or impactful. This strengthens their ability to prioritize and make decisions about what matters most in their writing.

For example:
Sentence: *Their going to the concert tommorow, but no one brang tickets.*
Answer Choices:
A. Change *Their* to *They're*
B. Change *brang* to *brought*
C. Change *tommorow* to *tomorrow*
D. No change needed

Students must decide which error affects the sentence most significantly. The **pronoun error (They're)** affects meaning more than spelling or verb choice. This decision-making process reinforces **effective editing skills**.

3. Tests Multiple Writing Standards in One Question

Mixed-concept questions allow assessments to cover multiple areas of language conventions efficiently. In one question, students may need to apply knowledge of:

- Grammar (verb tense, subject-verb agreement)
- Punctuation (commas, apostrophes)
- Word choice (correct homophones)
- Sentence structure (fragments, run-ons)

This ensures a more comprehensive evaluation of a student's language proficiency.

---

4. Prepares Students for Complex Writing and Revision

In real-world writing, students won't be tasked with fixing **just one type of mistake** at a time. Mixed-concept questions simulate real editing scenarios where they need to **apply multiple editing strategies simultaneously** to improve their writing. This mirrors what they will encounter in higher-level writing assignments and professional tasks.

---

5. Promotes Transferable Skills

By practicing with mixed-concept questions, students develop skills that extend beyond the classroom. These include:

- **Critical reading and evaluation**
- **Attention to detail**
- **Logical reasoning**
- **Prioritization and accuracy**

In professional and academic settings, these skills will help them identify and correct errors while maintaining clear and polished communication.

In summary, mixed-concept answer choices are a powerful tool for teaching students how to apply their knowledge holistically, sharpen their decision-making, and refine their writing into its clearest and most correct form. They create confident, well-rounded editors who can tackle writing challenges with ease!

A Three-Step Strategy for Tackling Editing Questions with Mixed-Concept Answer Choices

Does Your Answer Have PEP?

When students face a question with answer choices that cover **multiple revision and editing angles**, it can be tricky. One answer might correct **capitalization**, while others address **spelling, word replacement, punctuation, tense and agreement**, or **sentence structure**. Teaching students how to confidently approach these mixed-concept questions is essential.

In editing questions, students often need to choose the best answer from **multiple angles**—capitalization, punctuation, word replacement, tense and agreement, or sentence structure. **PEP** is a strategy to help students confidently navigate these questions and choose the best answer. **PEP** stands for:

- **P – Point Out or Identify the Focus of the Question**
- **E – Eliminate Irrelevant or Incorrect Answer Choices**
- **P – Plug It Back into the Passage**

P – Point Out or Identify the Focus of the Question

The first step is to figure out what the question is really asking. Some questions require students to analyze a sentence for multiple possible errors. **Identify what the focus is**—is it capitalization, spelling, punctuation, word choice, or sentence structure?

Strategy:
"Read the sentence once to understand its meaning, then read it again slowly, checking for one type of error at a time."

Common Errors to Check For:

- Capitalization
- Spelling
- Punctuation
- Word replacement (e.g., *their* vs. *they're*)
- Tense and agreement (subject-verb or pronoun-antecedent)
- Sentence structure (fragments, run-ons)

E – Eliminate Irrelevant or Incorrect Answer Choices

Once you've identified the focus, **use the process of elimination**. Cross out any choices that are clearly incorrect or unrelated to the error in the sentence.

Example:

Sentence: *Their going to the carnival after school.*
Question: What correction should be made to the sentence?

Answer Choices:
A. Change *Their* to *They're*
B. Change *carnival* to *Carnival*
C. Add a comma after *school*
D. No change needed

Elimination Process:

- **D** is incorrect because there's clearly an error in the sentence.
- **B** is incorrect because *carnival* doesn't need to be capitalized.
- **C** is unnecessary; no comma is needed after *school.*
- **A** is correct because *Their* should be changed to *They're* for proper subject-pronoun agreement.

P – Plug It Back into the Passage

Before finalizing your answer, **plug your choice back into the sentence** and read it in context. This step ensures the sentence flows naturally and remains grammatically correct.

Corrected Sentence: *They're going to the carnival after school.*

By plugging it back in, you confirm that the correction fixes the error and makes the sentence clear and logical.

Conclusion: Use PEP to Stay Focused

PEP—Point Out, Eliminate, and Plug It Back In—is a simple and effective strategy to help students tackle mixed-concept editing questions. With practice, students will feel more confident, choose the correct answer, and improve their overall editing skills!

PEP Song: "Row, Row, Row Your Boat" Tune ♫

This song will help students focus on **understanding the question, eliminating wrong answers, and plugging in the selected answer** to check its accuracy.

♫ Verse 1: Identify the Point

Read, read, read the question,
Find what it's about.
What's the focus? What's the point?
Now go check it out! ♫

♫ Verse 2: Eliminate the Wrong

Look, look at every choice,
One by one, you'll see.
Cross off answers that are wrong,
Then check carefully! ♫

♫ Verse 3: Plug It In and Check

Plug, plug, plug it in,
Read it one more time.
Does it fit? Does it flow?
If it works, it's fine! ♫

♫ Chorus (Repeat as Needed)

Read and check, eliminate,
Find the best one there!
Plug it in, check it twice,
Now you're fully prepared! ♫

PEP Song with Hand Motions: "Row, Row, Row Your Boat" Tune ♫

These **hand motions** will help students actively engage with the song while reinforcing the steps for **identifying the question, eliminating wrong answers, and plugging in the correct one**.

♫ Verse 1: Identify the Point

Read, read, read the question, (Pretend to hold a book and move your head like you're reading)
Find what it's about. (Put one hand above your eyes as if searching)
What's the focus? What's the point? (Point your finger in front of you twice)
Now go check it out! (Make a "thumbs up" motion)

♫ Verse 2: Eliminate the Wrong

Look, look at every choice, (Shade your eyes with one hand and pretend to search left to right)
One by one, you'll see. (Hold up one finger, then two, then three)
Cross off answers that are wrong, (Pretend to draw an "X" in the air)
Then check carefully! (Hold your hands out in a "wait and think" gesture)

♫ Verse 3: Plug It In and Check

Plug, plug, plug it in, (Pretend to plug something into an outlet)
Read it one more time. (Pretend to turn pages of a book)
Does it fit? Does it flow? (Hold your arms out like balancing scales)
If it works, it's fine! (Give a double thumbs-up)

♫ Chorus (Repeat as Needed)

Read and check, eliminate, (Point to your head, then cross arms in front of you like an "X")
Find the best one there! (Pretend to circle something with your finger)
Plug it in, check it twice, (Pretend to plug in again and count with your fingers)
Now you're fully prepared! (Stretch your arms wide with a big smile)

Reader's Theater: "The PEP Detectives"

Objective: Teach students how to apply the **PEP Strategy (Point Out, Eliminate, Plug It In)** when answering editing questions with mixed-concept answer choices.

Characters:

- **Narrator** – Guides the story
- **Emily** – A confident, thoughtful student
- **Jaden** – A curious problem-solver
- **Aisha** – A detail-oriented student
- **Luis** – A fun and energetic classmate
- **Chen** – The logical and organized thinker

Setting:

The scene takes place in a classroom where the teacher has just introduced a challenging editing question. The students are working together to solve the question using the **PEP Strategy**. There's a large whiteboard with an editing question written on it.

Script:

Narrator:
It's a bright afternoon in Room 204. The students are gathered around a whiteboard, trying to solve a tricky editing question. Their teacher has just taught them a new strategy called ***PEP***—*Point Out, Eliminate, and Plug It In. Emily, Jaden, Aisha, Luis, and Chen are ready to work together and become editing detectives.*

Emily: (pointing at the board)
"Okay, here's the question. It says, 'What correction should be made to the sentence?' The sentence is: *Their going to the carnival after school.* Hmm, something doesn't look right."

Luis: (scratching his head)
"Yeah, that sounds weird. *Their going?* I think something's wrong with that word *Their.*"

Aisha: (nodding)
"Let's use the **P in PEP—Point Out the focus of the question**. We need to figure out what kind of error we're dealing with. Is it capitalization, spelling, punctuation, or something else?"

Chen: (raising his hand)
"I think it's subject-pronoun agreement. The word *Their* is wrong because it's supposed to show they are going somewhere, not possession."

Narrator:
The students nod in agreement. They've successfully pointed out the focus: it's a pronoun error.

Emily:
"Now let's move to the **E—Eliminate irrelevant or incorrect answer choices**. What are the options?"

(Aisha reads the answer choices aloud from the board.)

Aisha:
"A. Change *Their* to *They're.*
B. Change *carnival* to *Carnival.*
C. Add a comma after *school.*
D. No change needed."

Jaden: (laughing)
"Well, D is definitely wrong. There's an error for sure."

Luis:
"And B doesn't make sense either—*carnival* doesn't need to be capitalized unless it's the name of something specific."

Chen:
"C isn't right either. There's no reason for a comma after *school.*"

Emily: (clapping her hands)
"So, the only one left is A: Change *Their* to *They're.* That makes sense because it fixes the pronoun error!"

Narrator:
The group has eliminated the incorrect answers, and only one remains. But they're not done yet!

Aisha:
"Now it's time for the last P—**Plug It In!** Let's read the sentence with the correction and see if it works."

Luis:
"I'll read it: *They're going to the carnival after school.*"

Chen:
"That sounds perfect! It's clear and correct. We plugged it in, and it flows naturally."

Jaden:
"So, the correct answer is definitely A. We used PEP and nailed it!"

Emily: (pretending to hold a detective's magnifying glass)
"We're officially editing detectives. PEP helped us solve the case!"

Narrator:
The students celebrate their success. They've learned how to apply the PEP strategy: Point Out the focus of the question, Eliminate irrelevant answers, and Plug It In to double-check their choice. From now on, they're ready to tackle even the trickiest editing questions!

End of Play

Narrator:
"And remember, whenever you're faced with a tough editing question, just ask yourself: Does your answer have PEP?"

Exemplar Editing Questions

(1) What change, if any, should be made to sentence (1)?

A. Change **abraham lincoln** to **Abraham Lincoln** ✅ *(Correct – Names should be capitalized.)*
B. Change **leaders** to **leader's** ✕ *(Incorrect – No possessive is needed.)*
C. Change **was** to **were** ✕ *(Incorrect – Subject-verb agreement is correct as written.)*
D. No change needed ✕ *(Incorrect – The name should be capitalized.)*

---

(2) What change, if any, should be made to sentence (4)?

A. Change **gettysburg address** to **Gettysburg Address** ✅ *(Correct – Proper noun titles should be capitalized.)*
B. Add a comma after **history** ✕ *(Incorrect – No comma is necessary.)*
C. Change **which** to **who** ✕ *(Incorrect – "Which" correctly refers to the speech, not a person.)*
D. No change needed ✕ *(Incorrect – The title should be capitalized.)*

---

(3) What change, if any, should be made to sentence (8)?

A. Change **believe** to **believed** ✅ *(Correct – The past tense is needed to match the rest of the passage.)*
B. Change **should** to **shall** ✕ *(Incorrect – "Should" correctly expresses Lincoln's belief.)*
C. Change **men** to **man** ✕ *(Incorrect – "Men" correctly refers to all people.)*
D. No change needed ✕ *(Incorrect – "believe" is in the wrong tense.)*

---

(4) What change, if any, should be made to sentence (12)?

A. Change **assasinated** to **assassinated** ✅ *(Correct – "Assasinated" is a spelling error.)*
B. Change **watching** to **watched** ✕ *(Incorrect – "Watching" is correct in this context.)*
C. Change **Fords Theatre** to **Ford's Theatre** ✅ *(Correct – "Fords" should have an apostrophe for possession.)*
D. No change needed ✕ *(Incorrect – Two errors need to be corrected.)*

(5) What change, if any, should be made to sentence (14)?

A. Change **Lincolns** to **Lincoln's** ✅ *(Correct – Possessive form is needed.)*
B. Change **remains** to **remained** ❌ *(Incorrect – Present tense is correct to show Lincoln's ongoing influence.)*
C. Change **today** to **yesterday** ❌ *(Incorrect – "Today" is correct in this context.)*
D. No change needed ❌ *(Incorrect – The possessive apostrophe is missing.)*

Lesson 1: P – Point Out the Focus of the Question

Objective:

Students will identify the focus of editing questions by recognizing different types of errors (capitalization, spelling, punctuation, word replacement, tense and agreement, sentence structure).

Materials:

- Sentences with different types of errors (printed on strips of paper)
- Whiteboard and markers
- Labels for different categories: **Capitalization**, **Spelling**, **Punctuation**, **Tense/Agreement**, **Sentence Structure**, **Word Replacement**

Teacher Script:

"When we edit sentences, the first thing we need to do is figure out what kind of error we're looking for. Is it a problem with capitalization? Spelling? Punctuation? We can't fix it if we don't know what's wrong first! Today, we're going to become 'Error Detectives' and identify the focus of each question by recognizing common errors."

Activity: Error Detective Walk

1. Post **sentence strips** with different types of errors around the room.
2. Divide students into small groups. Give each group a clipboard and worksheet with the following categories: **Capitalization**, **Spelling**, **Punctuation**, **Tense/Agreement**, **Sentence Structure**, **Word Replacement**. Use the **SCRiPT**S acronym to help you.
3. Students walk around the room, read each sentence, and write down which type of error they believe it contains.
4. Once they've identified the focus for each sentence, groups return to their seats and discuss their answers with the class.

Example Sentences:

1. *their going to the carnival after school.* (Tense/Agreement)
2. *The principal said, "School starts at Eight AM."* (Capitalization)
3. *I've always wanted to meat a famous author.* (Spelling)
4. *The teacher hand out the tests yesterday.* (Tense/Agreement)

Lesson 1: Point Out the Focus of the Question

Name:________________________ Date:________________________

Instructions:

In each sentence below, there is an error. Your job is to identify the type of error by pointing out the focus of the question. Write whether the error is related to **Capitalization, Spelling, Punctuation, Word Replacement, Tense/Agreement,** or **Sentence Structure.**

Example:

their going to the carnival after school.
Answer: Tense/Agreement (Their should be They're)

Part 1: Identify the Error Focus

For each sentence below, write the type of error:

1. *The principal said, "School starts at Eight AM."*

2. *I've always wanted to meat a famous author.*

3. *The teacher hand out the tests yesterday.*

4. *their going to the game after school.*

5. *My friend lives on Apple street.*

Lesson 2: E – Eliminate Irrelevant or Incorrect Answer Choices

Objective:

Students will practice the process of elimination by crossing out irrelevant or incorrect answer choices in multiple-choice editing questions.

Materials:

- Multiple-choice questions with mixed-concept answer choices
- Chart paper for group work
- Markers

Teacher Script:

"After we know what kind of error we're looking for, the next step is to get rid of the wrong answers. Sometimes you'll see answers that have nothing to do with the error in the sentence. Other times, two answers might seem right, but one is better. Today, we'll practice crossing out irrelevant choices and finding the best one!"

Activity: Answer Choice Relay

1. Divide students into small groups and give each group a chart paper with three multiple-choice editing questions.
2. Each group works together to eliminate incorrect answers and explain why those answers don't fit.
3. Once they've chosen their final answer, they run to the whiteboard to record their group's choice.
4. Discuss the correct answers as a class, highlighting why certain choices were eliminated.

Example Question:
Sentence: *Their going to the carnival after school.*
Answer Choices:
A. Change *Their* to *They're.*
B. Change *carnival* to *Carnival.*
C. Add a comma after *school.*
D. No change needed.

Lesson 2: Eliminate Irrelevant or Incorrect Answer Choices

Name:_________________________ **Date:**_________________________

Instructions:

Each question below contains four answer choices. Use the process of elimination to cross out irrelevant or incorrect answers and choose the best one. Explain why you chose the correct answer.

Example Question:

Sentence: *Their going to the carnival after school.* **Answer Choices:** A. Change *Their* to *They're*
B. Change *carnival* to *Carnival*
C. Add a comma after *school*
D. No change needed

Correct Answer: A. Change *Their* to *They're*. **Explanation:** This fixes the subject-pronoun agreement.

Part 1: Eliminate Incorrect Choices

1. **Sentence:** *The dog wagged it's tail happily.*
   A. Change *it's* to *its*
   B. Change *dog* to *Dog*
   C. Add a comma after *wagged*
   D. No change needed
   Correct Answer: __________________________________ **Explanation:** __________________________________
2. **Sentence:** *We are going to the movies on friday.*
   A. Change *friday* to *Friday*
   B. Change *are* to *were*
   C. Add a period after *movies*
   D. No change needed
   Correct Answer: __________________________________ **Explanation:** __________________________________
3. **Sentence:** *She seen the movie yesterday.*
   A. Change *seen* to *saw*
   B. Change *movie* to *Movie*
   C. Add a comma after *she*
   D. No change needed
   Correct Answer: __________________________________ **Explanation:**

Lesson 3: P – Plug It Back into the Passage

Objective:

Students will practice plugging their selected answer back into the sentence or passage to ensure it fits and maintains clarity and flow.

Materials:

- Sentences with possible corrections
- Index cards with corrected versions of sentences
- Red and green cards for student responses

Teacher Script:

"Our final step is the most important—plug it back in! Once we've chosen our answer, we need to make sure it fits into the sentence or passage. Does it make sense? Does it sound right? If it flows smoothly, we've got the right answer. If not, we may need to double-check."

Activity: Red or Green Check-In

1. Read a sentence with a correction aloud.
2. Provide two possible corrected versions on index cards and read them aloud.
3. Students hold up a **green card** if the correction works or a **red card** if it doesn't.
4. Discuss as a class why the correction works or doesn't.

Example Sentence:
Original: *Their going to the carnival after school.*
Corrected Options:

- A. *They're going to the carnival after school.*
- B. *Their going to the Carnival after school.*

Assessment:

Give students a short passage with highlighted errors. After they choose the correct answers, they must rewrite the passage with the corrections plugged in to confirm that it flows smoothly.

Lesson 3: Plug It Back into the Passage

Name:________________________ **Date:**________________________

Instructions:

Choose the best correction for each sentence and then plug it back into the passage to make sure it fits. Read the corrected sentence aloud to confirm that it flows and makes sense.

Example:

Sentence: *Their going to the carnival after school.*
Correction: Change *Their* to *They're.*
Plugged-In Sentence: *They're going to the carnival after school.*

Plug It In

1. **Sentence:** *The childs toy was broken.*
   Correction Options:
   A. Change *childs* to *child's*
   B. Change *toy* to *Toy*
   C. Add a period after *broken*
   Corrected Sentence: ______________________________
2. **Sentence:** *She runned to the store quickly.*
   Correction Options:
   A. Change *runned* to *ran*
   B. Change *store* to *Store*
   C. Add a comma after *store*
   Corrected Sentence: ______________________________
3. **Sentence:** *There going to meet us at noon.*
   Correction Options:
   A. Change *There* to *They're*
   B. Change *meet* to *meets*
   C. Add a semicolon after *noon*
   Corrected Sentence: **Part 2: Group Practice**

Bridge Between Editing and Revising

Difference Between Editing and Revising Questions on State Assessments

On the STAAR assessment, **editing** and **revising** questions are two distinct categories, each focusing on different aspects of writing. While both are essential for improving a passage, they have **unique goals and question formats**. Understanding their differences helps students approach them with the right strategies.

---

1. Revising Questions

Goal: Improve the content, organization, and clarity of a passage.
Focus: Revising questions test a student's ability to make higher-level changes that affect the **meaning, structure, or style** of the writing.

Defining Characteristics:

- Ask students to enhance or rewrite parts of a passage for better **flow, coherence, word choice, tone, and organization**.
- May involve adding, deleting, or exchanging information for stronger, more relevant details.
- Require students to understand **how ideas connect** within the passage.
- Often involve identifying the **best way to combine or rearrange sentences** or **replace vague words with more specific ones**.

Examples of Revising Questions:

- *Which sentence would best introduce this paragraph?*
- *What is the most effective way to combine these two sentences?*
- *Which sentence should be added to improve the flow of the paragraph?*

2. Editing Questions

Goal: Correct grammatical, spelling, punctuation, and sentence structure errors.
Focus: Editing questions focus on the **technical accuracy** of a passage.

Defining Characteristics:

- Test a student's understanding of **grammar rules, capitalization, punctuation, spelling, and subject-verb agreement**.
- Often ask students to correct **errors** in sentence structure, verb tense, or pronoun-antecedent agreement.
- More **objective** than revising questions—there is a clear right or wrong answer.
- Require attention to **details**, such as **commas, apostrophes, quotation marks, and verb tense consistency**.

Examples of Editing Questions:

- *What change should be made to sentence 3?*
- *Which word is spelled incorrectly in this sentence?*
- *What punctuation is needed to correct sentence 5?*

Summary of Differences:

Feature	Revising	Editing
Focus	Content, organization, word choice	Grammar, punctuation, spelling
Goal	Improve meaning and clarity	Ensure technical accuracy
Type of Changes	Add, delete, exchange ideas	Correct errors in sentence form
Higher/Lower Order	Higher-order thinking	Lower-order correction skills
Examples of Skills	Combining sentences, improving flow	Fixing run-ons, correcting verb tense

---

Why This Distinction Matters

- **Revising** questions require more creative and analytical thinking. Students must **evaluate the context** and decide how to improve overall coherence.
- **Editing** questions are about **attention to detail**, applying grammar and punctuation rules consistently.

Part 5

REVISING

Scope and Sequence for Revising Components Using the READ Framework

This scope and sequence outlines the progressive steps to teach revising, using the READ framework (Reorganize, Exchange, Add, Delete). The goal is to develop students' ability to assess and improve their writing with clarity, organization, and precision. The sequence starts with foundational concepts and moves toward advanced revising strategies.

Unit 1: Introduction to Revising and the READ Framework

Objective: Students will understand the purpose of revising and the READ framework as a tool for improvement.
Key Skills:

- Define and differentiate between revising and editing.
- Introduce the READ framework: Rearranging, Exchanging, Adding, and Deleting.

Activities:

- Analyze a sample text with errors in organization, word choice, or details and identify areas needing revision.
- Group discussion: Which READ strategy applies to specific revision needs?

Unit 2: Rearranging Information (R)

Objective: Students will learn how to assess and improve the organization of their writing.
Key Skills:

- Recognizing logical order (chronological, problem-solution, cause-effect).
- Using transitions to enhance flow.
- Identifying sections that disrupt coherence.

Activities:

- Practice rearranging paragraphs or sentences in sample texts.
- Use graphic organizers to visualize the structure of a piece before and after revision.

Unit 3: Exchanging Information (E)

Objective: Students will practice replacing weak or ineffective content with stronger alternatives.
Key Skills:

- Identifying vague or repetitive words and replacing them with precise vocabulary.
- Substituting weak examples or evidence with stronger, more relevant ones.
- Revising tone and word choice for audience and purpose.

Activities:

- Compare versions of a sentence with varied word choices and discuss their impact.
- Swap out weak arguments or details in provided paragraphs with improved content.

Unit 4: Adding Information (A)

Objective: Students will recognize gaps in their writing and learn to add missing details or explanations.
Key Skills:

- Identifying areas where additional evidence or examples are needed.
- Using sensory details and descriptive language to enhance clarity.
- Adding transitions to connect ideas smoothly.

Activities:

- Review a sample essay and brainstorm missing details that would improve it.
- Write a paragraph, intentionally leaving gaps, and have peers suggest what to add.

Unit 5: Deleting Information (D)

Objective: Students will identify and remove irrelevant, redundant, or off-topic content.
Key Skills:

- Recognizing unnecessary repetition.
- Evaluating whether details support the central idea.
- Maintaining focus by cutting unrelated tangents.

Activities:

- Highlight and remove extraneous sentences in sample texts.
- Conduct peer reviews focusing on identifying unnecessary content.

Unit 6: Sequencing and Word Order

Objective: Students will improve sentence structure and paragraph flow by rearranging word order for clarity and emphasis.
Key Skills:

- Understanding correct word order within sentences (subject-verb-object).
- Rearranging sentences to improve overall flow and coherence.
- Recognizing adjective order and logical sequencing.

Activities:

- Rearrange jumbled sentences for proper word order.
- Practice identifying and correcting awkward sentence constructions.
- Create coherent paragraphs by sequencing mixed-up sentences.

Unit 7: Combining READ Strategies

Objective: Students will integrate all four READ strategies to perform comprehensive revisions.
Key Skills:

- Applying multiple strategies to the same piece of writing.
- Recognizing when to rearrange, exchange, add, or delete information.
- Evaluating their own work critically.

Activities:

- Revise a full-length draft using the READ framework.
- Peer review: Use the READ framework to provide constructive feedback on a partner's draft.
- Reflection activity: Write about how each READ strategy improved their final product.

Unit 8: Self-Assessment and Revising for Purpose

Objective: Students will revise with a focus on audience, purpose, and tone.
Key Skills:

- Tailoring revisions to specific genres or audiences (e.g., persuasive, narrative, informational).
- Reflecting on revisions made and their impact on the writing.

Activities:

- Compare drafts to identify improvements made through the READ framework.
- Revise a piece of writing to suit a different audience or purpose (e.g., formal vs. informal).

Culminating Project

Objective: Students will demonstrate mastery of the READ framework by revising a piece of writing through multiple drafts.
Key Skills:

- Independent application of READ strategies.
- Integrating feedback from peers and teachers.
- Producing polished, well-organized, and impactful writing.

Activities:

- Submit a "revision log" that documents how the READ framework was used for each draft.
- Showcase before-and-after versions of a piece with explanations of changes.

Assessment

Evaluate students' ability to:

- Identify and explain which READ strategy applies to specific revision needs.
- Apply READ strategies effectively in their own writing.
- Provide constructive feedback using the READ framework during peer reviews.

Unit 1

R.E.A.D. Revising Framework

Introduction to Revising Using the READ Framework

Revising is a critical step in the writing process, where the goal is to refine and enhance a piece of work to meet its full potential. While there are many facets to effective revising—ranging from improving clarity and organization to strengthening arguments and eliminating redundancies—they can all be grouped under the **READ framework**. This acronym simplifies the process by categorizing revision actions into four essential techniques:

- **R** stands for **Rearranging information**: This involves adjusting the order of ideas, paragraphs, or sentences to improve the logical flow and structure of the piece.
- **E** stands for **Exchanging information**: Here, weaker ideas, words, or examples are replaced with stronger, more specific, or relevant ones.
- **A** stands for **Adding information**: Revising often requires inserting missing details, transitions, or evidence to clarify points or strengthen arguments.
- **D** stands for **Deleting information**: Cutting out irrelevant, redundant, or off-topic content ensures the writing remains focused and concise.

For teachers, the key to guiding students through successful revision lies in **helping them identify what needs to be done** at each stage. This means asking the right questions about the text. For example:

- Does the information flow logically, or does it need **rearranging (R)**?
- Are there weak areas that require **exchanging (E)** for better ideas or examples?
- Are key details or explanations missing, requiring **adding (A)** to make the text complete?
- Is there irrelevant or redundant content that should be **deleted (D)**?

By teaching students to analyze their writing with these questions in mind, educators empower them to make thoughtful and effective revisions. The READ framework provides a clear, actionable structure for revising, helping students focus their efforts on what matters most in improving their work.

Revising is a critical stage in the writing process that focuses on improving the overall content, structure, and clarity of a piece. Here are the **major components of revising**:

1. Content Development

- **Ensure Completeness:** Check that all ideas are fully developed and that the piece answers any questions or fulfills the purpose of the writing.
- **Clarify Ideas:** Make sure the main ideas and supporting details are clear and well-explained.
- **Remove Irrelevant Content:** Eliminate anything that distracts from the main points or purpose.
- **Enhance Examples and Evidence:** Add stronger or more specific examples, facts, or data if needed.

---

2. Organization

- **Check Logical Flow:** Ensure the writing follows a logical sequence. Ideas should progress naturally from one to the next.
- **Revise Paragraph Structure:** Each paragraph should have a clear topic sentence and supporting details.
- **Transitions:** Add or refine transition words and phrases to improve the connections between paragraphs or sections.
- **Introduction and Conclusion:** Ensure the introduction effectively sets the stage and the conclusion provides a satisfying end.

---

3. Clarity and Style

- **Simplify Complex Sentences:** Rewrite awkward or overly complicated sentences for readability.
- **Eliminate Redundancies:** Remove repetitive words or phrases.
- **Improve Word Choice:** Replace vague, weak, or imprecise words with stronger, more specific ones.
- **Maintain Consistency:** Ensure consistent tone, voice, and point of view throughout the piece.

4. Audience and Purpose

- **Adapt to the Audience:** Revise language, tone, and level of detail to match the intended audience.
- **Focus on Purpose:** Ensure the piece achieves its intended purpose, whether to inform, persuade, entertain, or explain.

---

5. Coherence

- **Unify Themes:** Ensure all sections and paragraphs contribute to the central idea or thesis.
- **Eliminate Contradictions:** Resolve any inconsistencies in arguments or details.
- **Strengthen Argument:** If applicable, address counterarguments or gaps in reasoning.

---

6. Feedback Incorporation

- **Respond to Feedback:** Use suggestions from peers, teachers, or editors to identify weak areas.
- **Evaluate Suggestions Critically:** Accept only feedback that aligns with the purpose and vision of the piece.

---

7. Grammar and Mechanics

- Although more prominent during the editing phase, revising also includes checking for significant grammatical or mechanical issues that affect meaning, such as sentence fragments, run-ons, or incorrect punctuation.

Revising is an iterative process, and writers often revisit multiple components to refine and polish their work.

Here is how the READ acronym applies to the revising techniques outlined above:

1. Content Development

- **E (Exchanging):** Replace weaker examples or evidence with stronger, more specific ones.
- **A (Adding):** Add details to clarify ideas or strengthen arguments.
- **D (Deleting):** Remove irrelevant or distracting content.

---

2. Organization

- **R (Rearranging):** Ensure ideas follow a logical sequence and rearrange sections or paragraphs if necessary.
- **A (Adding):** Add transitions to improve flow between ideas.
- **D (Deleting):** Eliminate redundant or misplaced sentences that disrupt flow.

---

3. Clarity and Style

- **E (Exchanging):** Replace vague or weak words with stronger, more precise vocabulary.
- **D (Deleting):** Remove redundancies or overly complicated sentences.

---

4. Audience and Purpose

- **E (Exchanging):** Adapt language or tone to better suit the intended audience.
- **A (Adding):** Include additional details or explanations to clarify the purpose.

---

5. Coherence

- **R (Rearranging):** Restructure paragraphs or sections to better unify themes.
- **E (Exchanging):** Revise arguments or points to resolve contradictions and strengthen coherence.
- **A (Adding):** Include missing counterarguments or explanations for completeness.
- **D (Deleting):** Remove any points that conflict with the central theme or thesis.

6. Feedback Incorporation

- **R (Rearranging):** Apply feedback that suggests moving sections for better flow.
- **E (Exchanging):** Replace weaker ideas or arguments based on feedback.
- **A (Adding):** Add clarifications or details as suggested by reviewers.
- **D (Deleting):** Remove parts that reviewers find unclear or unnecessary.

---

7. Grammar and Mechanics

- **E (Exchanging):** Replace incorrect grammar or punctuation with correct usage.
- **D (Deleting):** Eliminate extra or incorrect punctuation that hinders understanding.

This labeling helps connect revising strategies to the READ framework, making it easier to remember and apply.

Unit 2

Rearranging Sentences

In writing, **how sentences are structured internally** can make a big difference in how clear, smooth, and engaging they sound. Rearranging parts within a sentence—such as phrases, clauses, or word order—helps writers create stronger, more polished sentences. In this unit, you'll learn how to revise and **rearrange sentence structure** to improve clarity, flow, and overall impact using the **CRISSSP** strategy.

Sometimes sentences feel awkward or confusing because their parts are not in the best order. Rearranging internal elements can solve that problem. For instance, if the subject and verb are too far apart, the sentence may be hard to follow. Moving an adjective closer to the noun it describes makes the sentence clearer. Rearranging also helps eliminate **repetitive patterns**, creating a more natural and varied rhythm.

The **CRISSSP** strategy will guide your revisions. **Clarity and Conciseness (C)** helps you get rid of extra words and place key details where they stand out. **Relevance and Focus (R)** ensures that only essential parts remain in the sentence. **Intentional Organization (I)** means placing words and phrases in an order that makes logical sense. **Sentence Variety (S)** ensures that the added sentence provides variety based on sentences that are already in the passage. **Sentence Structure (S)** focuses on building grammatically correct sentences. **Style and Tone (S)** emphasize that the answer should match that of the passage. **Precision (P)** replaces vague phrasing with sharp, specific language.

In this unit, you'll explore different ways to rearrange sentences internally to make them more powerful and precise. Let's get started and create sentences that are **clear, concise, and CRISSSP!**

Characteristics of the BEST Answer in Revising:

1. **Clarity and Conciseness**
   - **Best Answer:** Is clear, direct, and avoids unnecessary words or repetition.
   - **Good Answer:** May be correct but wordy, awkward, or less polished.
     Example:
   - Good: *Due to the fact that he was tired, he went to bed early.*
   - Best: *Because he was tired, he went to bed early.*
2. **Precision and Specificity**
   - **Best Answer:** Uses more precise vocabulary or details to enhance meaning.
   - **Good Answer:** Uses general or less descriptive language.
     Example:
   - Good: *The dog ran fast.*
   - Best: *The dog sprinted across the yard.*
3. **Consistency in Tone and Style**
   - **Best Answer:** Matches the tone, voice, and style of the passage.
   - **Good Answer:** May introduce a slight shift in tone or formality.
     Example: In a formal essay:
   - Good: *This proves that the experiment works.*
   - Best: *This demonstrates that the experiment is successful.*
4. **Logical Flow and Organization**
   - **Best Answer:** Enhances the overall structure and flow of the passage, creating smoother transitions.
   - **Good Answer:** May improve a sentence but not contribute as much to the flow.
     Example:
   - Good: *First, she brushed her teeth. She put on her shoes after.*
   - Best: *First, she brushed her teeth, then she put on her shoes.*
5. **Relevance and Focus**
   - **Best Answer:** Stays focused on the main idea without introducing irrelevant details.
   - **Good Answer:** Might add related information but doesn't improve the overall focus.
     Example:
   - Good: *The author talks about how much he likes running and swimming.*
   - Best: *The author describes his passion for running.*
6. **Variety in Sentence Structure**
   - **Best Answer:** Improves sentence variety, avoiding repetition of sentence patterns.
   - **Good Answer:** Corrects the problem but may still result in repetitive structure.
     Example:
   - Good: *The car was fast. The car was blue.*
   - Best: *The fast car was blue.*

Habits for Students to Identify the BEST Answer:

1. **Reread the Entire Sentence or Paragraph** – Ensure the answer fits the overall meaning and tone.
2. **Eliminate Options That Don't Fully Improve the Text** – If two choices seem correct, ask: *Which one is clearer, more precise, and better aligned with the passage?*
3. **Look for Redundancy and Wordiness** – Best answers are often shorter and more direct.
4. **Check for Logical Flow** – The best option will make the sentence or paragraph flow more naturally.
5. **Match the Tone and Style** – Ensure the answer maintains the voice of the original passage.

CRISSSP Revision Techniques when Deciding Between Good and BEST

- **C – Clarity and Conciseness**
  Keeps writing clear, direct, and free of unnecessary words.
- **R – Relevance and Focus**
  Stays on topic and avoids unrelated details to the passage.
- **I – Intentional Organization**
  Ensures ideas are presented in a logical order with smooth transitions for that passage.
- **S – Sentence Variety**
  Avoids repetitive patterns already found in the passage to create more engaging writing.
- **S – Sentence Structure**
  Builds grammatically sound sentences with proper punctuation and word order.
- **S – Style and Tone**
  Maintains a consistent tone, voice, and level of formality found in the passage.
- **P – Precision**
  Uses accurate language to paint a picture, to improve meaning, or enhance understanding necessary for the passage.

Why CRISSSP?

- **Memorable** – "CRISSSP" sounds like **"crisp,"** symbolizing clear and polished writing.
- **Comprehensive** – Covers all essential aspects of revising, from content and structure to grammar and style.

Mentor Revising Passage

(1) Joining the school garden club is a fun activity, it helps students learn how to grow vegetables and flowers. (2) Students plant seeds, water them, and watch them grow into plants that can be eaten or just look nice. (3) One time, we grew a lot of tomatoes, it was the most tomatoes we ever grew in a single season. (4) The club is open for kids in fourth and fifth grade, and everyone who joins will have lots of fun. (5) Also, we learned about bugs, weather, and teamwork, which are things that help us in school and life. (6) Growing things is an important skill that takes patience.

Revision Questions

(1) What is the BEST way to revise sentence (1)?

A. Joining the school garden club is a fun activity because it helps students learn how to grow vegetables and flowers.
B. The school garden club is fun and helps students, it teaches them to grow vegetables and flowers.
C. The school garden club is a fun activity; students learn to grow vegetables and flowers from it.
D. The school garden club is fun and helps with learning how vegetables and flowers are grown.

Best Answer: A. It combines the ideas clearly and avoids the comma splice.

---

(2) What is the BEST way to revise sentence (3)?

A. One time, we grew a lot of tomatoes. This was the most tomatoes we ever grew in a single season.
B. One time, we grew a lot of tomatoes because it was the most tomatoes we ever grew.
C. We grew so many tomatoes once; it was the most tomatoes ever grown.
D. One time, we grew tomatoes, it was the most tomatoes ever.

Best Answer: A. It breaks the sentence into two shorter sentences for better variety.

(3) How can sentence (5) be improved?

A. Also, we learned about bugs, weather, and teamwork, which are helpful in school and life.
B. We also learned about bugs and teamwork; they help with life and stuff.
C. Bugs, weather, and teamwork are good things to know.
D. We learned some cool things like bugs and weather and stuff for life.

Best Answer: A. It maintains a formal and consistent tone.

---

(4) What is the BEST way to improve sentence (4)?

A. The club is open for kids in fourth and fifth grade, and students can have fun learning about gardening.
B. The club is open for kids in fourth and fifth grade, and they get to enjoy planting seeds.
C. The club is open for kids in fourth and fifth grade, and everyone who joins will have fun learning.
D. The club is for fourth and fifth graders who want to learn science, gardening, and teamwork.

Best Answer: D. It improves focus by clearly specifying the club's purpose and benefits.

Revision Questions with CRISSSP Labels

(1) What is the BEST way to revise sentence (1)?

Original Sentence: *The school garden club is a fun activity, it helps students learn how to grow vegetables and flowers.*

A. Joining the school garden club is a fun activity because it helps students learn how to grow vegetables and flowers. *(S – Sentence Structure)*
B. The school garden club is fun and helps students, it teaches them to grow vegetables and flowers. *(S – Sentence Structure; contains a comma splice)*
C. The school garden club is a fun activity; students learn to grow vegetables and flowers from it. *(C – Clarity and Conciseness)*
D. The school garden club is fun and helps with learning how vegetables and flowers are grown. *(C – Clarity and Conciseness, but less effective than A)*

---

(2) What is the BEST way to revise sentence (3)?

Original Sentence: *One time, we grew a lot of tomatoes, it was the most tomatoes we ever grew in a single season.*

A. One time, we grew a lot of tomatoes. This was the most tomatoes we ever grew in a single season. *(S – Sentence Variety)*
B. One time, we grew a lot of tomatoes because it was the most tomatoes we ever grew. *(S – Sentence Structure; lacks sentence variety)*
C. We grew so many tomatoes once; it was the most tomatoes ever grown. *(C – Clarity and Conciseness)*
D. One time, we grew tomatoes, it was the most tomatoes ever. *(S – Sentence Structure; comma splice present)*

(3) How can sentence (5) be improved?

Original Sentence: *Also, we learned about bugs, weather, and teamwork, which are things that help us in school and life.*

A. Also, we learned about bugs, weather, and teamwork, which are helpful in school and life. *(S – Style and Tone)*
B. We also learned about bugs and teamwork; they help with life and stuff. *(S – Style and Tone; inconsistent tone)*
C. Bugs, weather, and teamwork are good things to know. *(C – Clarity and Conciseness, but lacks proper tone)*
D. We learned some cool things like bugs and weather and stuff for life. *(S – Style and Tone; informal and inconsistent)*

---

(4) What is the BEST way to improve sentence (4)?

Original Sentence: *The club is open for kids in fourth and fifth grade, and everyone who joins will have lots of fun.*

A. The club is open for kids in fourth and fifth grade, and students can have fun learning about gardening. *(R – Relevance and Focus)*
B. The club is open for kids in fourth and fifth grade, and they get to enjoy planting seeds. *(R – Relevance and Focus)*
C. The club is open for kids in fourth and fifth grade, and everyone who joins will have fun learning. *(S – Style and Tone; general but not focused)*
D. The club is for fourth and fifth graders who want to learn science, gardening, and teamwork. *(R – Relevance and Focus; Best – more specific and focused)*

Teacher Training Script: Rearranging Information to Revise

Lower Level Script (Elementary)

"Rearranging information helps make our writing easier to understand. Sometimes the order of words or ideas in a sentence can be confusing. When this happens, we need to move things around so they make sense. Think of it like a puzzle—if the pieces are in the wrong place, the picture doesn't look right. But when you put the pieces in the right order, everything becomes clear. So, when we rearrange, we're making sure the sentence flows smoothly and the reader can follow our ideas easily."

Upper Level Script (Middle/High School)

"Rearranging information is a powerful revision tool that improves clarity and flow. Sometimes, even though a sentence is grammatically correct, its structure might feel awkward or disorganized. Rearranging parts of the sentence—such as moving a phrase closer to the noun it describes or changing the order of clauses—can make the sentence clearer and more logical. Think of rearranging as adjusting the building blocks of a sentence to create stronger, more readable writing. Remember, the goal is to make the sentence flow smoothly while keeping its meaning intact."

Lesson 1: C – Clarity and Conciseness

Objective: Students will identify and revise sentences to make them more clear and concise.
Materials: Practice passage, index cards with wordy sentences, markers, whiteboard.

Scripted Explanation:

"Writers can make their ideas easier to understand by keeping their sentences clear and concise. This means saying what you need to say without extra or unnecessary words. Think of it like packing a suitcase—you only pack what you need!"

Practice Passage:

"Due to the fact that it was raining heavily, the baseball game was canceled. The players who were going to play the game were very disappointed and went home sadly."

Activity (Whole Group – Editing Relay Race):

1. Divide the class into small teams (3-4 students each).
2. Give each team an index card with a long, wordy sentence.
3. Teams race to rewrite the sentence on a whiteboard, making it shorter and clearer.
4. The first team to create a concise sentence gets a point, but all teams must read their sentence aloud for feedback.

Assessment:

Have students rewrite the practice passage individually, aiming to make it more concise. Share some examples with the class.

Here's a list of 10 wordy sentences **for students to practice revising for** clarity and conciseness:

1. Due to the fact that it was raining outside, the outdoor soccer game that was scheduled to take place had to be postponed until a later date.
2. The student who was sitting in the third row from the front of the classroom decided to raise his hand in order to ask the teacher a question that he was curious about.
3. At this point in time, it is necessary for all students who are planning to attend the field trip to turn in their signed permission slips by the end of the school day tomorrow.
4. The dog, which was extremely large and had a very fluffy tail, ran quickly through the green grassy park while barking loudly at the birds flying overhead.
5. In the event that you happen to forget your homework assignment at home, it will be essential for you to bring it in the next time you come to class.
6. The principal of the school announced over the intercom that all students who were interested in signing up for the spelling bee should make sure to write their names on the signup sheet located outside of the front office.
7. It is my opinion that we should probably think about the possibility of discussing this topic further before we make any decisions on it.
8. The library has a large collection of books that cover many different topics, and if you take some time to look around, you will probably find something interesting to read.
9. In order to finish the science project on time, it is important that each group member takes responsibility for their part of the work and completes it by the agreed-upon deadline.
10. When I was walking down the street on my way to school, I saw a cat that was sitting on top of a fence, and it was looking at me with curious eyes.

Lesson 2: R – Relevance and Focus

Objective: Students will determine whether sentences in a passage are relevant and focused on the main idea.
Materials: Practice passage, red and green paper strips, tape.

Scripted Explanation:

"Good writing stays focused on the topic and doesn't wander off. If a sentence doesn't fit the main idea, it's like a puzzle piece in the wrong box—it just doesn't belong!"

Practice Passage:

"The school carnival was the most exciting event of the year. Everyone in the school looked forward to it for weeks. There were games, prizes, and lots of delicious snacks. **My dog is really good at doing tricks.** We started by playing ring toss, trying to win stuffed animals. The smell of fresh popcorn filled the air as kids gathered around the snack booth. **I love playing soccer after school.** One of my favorite snacks was the cotton candy—it was fluffy and sweet. We also tried the beanbag toss, where the goal was to hit the target and win a prize.

The carnival was held on the school field, with colorful tents set up everywhere. **My cousin has a huge trampoline in her backyard.** Music played in the background while kids danced and sang along. My friends and I entered a pie-eating contest and laughed the whole time. It was messy, but it was so much fun! **My family went to the zoo last weekend to see the giraffes.** There was also a photo booth where we dressed up in silly hats and took pictures.

Some students volunteered to run the booths and hand out prizes. The bounce house was one of the busiest attractions, with kids jumping and laughing nonstop. We ended the day with a raffle, and one lucky student won a brand-new bike! The principal even got dunked in the dunk tank, which was a highlight of the event. **My mom makes the best lasagna for dinner on Fridays.** After the carnival, everyone was tired but happy, already talking about next year's event."

Activity (Physical Sorting – Sentence Match Up):

1. Post sentences from the practice passage on strips of paper around the room.
2. Label one side of the room **"Relevant"** and the other side **"Not Relevant."**
3. Students walk around and decide if each sentence is relevant to the carnival story.
4. They place each strip on the correct wall. Discuss their choices.

Assessment: Provide a short passage with a mix of relevant and irrelevant sentences. Students underline the relevant ones and cross out the irrelevant ones.

Lesson 3: I – Intentional Organization

Objective: Students will organize sentences to create a logically flowing paragraph.
Materials: Practice passage, sentence strips, timer.

Scripted Explanation:

"When writing, the order of your sentences matters! Imagine telling a story about how you baked a cake—if you start with 'I ate the cake,' it wouldn't make sense! Organizing your ideas in the right order makes your writing stronger."

Practice Passage (Scrambled):

1. I frosted the cake and added sprinkles.
2. I mixed the ingredients in a big bowl.
3. First, I preheated the oven.
4. Then, I poured the batter into a pan and baked it.

Activity (Group Sequencing Race):

1. Give each group a set of sentence strips (one sentence per strip).
2. Groups race to arrange the sentences in the correct order.
3. The first group to get the order right wins.

Assessment:

Students write their own "How-To" paragraph and ensure their steps are in logical order.

Lesson 4: S – Sentence Variety

Objective: Students will improve sentence variety in their writing by combining short, choppy sentences.
Materials: Practice passage, dice, sentence cards.

Scripted Explanation:

"If all your sentences are the same length and style, it can be uninteresting to read. Variety makes your writing more intruging—like adding spices to a recipe!"

Practice Passage:

The cat sat on the mat. The mat was blue. The mat was soft. The cat slept.

The dog barked. The dog ran. The dog chased a ball. The dog was happy.

The sun was bright. The sky was blue. The wind was cold. The leaves fell.

The boy read a book. The book was long. The book was interesting. The boy smiled.

The pizza was hot. The pizza smelled good. The pizza had cheese. The pizza was delicious.

Activity (Dice Sentence Challenge – Whole Group):

1. Write short sentences on cards and assign each a number (1–4).
2. Roll a die to determine which sentence students will combine or rewrite for variety.
3. Take turns rolling and sharing the new versions of the sentences.

Assessment:

Students rewrite the practice passage to combine and vary the sentences for smoother reading.

Lesson 5: S – Sentence Structure

Objective: Students will identify and correct sentence structure errors (fragments, run-ons).
Materials: Practice passage, highlighters, worksheet.

Scripted Explanation:

"A strong sentence needs a subject and a verb. If it's missing one, it's a fragment. If it has too much going on without punctuation, it's a run-on. We're going to make sure our sentences are just right!"

List 1: 10 Sentence Fragments

1. Because it was raining outside.
2. Running through the park without stopping.
3. The cat on the windowsill.
4. When we got to the carnival.
5. After the long day at school.
6. Jumping over the puddles and laughing.
7. The best part of the movie.
8. While eating lunch with my friends.
9. In the middle of the crowded room.
10. Hoping to win the game.

List 2: 10 Run-On Sentences

1. The sun was shining we went to the beach.
2. I love pizza it is my favorite food.
3. The dog barked the baby cried the doorbell rang all at once.
4. We ran to the park we played soccer we went home.
5. She likes to sing she also plays the piano and dances.
6. I woke up late I missed the bus I had to walk to school.
7. My brother ate the last cookie I was so mad at him.
8. The storm was loud it knocked out the power for hours.
9. We visited the zoo we saw lions we ate lunch at the café.
10. He studied all night for the test he was so tired the next day.

Activity (Fragment Fixer Walk – Physical Movement):

1. Post fragments and run-ons around the room.
2. Students walk around and rewrite each sentence on sticky notes to fix it.
3. Share corrections as a class.

Lesson 6: S – Style and Tone

Objective: Students will match sentences to the correct tone and style (formal/informal).
Materials: Sentence cards with different tones, T-chart.

Scripted Explanation:

"Writing style and tone can change the way your message sounds. Imagine texting a friend versus writing a letter to your principal—you wouldn't use the same words!"

Activity (Style and Tone Sorting – Physical Activity):

1. Create two sections of the room: **"Formal"**, **"Informal"**, and **"Family."**
2. Read a sentence aloud (e.g., "Hey dude, what's up?" vs. "Dear Sir, I hope this message finds you well.").
3. Students move to the side of the room that matches the sentence's tone.

Assessment:

Students revise sentences to match a specified tone (formal or informal).

List 1: 10 Formal Sentences

1. I sincerely appreciate your assistance with this matter.
2. Please submit your completed assignment by the end of the day.
3. The presentation will commence at 9:00 a.m.
4. Kindly refrain from using your phone during the meeting.
5. The results of the project were both significant and informative.
6. It is imperative that we address this issue immediately.
7. We look forward to your response at your earliest convenience.
8. The professor provided constructive feedback on the report.
9. The event will take place at the downtown conference center.
10. Your participation in this survey is greatly valued.

List 2: 10 Informal Sentences

1. Hey, what's up?
2. Can you help me with this real quick?
3. I'll text you later about the party.
4. This food is amazing!
5. We should totally hang out sometime.
6. You're not gonna believe what just happened!
7. I need to grab a coffee before we go.
8. Let's take a selfie!
9. That movie was crazy good!
10. No worries, it's all good.

List 3: 10 Sentences You Would Say to Your Family

1. What's for dinner tonight?
2. Can you help me find my keys?
3. I love you—have a great day!
4. Don't forget to take the dog out.
5. Did you put the laundry in the dryer?
6. Let's watch a movie together later.
7. Can you pass me the remote?
8. Do we have any snacks left?
9. I'll clean my room after dinner, I promise.
10. Thanks for always being there for me.

Lesson 7: P – Precision

Objective: Students will replace vague words with precise, descriptive vocabulary.
Materials: Practice passage, thesauruses.

Scripted Explanation:

"Precise language helps paint a clear picture. Instead of saying 'big dog,' you could say 'giant Great Dane.' Specific words make your writing stronger!"

Practice Passage:

"The food was good. The dog was big. We had a fun time at the park."

Activity (Precise Word Scavenger Hunt – Independent):

1. Give students a list of vague words (e.g., good, big, fun).
2. Students search the room for cards with more precise alternatives.
3. Replace the vague words in the practice passage with the precise ones they find.

List 1: 20 Ambiguous or Vague Words

1. Good
2. Big
3. Fun
4. Exciting
5. Nice
6. Bad
7. Small
8. Fast
9. Slow
10. Happy
11. Sad
12. Pretty
13. Scary
14. Hot
15. Cold
16. Loud
17. Quiet
18. Old
19. New
20. Delicious

List 2: 20 Precise Words (Matching the Vague List)

1. **Excellent** (for good)
2. **Enormous** (for big)
3. **Entertaining** (for fun)
4. **Thrilling** (for exciting)
5. **Kind** (for nice)
6. **Terrible** (for bad)
7. **Tiny** (for small)
8. **Swift** (for fast)
9. **Sluggish** (for slow)
10. **Joyful** (for happy)
11. **Heartbroken** (for sad)
12. **Elegant** (for pretty)
13. **Frightening** (for scary)
14. **Scorching** (for hot)
15. **Freezing** (for cold)
16. **Deafening** (for loud)
17. **Whisper-soft** (for quiet)
18. **Ancient** (for old)
19. **Modern** (for new)
20. **Savory** (for delicious)

Rearranging Sentence Structure: How to Identify the BEST Revision

Another type of revising question you'll encounter focuses on **rearranging sentence structure**. These questions may ask:

- **What is the best way to rewrite the following sentences?**
- **What is the best way to revise the following sentences?**
- **What is the best way to combine the following sentences?**

In these questions, your primary focus is **sentence structure**. All options might appear grammatically correct at first glance, but your job is to determine which option is the clearest, most concise, and logically arranged.

Simple Sentence Chant

Definition: A simple sentence contains one independent clause. It has a subject (noun) and a predicate (verb) and expresses a complete thought.

Chant:
"One noun, verb pair—a simple sentence is there!"

Compound Sentence Chant

Definition: A compound sentence contains two or more independent clauses joined by a coordinating conjunction (FANBOYS: for, and, nor, but, or, yet, so) or a semicolon. Each clause can stand on its own as a complete sentence.

Chant:
"Complete on the left, complete on the right, it takes two to make it right!"

Complex Sentence Chant

Definition: A complex sentence contains one independent clause and one or more dependent clauses. The dependent clause cannot stand alone and often starts with a subordinating conjunction (because, although, since, when, etc.).

Chant:
"1-1-1, my job is done!"

When you've eliminated the clearly incorrect options and are left with two sentences that **both appear correct and punctuated properly**, you'll need to rely on **tiebreakers** to select the best answer.

Tiebreakers for Sentence Rearranging Questions:

1. **Verb Tense Consistency:**
   Ensure that the verb tense in the sentence matches the verb tense of the rest of the passage. For example, if the passage is written in past tense, the correct answer should also be in past tense.

   Example:
   Incorrect: *He walks to the store and bought milk.*
   Correct: *He walked to the store and bought milk.*

2. **Antecedent Agreement:**
   This means that the **pronoun correctly refers to its noun** in both number and gender. Singular nouns need singular pronouns, and plural nouns need plural pronouns.

   Example:
   Incorrect: *Each student must bring their lunch.*
   Correct: *Each student must bring his or her lunch.*

3. **Content Accuracy:**
   When all else is equal, choose the sentence that presents the most **accurate and logical content**. This ensures the information is factually correct and makes sense within the context of the passage.

   Example:
   Incorrect: *The sun sets in the east.*
   Correct: *The sun sets in the west.*

Sentence Types Circle Chants

Simple Sentence Chant:

"One noun, verb pair—
A simple sentence is there!"

Compound Sentence Chant:

"Complete on the left, complete on the right
-It takes two to make it right!"

Complex Sentence Chant:

"1-1-1, my job is done!"

7 Synonyms for Rearrange

Reorganize

Restructure

Reorder

Revise

Adjust

Combine

Modify

When to Use Answer Anchors "CRISSSP" and "ROCKS"

CRISSSP for revising sentence structure and grammar-based decisions that require **Rearranging.**

ROCKS for revising questions involving **Exchanging, Adding,** and **Deleting** questions.

The Circling Chants: A Strategy for Identifying and Punctuating Simple, Compound, and Complex Sentences

The **Circling Chants** strategy provides a structured, hands-on approach for helping students identify whether a sentence is **simple, compound, or complex** and determine if it is **correctly written and punctuated**. By marking conjunctions, punctuation, and clauses, students gain a clear and visual understanding of sentence structure. Let's break down how to use this process and how the **three chants** will help students self-check their work.

The **Circling Chants** process is a critical tool for students because it transforms the often **abstract concepts of sentence structure, grammar, and punctuation into something visual, physical, and memorable**. This process addresses **all learning styles—visual, auditory, and kinesthetic—ensuring that every type of learner benefits**. Visual learners engage by circling conjunctions, commas, and marking clauses with checks and Xs, allowing them to literally see the structure of a sentence unfold. **Auditory learners thrive on the chants**, which serve as rhythmic, easy-to-remember cues for determining whether a sentence is simple, compound, or complex. For **kinesthetic learners**, the act of marking the sentence becomes a physical activity that reinforces the lesson in a hands-on way.

This multi-sensory approach makes an **intangible idea, like identifying clause relationships or punctuation patterns, tangible and accessible**. Circling Chants also help **reduce cognitive overload** during assessments by breaking complex tasks into manageable steps, offering a clear structure for analysis and self-checking. The process promotes **confidence and independence**, as students can rely on a system that provides instant feedback. In the learning process, **making grammar concrete and interactive bridges the gap between theory and practice**, enabling deeper understanding and long-term retention.

Step-by-Step Process For Circling Chants

1. **Identify and Circle Conjunctions and Commas**
   - Circle any **coordinating conjunctions** (FANBOYS: *for, and, nor, but, or, yet, so*) or **subordinating conjunctions** (*because, although, when, while, if, since, etc.*) that appear in the middle of the sentence.
   - Circle any **commas** that serve as **conjunction helpers** (e.g., a comma before a coordinating conjunction).
2. **Mark Clauses and Phrases**
   - Look to the **left and right of each circle** (conjunction). Determine if the words form:
     - **Independent Clause** (A complete sentence that can stand alone)—Mark with a ✔ **above the clause.**
     - **Dependent Clause or Phrase** (Cannot stand alone as a sentence)—Mark with an ✖ **above the clause or phrase.**
3. **Apply the Circling Chants** Based on the number of circles and how the clauses are arranged, apply one of the following chants to determine sentence type and punctuation correctness:

1. Simple Sentence (No Circles)

- **Chant:** *"One noun-verb pair, a simple sentence is there."*
- **Verification:** If there are **no conjunctions** in the sentence and **only one noun-verb pair**, it's a simple sentence.

2. Complex Sentence (One Circle)

- **Chant:** *"1-1-1, my job is done."*
- **Verification:**
  - If there is **one circle** (a subordinating conjunction) and an **X** on one side and a ✔ **on the other**, it's a complex sentence.
  - If the **X** marks a **prepositional phrase**, the sentence remains a **simple sentence** because it only has **one noun-verb pair**.

3. Compound Sentence (Two Circles)

- **Chant:** *"Complete on the left, complete on the right, it takes two to make it right."*
- **Verification:**
  - If there are **two circles** and ✔ **marks on both sides**, it's a **compound sentence**—each clause is independent.

Example Sentences Using Circling Chants

1. Simple Sentence (No Circle)

Sentence: *The dog barked at the mailman.*

- **Chant:** *"One noun-verb pair, a simple sentence is there."*
- **Noun-Verb Pair:** *dog barked*
- **Verification:** No conjunctions or additional clauses are present. It is a simple sentence.

2. Complex Sentence (One Circle)

Sentence: *Because it rained, the game was canceled.*

- **Circle:** *Because*
- **Marks:** ✕ (dependent clause on the left), ✔ (independent clause on the right)
- **Chant:** *"1-1-1, my job is done."*
- **Verification:** It's a complex sentence with one subordinating conjunction.

3. Compound Sentence (Two Circles)

Sentence: *The dog barked, and the cat ran away.*

- **Circle:** *and*
- **Marks:** ✔ on both sides of the conjunction
- **Chant:** *"Complete on the left, complete on the right, it takes two to make it right."*
- **Verification:** Both sides are independent clauses. It is a compound sentence.

Why This Process Works

- **Visual Cues:** Circling conjunctions and commas makes sentence structure more apparent.
- **Chants Reinforce Patterns:** The chants serve as auditory tools to help students remember the sentence types.
- **Clause Identification Practice:** Marking independent and dependent clauses builds students' grammatical awareness.
- **Connection to Punctuation:** Students learn how punctuation supports sentence structure, reducing errors.

Assessment and Practice

1. **Sentence Sorting Game:** Give students a mix of simple, compound, and complex sentences and have them apply the **Circling Chants** to identify each one.
2. **Peer Review Exercise:** Have students exchange their writing and mark each other's sentences using the strategy.
3. **Exit Ticket:** Ask students to create and mark their own sentence using the Circling Chants process, then explain how they identified its type.

The Circling Chants Process: A Lifeline for Students in Stressful Assessment Situations

In high-pressure assessment environments—whether it's a multiple-choice question or a short constructed response—students often experience **stress and mental fatigue**. This stress can lead to confusion, causing even confident students to miss simple errors in sentence construction. The **Circling Chants Process** serves as an **anchor**, helping students focus on clear, actionable steps to analyze and revise sentences logically and systematically.

By teaching students how to identify **sentence types (simple, compound, complex, and compound-complex)** and verifying their punctuation and structure using visual and auditory cues, Circling Chants can transform an overwhelming revising question into a **manageable task**. Here's how:

Benefits in High-Stress Situations

1. **Reduces Cognitive Overload**
   In a stressful situation, students may struggle to recall grammar rules or punctuation guidelines. Circling Chants simplifies the process into **three chants** that act as **mental shortcuts**:
   - **Simple Sentence:** *"One noun-verb pair, a simple sentence is there."*
   - **Complex Sentence:** *"1-1-1, my job is done."*
   - **Compound Sentence:** *"Complete on the left, complete on the right, it takes two to make it right."*
     This reduces the cognitive load and allows students to **focus on identifying conjunctions and clauses** without second-guessing themselves.
2. **Encourages Visual and Kinesthetic Learning**
   Circling conjunctions and commas engages **visual learners**, while marking independent and dependent clauses provides a **kinesthetic, hands-on approach**. These physical actions help **ground students** during moments of test anxiety, giving them something tangible to do.
3. **Supports Logical Reasoning and Self-Checking**
   Each chant serves as a built-in **verification tool**. Once students apply the chant, they can quickly determine if their sentence is correctly punctuated and constructed. This self-checking process gives them the **confidence** to move forward without second-guessing their answers.

Circling Chants in Multiple-Choice Revising Questions

In a multiple-choice question that asks students to **revise, combine, or rewrite sentences**, the Circling Chants strategy can be applied to **eliminate incorrect answers and select the best revision option**.

Example Question:
What is the best way to combine these sentences?

- The storm was intense. It caused flooding in several neighborhoods.

Answer Choices:
A. The storm, which was intense caused flooding.
B. The storm was intense, it caused flooding.
C. The intense storm caused flooding in several neighborhoods.
D. Because the storm was intense, flooding occurred in several neighborhoods.

How Circling Chants Helps:

1. **Circle the conjunctions or commas in each answer.**
   - Option A: Incorrect—missing a comma after *intense.*
   - Option B: Comma splice.
   - Option C: Correct—concise and combines the idea logically.
   - Option D: Correct—complex sentence with a dependent clause.
2. **Apply the Complex Sentence Chant:** *"1-1-1, my job is done."*
   - This chant confirms that Option D is a valid complex sentence.
3. **Eliminate Redundant or Incorrect Answers:**
   Using Circling Chants ensures students don't fall for **comma splice traps** or awkward phrasing.

Circling Chants in Constructed Responses

In short constructed response questions where students must **revise or combine multiple sentences**, the Circling Chants process guides them through **logical revision**:

1. **Mark conjunctions and punctuation.**
2. **Identify independent and dependent clauses.**
3. **Apply the appropriate chant.**

Why This Process Is Crucial for Revising Tasks

1. **Rearranging Revising Questions:** Often, students are asked to **rearrange ideas** within or between sentences for clarity. Circling Chants makes it easier to visualize how different clauses fit together.
2. **Combining Sentences:** Circling conjunctions helps students choose the best way to combine two independent ideas without creating fragments or run-ons.
3. **Short Constructed Responses:** It builds students' confidence in **editing their own writing**, ensuring that their responses are clear, correctly punctuated, and grammatically sound.

In Summary

Circling Chants is more than just a method; it's a **safety net** for students during high-stakes assessments. It empowers them to approach complex grammar and punctuation questions with **clarity, structure, and confidence**, ensuring that their sentence construction and punctuation are as polished as their ideas.

Unit 3

Exchanging Words or Sentences

E – Exchanging Information: The Key to Stronger Writing

In the **READ revising acronym**, the letter **E stands for Exchanging Information**. This step focuses on identifying weaker ideas, words, or examples in a passage and **replacing them with stronger, more relevant, and specific ones**. Exchanging information is essential for making writing more precise, engaging, and effective.

When you first write a passage, some sentences may be vague or lack the detail needed to help the reader fully understand the message. Words like "big," "fun," or "nice" may feel easy to use, but they don't paint a clear picture. By **exchanging general words for more specific ones**, you give your writing more power and clarity. For example, replacing "big house" with "three-story brick mansion" creates a clearer and more vivid image for the reader.

Exchanging weaker ideas also helps keep the passage focused and relevant. Sometimes, a sentence may drift away from the main idea or repeat information unnecessarily. Instead of cutting it completely, you can **replace it with an idea that supports the topic** more effectively. This keeps your writing organized and meaningful.

In addition to exchanging individual words and phrases, you can **replace weak examples with stronger, more detailed ones**. If a passage simply says, "The boy worked hard," exchanging that for "The boy spent hours solving math problems until he mastered them" gives the reader a clearer understanding of his effort.

Ultimately, exchanging information makes your writing **more specific, descriptive, and impactful**. It helps your reader see, hear, and understand what you're trying to communicate, leaving no room for confusion. This step in revising ensures that your writing is not only accurate but also polished and powerful, bringing out the best in every sentence.

Let's practice exchanging information to take your writing to the next level!

Understanding the ROCKS Strategy for Revising Questions

When answering **revising questions** that focus on **Exchanging, Adding, or Deleting** information in a passage, specific types of answer choices appear consistently. These answer choices can be categorized using the acronym **ROCK**: **R – Repeat, O – Off Topic, C – Connection, K – Key Knowledge**. Understanding these answer types will help you identify the best revision option and avoid common traps.

- **R – Repeat:** These answer choices contain information that is already mentioned in the passage. Adding or keeping repetitive details makes the writing redundant and weakens the passage. When you spot repetition, it's a clear sign that the information should be exchanged or deleted.
- **O – Off Topic:** These answer choices introduce information that doesn't fit the main idea of the passage. Off-topic details can distract the reader and confuse the message. These should be deleted or replaced with relevant information that supports the passage's focus.
- **C – Connection:** This type of answer choice is the best option for improving the flow of ideas. Strong answers create logical connections between sentences and paragraphs, ensuring that the information fits smoothly into the context of the passage.
- **K – Key Knowledge:** These answers offer specific, important details that enhance the passage's meaning. Strong revision choices often introduce key knowledge that clarifies or expands on the main idea without unnecessary elaboration.

For **Exchanging, Adding, and Deleting** questions, thinking about **ROCK** will help you evaluate each answer carefully and avoid common pitfalls.

Adding S – Sequencing

The letter **S stands for Sequencing**, which focuses on the order of ideas. This type of answer choice ensures that the information flows logically within a paragraph or passage. Poor sequencing can confuse readers, while strong sequencing guides them smoothly from one idea to the next.

Together, **ROCKS** is a powerful tool for identifying the most effective revision choices in **Exchanging, Adding, and Deleting** questions. Mastering this strategy will help you quickly recognize strong answers and avoid weaker ones. Let's start revising like a ROCKS star!

ROCKS Strategy for Revising: Exchange, Add, and Delete Questions

When answering **revising questions** that focus on **Exchanging, Adding, or Deleting**, it's important to understand how the **ROCKS** acronym helps identify the best answer. However, not all parts of **ROCKS** apply to every type of revising question. Here's how to determine which answer choices are relevant and how to select the best one.

Exchange or Add Revision Questions

In **Exchange** or **Add** questions, you are asked to replace or insert information that strengthens the passage. The only relevant parts of **ROCKS** in these questions are:

· **C – Connection:** The best answers create a logical connection between ideas or improve the flow of the passage. This ensures that the added or exchanged information fits naturally and enhances the overall meaning.
· **K – Key Knowledge:** These answers provide specific, relevant details that clarify or expand on the topic. Key knowledge adds depth and makes the passage more informative.
· **S – Sequencing:** Sometimes, the added or exchanged information must be arranged in the correct order to ensure logical flow. Proper sequencing keeps the reader from becoming confused.

In these questions, **Repeat (R)** and **Off Topic (O)** answer choices will **always be wrong** because they either repeat information already mentioned or introduce irrelevant details.

When you have two possible correct answers—one offering a **connection** and the other offering **key knowledge**—it's typically better to choose the **connection**. However, if two connection answers or two key knowledge answers seem correct, you can apply **tiebreakers** to decide which one is best:

· **Verb Tense:** The correct answer will match the verb tense used throughout the passage.
· **Antecedent Agreement:** Ensure the pronoun in the answer choice agrees with its noun in number and gender (e.g., *they* for plural nouns, *it* for singular nouns).
· **Sentence Structure:** Choose the answer with stronger, more varied sentence structure that avoids fragments or run-ons.

Delete Revision Questions

In **Delete** questions, the only relevant parts of **ROCKS** are:

- **R – Repeat:** If the sentence repeats information already stated, it should be deleted to avoid redundancy.
- **O – Off Topic:** If the sentence introduces unrelated information that strays from the passage's main idea, it should be deleted.

These answers help streamline the passage, keeping it focused and concise.

By mastering how to use **ROCKS** for different types of revising questions, you'll know exactly what to look for and how to select the best answer every time!

Teacher Training Script: Exchanging Information to Revise

Lower Level Script (Elementary)

"Exchanging information means trading weaker words or ideas for stronger ones. Sometimes our first word choice isn't the best, and that's okay! We can go back and make it better. For example, instead of saying, 'The dog was big,' we can exchange the word 'big' for something more exciting, like 'huge' or 'giant.' Exchanging makes our writing more interesting and gives the reader a clearer picture of what we mean."

Upper Level Script (Middle/High School)

"Exchanging information is about replacing weaker words, phrases, or ideas with stronger, more specific, or relevant ones. This is key when revising to improve precision and focus. For example, instead of writing, 'She had a good time at the party,' you could exchange 'good' for a more vivid word like 'fantastic' or 'memorable.' We can also exchange whole sentences if they don't add much value or aren't as clear as they could be. The goal of exchanging is to refine the writing so it's more precise, engaging, and relevant."

7 Synonyms for Exchange

Replace

Swap

Switch

Trade

Substitute

Adjust

Change

Lesson Plan 1: Exchanging Information for Specific Words and Phrases

Grade Level: 6th–8th Grade
Duration: 60 minutes

Objective:

Students will learn how to exchange general or vague words for more specific, descriptive, and impactful language, enhancing the quality and clarity of their writing.

Materials Needed:

- Whiteboard and markers
- Sample sentences with vague words
- Word exchange cards (with weak words and stronger alternatives)
- Writing journals or notebooks
- Assessment rubric

Introduction (10 minutes)

Teacher Script (Italicized):
"Today, we're focusing on a revising strategy called exchanging information. Imagine you're a chef creating a delicious meal. If you use plain, boring ingredients, your dish won't taste very good. But if you swap those ingredients for fresher, more flavorful ones, the dish becomes something special. That's exactly what we'll do with our writing! We'll trade dull or vague words for more specific and powerful ones to create writing that leaves a lasting impression."

"For example, instead of writing, 'The big dog ran fast,' you can exchange it for, 'The massive Labrador sprinted down the field.' See how it paints a clearer picture? Let's try this together!"

Direct Instruction (15 minutes)

Explain the Rule:

· **Identify weak or vague words** like big, fun, nice, good, and bad.
· **Replace them with more descriptive and specific language** that helps the reader visualize or understand more clearly.
· Example: *Replace "big house" with "three-story brick mansion."*
· Example: *Replace "worked hard" with "spent hours solving complex equations."*

Teacher Script (Italicized):
"Vague words don't help readers create a clear image. But swapping in precise words adds life to your writing. Your goal is to find the weak spots and exchange them for stronger, more vibrant language."

Guided Practice (15 minutes)

Activity: Word Exchange Challenge

· Distribute **Word Exchange Cards** that list vague words on one side and stronger alternatives on the back.
· Students will work in small groups to identify vague words in sample sentences and swap them for more precise alternatives.
· Share revisions as a class.

Example Sentences for Practice:

· *The boy did a good job on the project.*
· Revision: *The boy created a detailed model of a solar system with labeled planets.*
· *We had a fun day at the park.*
· Revision: *We spent the afternoon flying kites and playing soccer at the park.*

Independent Practice (10 minutes)

Activity: Personal Writing Revision

· Students will choose a short paragraph from their own writing and underline any vague words or weak phrases.
· They will replace at least five weak words with more specific alternatives.

Assessment: Authentic Task (15 minutes)

Activity: Create a Before-and-After Writing Display

· Students will write two versions of a short descriptive paragraph—one with vague language and one with improved, specific language.
· Post the paragraphs on a "Writing Makeover" wall for students to compare and discuss.

Closure (5 minutes)

Teacher Script (Italicized):
"Great work! Remember, exchanging information makes your writing more powerful and clear. The next time you write, look for words that could be stronger and make those swaps to keep your reader engaged!"

Lesson Plan 2: Exchanging Information for Stronger Examples and Ideas

Grade Level: 6th–8th Grade
Duration: 60 minutes

Objective:

Students will learn how to identify weaker examples or ideas in writing and exchange them for stronger, more relevant, and specific ones.

Materials Needed:

- Whiteboard and markers
- Sample paragraphs with weak examples
- Task cards for group activity
- Student writing samples
- Assessment rubric

Introduction (10 minutes)

Teacher Script (Italicized):
"Have you ever told a story to someone and noticed they weren't really paying attention? Sometimes, it's because the details weren't strong enough to hold their interest. The same thing can happen in writing if we use weak or general examples. Today, we'll learn how to exchange weak examples for stronger ones that really connect with our readers and bring our writing to life!"

"For example, if you wrote, 'The boy worked hard,' that doesn't tell the reader much. But if you write, 'The boy spent hours solving math problems until he mastered them,' the reader can really picture his effort and determination."

Direct Instruction (15 minutes)

Explain the Rule:

· **Identify weak or vague examples** that don't add much detail.
· **Replace them with stronger, more specific examples** that clarify and enhance the main idea.
· Example: *Replace "She helped her community" with "She organized a food drive that collected 500 cans of food."*

Teacher Script (Italicized):
"Weak examples are like blurry pictures—they don't help the reader understand what you're trying to say. Strong examples are like high-definition images, making your writing clearer and more powerful."

Guided Practice (15 minutes)

Activity: Strong Example Swap

· Distribute **Task Cards** with weak examples in sample paragraphs.
· Students will work in small groups to brainstorm stronger, more specific replacements.
· Groups will share their new examples with the class.

Sample Paragraph:

· *Weak Example: The team did well in the tournament.*
· *Stronger Example: The team won three consecutive games, finishing first in the regional tournament.*

Independent Practice (10 minutes)

Activity: Strengthen Your Writing

· Students will choose one paragraph from their own writing and exchange at least two weak examples for stronger ones.
· Share one improved sentence with a partner.

Assessment: Authentic Task (15 minutes)

Activity: Writing Showcase

· Each student will write a short story that includes at least three strong examples.
· Create a gallery walk where students read each other's stories and leave sticky-note feedback on the strength of their examples.

Closure (5 minutes)

Teacher Script (Italicized):
"Fantastic job today! Remember, strong examples are key to great writing. Keep looking for ways to exchange weak ideas for more detailed ones, and your writing will always shine!"

Extensions:

· **Peer Review:** Partner students to review each other's writing and suggest stronger examples.
· **Real-World Connection:** Have students find strong examples in news articles or books and discuss what makes them effective.

Mentor EXCHANGE Passage: The History of the Bison

The bison is a big animal that lived on the Great Plains. Native Americans thought the bison was an important part of their life. They used it for food, clothes, and shelter. When European settlers arrived, the number of bison got smaller. People hunted them too much, and by the late 1800s, there were not many bison left. Today, bison live in protected areas and are a symbol of America's wild past.

Analysis of Sentences for Exchange

Several sentences in this passage can be revised for more specific language, stronger examples, and increased clarity. Here's a detailed explanation:

· **Original Sentence:**
The bison is a big animal that lived on the Great Plains.
Exchange:
The bison is a massive, shaggy-coated mammal that once roamed the Great Plains in enormous herds.
Reason for Exchange:
The original sentence uses "big," which is vague. "Massive" and "shaggy-coated" create a clearer picture, and mentioning "enormous herds" adds historical detail.
· **Original Sentence:**
Native Americans thought the bison was an important part of their life.
Exchange:
For Native Americans, the bison was a sacred animal, vital for survival and deeply woven into their cultural traditions.
Reason for Exchange:
The revised sentence adds more depth and specificity by highlighting the spiritual and cultural significance of the bison.
· **Original Sentence:**
They used it for food, clothes, and shelter.
Exchange:
Every part of the bison was used—its meat for food, hides for clothing and tepees, and bones for tools.
Reason for Exchange:
This revision provides more specific examples, helping the reader visualize how the bison was used in various aspects of life.
· **Original Sentence:**
When European settlers arrived, the number of bison got smaller.
Exchange:
As European settlers expanded westward, overhunting and habitat loss caused the bison population to plummet.
Reason for Exchange:
"Got smaller" is vague. "Plummeted" and "overhunting and habitat loss" give a more accurate and vivid description of what happened.

- **Original Sentence:**
Today, bison live in protected areas and are a symbol of America's wild past.
Exchange:
Today, bison thrive in national parks and reserves, symbolizing resilience and the enduring spirit of the American West.
Reason for Exchange:
This revision makes the sentence more specific and adds emotional resonance by emphasizing resilience and the symbolic importance of bison.

Summary of Suggested Exchanges

These sentence exchanges transform the passage from simple and somewhat vague to one that is engaging, informative, and vivid. By adding stronger examples, specific language, and deeper context, the revised passage provides a clearer and more powerful message about the history and importance of the bison.

Unit 4

Adding Words or Sentences

The Revision Technique: Adding

In revising, **adding information** can improve a passage by making it more complete, clear, and connected. Adding happens in two main ways: **adding key knowledge** and **adding connections**. Both techniques serve different purposes, and understanding when and how to use them will help you choose the best revision option.

· Adding Key Knowledge (Textual Evidence)

Adding key knowledge involves inserting **specific, relevant details** that provide essential information or clarify a concept. This type of addition strengthens the passage by making it more informative and vivid. Key knowledge often answers questions the reader might have or offers important evidence to support an argument.

Example:
Original: *The science project was a success.*
Revised with Key Knowledge: *The science project was a success because the experiment proved that plants grow faster with natural light than with artificial light.*

When to Add Key Knowledge:

· When a sentence is too vague or lacks detail.
· When the passage needs additional support for a claim or idea.
· When more evidence is required to strengthen the explanation or argument.

· Adding Connections

Adding connections focuses on **linking ideas** within the passage to create logical flow and unity. These connections can occur between two sentences, at the beginning of a paragraph, or in a closing sentence. **Connecting ideas** ensures that each part of the passage builds on the previous one, guiding the reader through the content smoothly.

Example:
Original: *We planted seeds. The plants grew quickly.*
Revised with a Connection: *After planting seeds, we observed that the plants grew quickly due to the rich soil and daily watering.*

Opening or Closing Sentences:
Sometimes, adding a **connecting sentence** at the start or end of a paragraph ties the entire paragraph together. An opening sentence introduces the main idea and sets up the details that follow, while a closing sentence reinforces the idea and leaves the reader with a final thought.

When to Add Connections:

- When sentences feel disconnected or jump abruptly from one idea to another.
- When a paragraph lacks an opening sentence to introduce its purpose.
- When a closing sentence is needed to summarize the main point.

Choosing Between Key Knowledge and Connections

When both options are available, **adding a connection** is often the better choice because it improves the **flow and cohesion** of the passage. Connections guide the reader naturally from one idea to the next, making the writing more polished and easier to follow.

By mastering the technique of adding, whether for **key knowledge** or **connections**, you'll make your writing clearer, stronger, and more engaging.

Teacher Training Script: Adding Information to Revise

Lower Level Script (Elementary)

"Sometimes, when we write, we leave out important details that help the reader understand what we mean. Adding information can make our writing more interesting and clear. Think about telling a story—if you just say, 'I saw a dog,' the reader won't know much. But if you add details like, 'I saw a big, fluffy dog running through the park,' it paints a picture in their mind. We add information to make our sentences stronger and help the reader see what we see or understand what we're explaining."

Upper Level Script (Middle/High School)

"Adding information during revision helps clarify and expand ideas. This can be done by adding key details, examples, or evidence that strengthen the main point. Sometimes our writing feels incomplete because it lacks specifics or connections between ideas. For example, instead of writing, 'The experiment was successful,' you could add details like, 'The experiment was successful because the results showed a 20% increase in plant growth under natural light.' Adding information not only makes writing more informative but also more engaging for the reader."

7 Synonyms for Add

Include

Insert

Would best follow

Should come before

Add on

Expand

Extend

Lesson Plan 1: Adding Key Knowledge (Textual Evidence)

Grade Level: 6th–8th Grade
Duration: 60 minutes

Objective:

Students will learn how to identify vague or incomplete sentences in a passage and add key knowledge to strengthen and clarify the writing.

Materials Needed:

- Whiteboard and markers
- Sample sentences with missing details
- Task cards with incomplete paragraphs
- Student journals
- Assessment rubric

Introduction (10 minutes)

Teacher Script (Italicized):
"Have you ever read something and felt like it didn't tell the whole story? Maybe you had questions like 'What happened?' or 'Why did that work?' Today, we're going to focus on a revising strategy called adding key knowledge. This means adding important facts or details to make your writing more complete and informative."

"For example, if you write, 'The science project was a success,' your reader might wonder, 'What made it a success?' You can make the sentence clearer by adding key knowledge: 'The science project was a success because the experiment proved that plants grow faster with natural light than with artificial light.' See how that sentence answers a question the reader might have?"

Direct Instruction (15 minutes)

Explain the Rule:

· **Identify sentences that are too vague** or don't give enough information.
· **Add specific facts, examples, or details** that clarify or strengthen the sentence.
· **Avoid unnecessary information**—only add what makes the meaning clearer.

Teacher Script (Italicized):
"Think about your reader. What questions might they ask? Look for sentences that feel too short or incomplete, and add details to answer those questions."

Guided Practice (15 minutes)

Activity: Sentence Expansion Challenge

· Distribute task cards with vague sentences.
· In small groups, students will add key knowledge to improve the sentences.
· Share and discuss their revisions.

Example Sentences for Practice:

· *The history project was interesting.*
· Revision: *The history project was interesting because we built a model of a Civil War battlefield.*
· *The team did well in the tournament.*
· Revision: *The team did well in the tournament, winning all three games and finishing in first place.*

Independent Practice (10 minutes)

Activity: Personal Writing Revision

· Students will choose a paragraph from their writing and underline at least two sentences that need key knowledge.
· They will revise those sentences by adding specific details.

Assessment: Authentic Task (15 minutes)

Activity: Key Knowledge Poster Presentation

· Students will write a short paragraph about a topic of their choice, ensuring they add at least two pieces of key knowledge.
· Present their revised paragraphs on posters, explaining what details they added and why.

Lesson Plan 2: Adding Connections for Logical Flow and Cohesion

Grade Level: 6th–8th Grade
Duration: 60 minutes

Objective:

Students will learn how to add connecting sentences to improve the logical flow and cohesion of a passage, making their writing more polished and easier to follow.

Materials Needed:

- Whiteboard and markers
- Sample paragraphs with missing connections
- Task cards with disconnected sentences
- Student journals
- Assessment rubric

Introduction (10 minutes)

Teacher Script (Italicized):
"Have you ever read something that felt choppy or disjointed, like the ideas were jumping around? That happens when sentences don't connect smoothly. Today, we're going to focus on adding connections—sentences that help link ideas together so your writing flows naturally."

"For example, look at these sentences: 'We planted seeds. The plants grew quickly.' It feels abrupt. By adding a connection, we can make it smoother: 'After planting seeds, we observed that the plants grew quickly due to the rich soil and daily watering.' That connection helps the reader understand how the two ideas are related."

Direct Instruction (15 minutes)

Explain the Rule:

- **Identify sentences that feel abrupt or disconnected.**
- **Add connecting phrases or sentences** to link ideas logically.
- **Use opening or closing sentences** to introduce or summarize the paragraph's main idea.

Teacher Script (Italicized):
"Think of adding connections as building a bridge between ideas. Each connection helps your reader travel smoothly from one thought to the next."

Guided Practice (15 minutes)

Activity: Sentence Connection Relay

- Divide the class into small groups.
- Each group receives a set of disconnected sentences on strips of paper.
- Their task is to add connecting sentences to create a coherent paragraph.
- Share and discuss their revisions.

Example Disconnected Sentences:

- *We arrived at the park.*
- *It started to rain.*
- *We decided to go home early.*

Revised with Connections:
- *We arrived at the park, excited for a picnic. Unfortunately, it started to rain, so we decided to go home early.*

Independent Practice (10 minutes)

Activity: Connecting Sentences in Your Writing

- Students will review a paragraph from their own writing and look for places where sentences feel abrupt.
- They will add at least two connecting sentences to improve the flow.

Assessment: Authentic Task (15 minutes)

Activity: Connection Map Challenge

· Students will create a visual connection map for a short story or passage, showing how each sentence relates to the next.
· Present their maps to the class, explaining the connections they added.

Closure (5 minutes)

Teacher Script (Italicized):
"Great work today! Adding connections makes your writing easier to read and understand. Keep practicing this strategy, and you'll see how it transforms your writing into something clear and polished!"

Mentor ADD Passage: Why People Study Insects

Many people think insects are just pests, but studying them is really important. Insects are found everywhere in the world. They do some things that are helpful and others that are harmful. Scientists collect bugs to put them in boxes and study them. Insects can pollinate flowers. Some bugs bite people. They have been around for millions of years. Some are even used in medicine. Butterflies are very pretty.

Analysis and Suggestions for Adding Information

· **Sentence to Add Key Knowledge:**
Original: *Insects can pollinate flowers.*
Suggested Addition: *Insects like bees and butterflies help pollinate crops, which is essential for growing fruits and vegetables.*
Reason: Adding key knowledge clarifies how pollination benefits humans, making the sentence more informative and relevant.

· **Sentence to Add a Connection:**
Original: *Scientists collect bugs to put them in boxes and study them.*
Suggested Addition: *By studying insects in controlled environments, scientists can learn how they affect ecosystems and discover new uses for them in medicine and agriculture.*
Reason: The original sentence is vague. Adding a connection explains the purpose of studying insects and how it impacts science.

· **Sentence to Add Key Knowledge:**
Original: *Some are even used in medicine.*
Suggested Addition: *For example, maggots are used to clean infected wounds, and bee venom is studied for treating arthritis.*
Reason: Specific examples make the sentence more vivid and informative, helping readers understand how insects contribute to medicine.

· **Sentence to Add a Closing Connection:**
Original: *Butterflies are very pretty.*
Suggested Addition: *In addition to their beauty, butterflies play an important role in pollination and serve as indicators of a healthy environment.*
Reason: The closing sentence ties the beauty of butterflies to their ecological importance, adding depth and relevance.

Revised Passage with Additions

Many people think insects are just pests, but studying them is really important. Insects are found everywhere in the world and play a critical role in the environment. Insects like bees and butterflies help pollinate crops, which is essential for growing fruits and vegetables. Scientists collect bugs to study them in controlled environments, learning how they affect ecosystems and discovering new uses for them in medicine and agriculture.

Insects have been around for millions of years and continue to impact human life in surprising ways. For example, maggots are used to clean infected wounds, and bee venom is studied for treating arthritis. Some insects can be harmful, but others are crucial for the health of our planet. Butterflies, for instance, are not only beautiful but also essential pollinators and indicators of a healthy environment.

Conclusion

Adding relevant information makes this passage more informative and engaging. Key knowledge clarifies vague sentences, while connecting sentences improve the logical flow. Each addition serves a purpose, enriching the reader's understanding of why insects are studied and their importance in our world.

Unit 5

Deleting Words or Sentences

The Revision Technique: Deleting

In revising, **deleting information** is just as important as adding or exchanging details. Deleting is a powerful tool that helps eliminate unnecessary or irrelevant information to make a passage **more concise, clear, and focused**. When you delete effectively, the passage becomes easier to read and understand, with every sentence serving a purpose. There are two primary reasons for deleting sentences: **repetition** and **off-topic information**. Let's explore each in detail.

1. Deleting Repetitive Information

Repetition occurs when the same idea is expressed more than once in slightly different ways. Repeated information makes the passage wordy and less engaging for the reader. By identifying and deleting repetitive sentences, you ensure that every detail adds something new and valuable to the passage.

Example of Repetition:
Original: *The science fair had many booths. There were a lot of different activities at the science fair. Students visited various booths to participate in activities.*
Revised: *The science fair had many booths with different activities for students to enjoy.*

Why Delete Repetition?

- It improves **clarity and conciseness**, helping the reader focus on the important points.
- It avoids redundancy, which can distract or bore the reader.
- It allows space for stronger, more meaningful details to be included.

2. Deleting Off-Topic Information

Off-topic sentences introduce ideas that don't fit the main idea of the passage. These sentences often feel random or unrelated and confuse the reader. Deleting off-topic information keeps the writing focused and coherent, ensuring every sentence supports the central theme.

Example of Off-Topic Information:
Passage about a school carnival:
The school carnival had games, snacks, and prizes. My dog learned a new trick yesterday. We played ring toss and ate popcorn.

In this example, the sentence about the dog learning a new trick is off-topic and should be deleted because it has nothing to do with the carnival.

Why Delete Off-Topic Information?

· It keeps the passage **relevant and focused** on its main purpose.
· It prevents reader confusion and maintains a smooth flow of ideas.
· It strengthens the overall organization of the writing.

How Deleting Makes a Passage Better

Deleting unnecessary sentences is not about reducing word count but about **refining the content**. Strong writing should be **concise and purposeful**, with every sentence contributing to the reader's understanding of the topic. By eliminating repetition and off-topic details, you create writing that is polished, clear, and impactful.

Remember, less is often more when it comes to effective revision!

Teacher Training Script: Deleting Information to Revise

Lower Level Script (Elementary)

"Deleting information is a way to clean up our writing and make it easier to read. Sometimes, we add extra words or sentences that aren't really needed. They might repeat what we already said or be off-topic. For example, if you're writing about a school carnival and suddenly talk about your dog, that sentence doesn't belong. We delete those sentences to stay focused and keep our writing clear and interesting for the reader."

Upper Level Script (Middle/High School)

"Deleting information during revision helps improve clarity and focus. When we write, we sometimes include sentences that repeat what we've already said or drift away from the main topic. These sentences can distract or confuse the reader. For example, if a passage is about a science experiment and suddenly mentions what someone had for lunch, that detail is off-topic and should be removed. Deleting unnecessary or irrelevant information makes the writing more concise, keeps it on track, and strengthens its overall impact."

7 Synonyms for Delete

Omit

Remove

Eliminate

Exclude

Cut

Extract

Cancel

Erase

Lesson Plan 1: Deleting Repetitive Information

Grade Level: 6th–8th Grade
Duration: 60 minutes

Objective:

Students will learn how to identify and delete repetitive information in a passage to improve clarity, conciseness, and focus.

Materials Needed:

- Whiteboard and markers
- Sample passage with repetitive information
- Task cards with short paragraphs containing repetition
- Student journals
- Assessment rubric

Introduction (10 minutes)

Teacher Script (Italicized):
"Have you ever read something that repeats the same idea over and over again? It feels boring and confusing, right? Today, we're going to practice a revising technique called deleting repetitive information. This helps make writing more concise and easier to read by removing extra details that don't add anything new."

"For example, look at this sentence: 'The science fair had many booths. There were a lot of different activities at the science fair. Students visited various booths to participate in activities.' That's the same idea repeated three times! Instead, we can delete the repetition and revise it to: 'The science fair had many booths with different activities for students to enjoy.'"

Direct Instruction (15 minutes)

Explain the Rule:

- **Read the passage carefully and underline repetitive ideas.**
- **Compare sentences to see which ones express the same idea.**
- **Delete the weaker or redundant sentence and keep the one that adds the most value.**

Teacher Script (Italicized):
"Remember, good writing is not about how many words you use but how meaningful those words are. Deleting repetition helps your reader focus on what really matters."

Guided Practice (15 minutes)

Activity: Repetition Hunt

- Provide students with a passage that contains multiple examples of repetition.
- In small groups, students will read the passage, underline repetitive sentences, and decide which ones to delete.
- Discuss their decisions as a class.

Example Passage for Practice:
"The summer festival was fun. There were many activities at the summer festival. We played games, ate snacks, and listened to music. There were games for all ages, and we enjoyed playing them."
Revised: "The summer festival was fun, with games, snacks, and music for all ages."

Independent Practice (10 minutes)

Activity: Personal Writing Revision

- Students will review a draft of their writing and identify at least two repetitive sentences.
- Delete or revise these sentences to make the writing clearer and more concise.

Assessment: Authentic Task (15 minutes)

Activity: Poster Presentation – Before and After

· Students will create a "before and after" poster showing a repetitive passage they revised by deleting repetition.
· Share with the class, explaining why they made their revisions.

Lesson Plan 2: Deleting Off-Topic Information

Grade Level: 6th–8th Grade
Duration: 60 minutes

Objective:

Students will learn how to identify and delete off-topic information to improve the relevance and coherence of a passage.

Materials Needed:

- Sample passage with off-topic sentences
- Task cards with short paragraphs containing unrelated details
- Student journals
- Assessment rubric

Introduction (10 minutes)

Teacher Script (Italicized):
"Have you ever read something that feels random or out of place, like it doesn't belong in the story? These are called off-topic sentences, and they can confuse your reader. Today, we're going to practice deleting off-topic information to make our writing more focused and clear."

"For example, imagine you're writing about a school carnival and suddenly include this sentence: 'My dog learned a new trick yesterday.' It has nothing to do with the carnival, right? That sentence is off-topic and should be deleted."

Direct Instruction (15 minutes)

Explain the Rule:

- **Identify the main idea of the passage.**
- **Read each sentence carefully and ask, 'Does this sentence support the main idea?'**
- **If it doesn't, delete it!**

Teacher Script (Italicized):
"Think of writing as a puzzle. Every sentence should fit together. If a piece doesn't belong, it makes the whole picture unclear. Deleting off-topic sentences helps your writing stay on track."

Guided Practice (15 minutes)

Activity: Off-Topic Sentence Challenge

- Provide students with a sample passage containing off-topic sentences.
- In pairs, students will identify and delete the off-topic information.
- Share and discuss their revisions.

Example Passage:
"The school carnival had games, snacks, and prizes. My dog learned a new trick yesterday. We played ring toss and ate popcorn."
Revised: "The school carnival had games, snacks, and prizes. We played ring toss and ate popcorn."

Independent Practice (10 minutes)

Activity: Off-Topic Sentence Hunt

- Students will review a piece of their own writing and identify one or two off-topic sentences.
- Delete these sentences and rewrite the passage to improve its focus.

Assessment: Authentic Task (15 minutes)

Activity: Editing Partner Challenge

- In pairs, students will swap drafts and identify off-topic sentences in each other's writing.
- Discuss the edits with their partner and justify the deletions.

Closure (5 minutes)

Teacher Script (Italicized):
"Great job today! Deleting unnecessary information makes your writing stronger and easier to follow. Remember, every sentence should serve a purpose. Keep practicing this strategy to make your writing shine!"

Passage: Why People Study Insects

Insects are among the most diverse creatures on Earth. They play a big role in nature, often going unnoticed. Some people think insects are only pests that cause problems. Others study them because they are curious. Scientists have been learning about insects for hundreds of years. Insects are useful for farming and the environment. Ants work together to build large colonies. Bees are fascinating creatures. Some insects are dangerous.

Unit 6

Word Order

Rules and Patterns for Word Order in English

In English, **word order** follows a set of rules that govern how different parts of speech (subject, verb, object, adjectives, adverbs, etc.) should be arranged to create clear, natural, and meaningful sentences. Understanding these patterns is essential for building grammatically correct and coherent sentences. Below are the key word order rules and patterns:

---

1. Basic Sentence Structure: SVO (Subject-Verb-Object)

The most common word order in English is **Subject-Verb-Object (SVO)**.

- **Subject:** Who or what is performing the action
- **Verb:** The action or state of being
- **Object:** The person or thing affected by the action

Example:

- **Correct:** *The boy (subject) eats (verb) the apple (object).*
- **Incorrect:** *Eats the boy the apple.*

2. Adjective Order

When multiple adjectives describe a noun, they follow a specific order. The correct sequence is:

1. **Determiner** (a, an, the, my, some)
2. **Opinion/Observation** (beautiful, amazing, lovely)
3. **Size** (big, small, tall)
4. **Shape** (round, square, flat)
5. **Age** (old, young, new)
6. **Color** (red, blue, green)
7. **Origin** (American, French, Chinese)
8. **Material** (wooden, silk, metal)
9. **Purpose** (sleeping [as in sleeping bag], cooking [as in cooking pot])

Example:

- Correct: *The small, round, red ball.*
- Incorrect: *The red, round, small ball.*

---

3. Adverb Placement

Adverbs can appear in different parts of the sentence, depending on what they modify (the verb, adjective, or the whole sentence). However, the general pattern is:

1. **Adverbs of manner** (how?) – *She spoke quietly.*
2. **Adverbs of place** (where?) – *He went outside.*
3. **Adverbs of time** (when?) – *We will meet tomorrow.*

Example Patterns:

- Before the verb: *She always drinks coffee.*
- After the verb: *She sings beautifully.*

Order When Combining Adverbs: Manner → Place → Time

- Correct: *He ran quickly (manner) to the park (place) yesterday (time).*
- Incorrect: *He ran yesterday quickly to the park.*

4. Questions: Inversion of Word Order

In questions, the subject and auxiliary verb (or modal) switch places:

Yes/No Questions: Auxiliary Verb + Subject + Main Verb

- **Example:** *Are you coming?*

Wh- Questions: Wh- word + Auxiliary Verb + Subject + Main Verb

- **Example:** *Where are you going?*

---

5. Prepositional Phrases

Prepositional phrases typically follow the structure: **Preposition + Object (noun)**
They modify verbs, adjectives, or nouns and are usually placed after the word they describe.

Example:

- *The cat is on the table.*
- *She spoke with confidence.*

---

6. Modifier Placement (Avoid Misplaced Modifiers)

Modifiers should be placed next to the word they describe to avoid confusion.

Example:

- Correct: *Running down the street, I saw a dog.* (The speaker is running.)
- Incorrect: *I saw a dog running down the street.* (The dog is running.)

---

7. Compound Sentences (Coordinating Conjunctions)

When combining independent clauses, use **coordinating conjunctions** (for, and, nor, but, or, yet, so) to connect them.

- **Example:** *I wanted to go to the park, but it started to rain.*

Conclusion

English word order may seem rigid, but these rules and patterns ensure sentences are clear, logical, and easy to understand. Whether arranging adjectives, placing adverbs, or avoiding misplaced modifiers, mastering word order helps create effective communication. Understanding these patterns will make your writing and speech sound more natural and polished!

Understanding the "Who, What, What, Where, When" Chant

The **"Who, What, What, Where, When"** chant is a simple, rhythmic tool that helps students understand **word order** in a sentence. It provides a **framework** for organizing key sentence elements in a logical, natural sequence. Here's how it works:

---

1. "Who" – The Subject

- This part answers the question: *Who is the sentence about?*
- The **subject** always comes first in a basic sentence. It's the person, place, or thing performing the action.
  Example:
- **Who:** *The teacher*

---

2. "What" (First What) – The Verb

- This part answers: *What is the subject doing?*
- The **verb** follows the subject and describes the action or state of being.
  Example:
- **What (action):** *is reading*

---

3. "What" (Second What) – The Object

- This part answers: *What is receiving the action?*
- The **object** (if there is one) follows the verb and tells what is affected by the action.
  Example:
- **What (object):** *a book*

4. "Where" – Place Information

- This part answers: *Where did the action happen?*
- Location words (adverbs or prepositional phrases) should appear after the time phrase or at the end of the sentence.
  Example:
- **Where:** *in the library*

---

5. "When" – Time Information

- This part answers: *When did the action happen?*
- Time words (adverbs or prepositional phrases) should generally come after the verb or object.
  Example:
- **When:** *in the morning*

Putting It All Together

Example Sentence:
"The teacher (Who) is reading (What) a book (What) in the library (Where) in the morning (When)."

This word order sounds natural and provides complete, clear information to the reader.

Why This Chant Works

1. **Logical Order:** The chant mirrors how we naturally build sentences in English.
2. **Simplifies Complex Ideas:** It breaks sentence construction into manageable steps.
3. **Supports Grammar Learning:** It reinforces subject-verb-object structure and the correct placement of time and location phrases.
4. **Encourages Full Sentences:** Students are less likely to write incomplete or disorganized sentences.

Classroom Use Example:

1. **Chant Together:** Start by having the class chant *"Who, What, What, Where, When"* aloud.
2. **Sentence Building:** Give students sentence elements on cards and have them arrange them in the correct order.
3. **Assessment:** Provide scrambled sentences and ask students to reorder them according to the chant.

The chant becomes a powerful **mental guide** for constructing clear, organized sentences!

Word Order Chant

Who

What

What

Where

When

Lesson 1: Basic Sentence Structure (SVO – Subject-Verb-Object)

Objective:

Students will understand that English follows a Subject-Verb-Object (SVO) word order in basic sentences.

Materials:

· Sentence strips with scrambled sentences
· Whiteboard and markers

Teacher Script:

"In English, the most common word order is Subject-Verb-Object (SVO). The subject tells who or what the sentence is about, the verb shows the action, and the object tells who or what receives the action. If these parts are out of order, the sentence can be confusing. Let's practice putting sentences in the correct order!"

Activity: Sentence Strip Scramble

· Give each group a set of sentence strips with scrambled sentences.
· Groups work together to rearrange the words into the correct SVO order.
· After each group finishes, they read their sentence aloud and explain how they identified the subject, verb, and object.

Example Sentence:

· Scrambled: *ate / the cat / the mouse*
· Correct Order: *The cat ate the mouse.*

Assessment:

Provide students with five scrambled sentences. Have them rewrite each in the correct SVO order.

Lesson 2: Adjective Order

Objective:

Students will learn and apply the correct order of adjectives in English sentences.

Materials:

- Adjective order chart (Determiner, Opinion, Size, Shape, Age, Color, Origin, Material, Purpose)
- Pictures of objects (e.g., a red, round ball)

Teacher Script:

"When we use multiple adjectives to describe a noun, they must follow a specific order. We don't say 'the blue big ball'; we say 'the big blue ball.' The order is important because it makes our descriptions sound natural. Let's learn the correct order!"

Activity: Adjective Relay

- Show students a picture of an object (e.g., a small, round, red ball).
- Write adjectives on the board in random order.
- In teams, students rearrange the adjectives in the correct order on the board.
- Discuss the correct order and why it sounds more natural.

Assessment:

Give students a list of jumbled adjectives and have them write the correctly ordered description for each noun.

Adjective Order Chart

Adjective Type	Examples	Explanation
1. Determiner	a, an, the, my, some	Specifies which noun or how many (articles, possessives, or quantifiers).
2. Opinion/Observation	beautiful, amazing, lovely	Describes general opinions or observations about the noun.
3. Size	big, small, tall	Indicates the size or dimension of the noun.
4. Shape	round, square, flat	Describes the shape or form of the noun.
5. Age	old, young, new	Specifies the age or stage of the noun.
6. Color	red, blue, green	Indicates the color of the noun.
7. Origin	American, French, Chinese	Shows where the noun comes from or its nationality/region.
8. Material	wooden, silk, metal	Describes what the noun is made of.
9. Purpose	sleeping (bag), cooking (pot)	Explains the function or intended use of the noun (usually a noun acting as an adjective).

Adjective Type

Determiner

Opinion/Observation

Size

Shape

Age

Color

Origin

Material

Purpose

Lesson 3: Adverb Placement

Objective:

Students will practice placing adverbs (manner, place, time) correctly within sentences.

Materials:

· Sentence cards with missing adverbs
· Adverb word cards (quickly, yesterday, at the park, etc.)

Teacher Script:

"Adverbs tell us how, when, or where something happens. Depending on what the adverb describes, it can go in different parts of the sentence. Let's practice placing adverbs correctly!"

Activity: Adverb Placement Game

· Distribute sentence cards with blanks for adverbs.
· Give each student an adverb card.
· Students walk around the room and match their adverb card to the appropriate blank in a sentence.
· As a class, discuss the correct placement.

Example:

· *She ran ______ (manner) at the park ______ (place) yesterday ______ (time).*
· Correct Order: *She ran quickly at the park yesterday.*

Assessment:

Provide sentences with misplaced adverbs. Have students rewrite the sentences with correct adverb placement.

Lesson 4: Questions and Inversion of Word Order

Objective:

Students will learn how to form yes/no and Wh- questions using correct word order.

Materials:

· Question word cards (who, what, where, when, why, how)
· Sentence strips

Teacher Script:

"In questions, the word order changes. For yes/no questions, the auxiliary verb comes before the subject. For Wh- questions, we start with a question word like 'where' or 'what.' Let's practice switching word order to form questions!"

Activity: Question Formation Race

· Divide students into small groups.
· Provide sentence strips in statement form (e.g., *You are going to the park*).
· Groups race to rearrange the sentence into a yes/no question and a Wh- question.
· Share answers with the class.

Example:

· Statement: *You are going to the park.*
· Yes/No Question: *Are you going to the park?*
· Wh- Question: *Where are you going?*

Assessment:

Provide five statements. Have students convert them into both yes/no and Wh- questions.

Lesson 5: Prepositional Phrases

Objective:

Students will understand how to use and position prepositional phrases in sentences.

Materials:

· Prepositional phrase cards (on the table, at noon, with a friend)

Teacher Script:

"Prepositional phrases show relationships in a sentence—where, when, or how something happens. They usually come after the word they describe. Let's practice using prepositional phrases!"

Activity: Preposition Walkabout

· Place prepositional phrase cards around the room.
· Give students sentence starters (e.g., *The book is...*) and have them walk around the room, adding a prepositional phrase to complete the sentence.
· Share sentences with the class.

Example:

· *The book is on the table.*

Assessment:

Provide incomplete sentences and have students add appropriate prepositional phrases.

Lesson 6: Modifier Placement

Objective:

Students will learn to place modifiers correctly to avoid confusion.

Materials:

- Sentences with misplaced modifiers

Teacher Script:

"Modifiers are words or phrases that describe something in the sentence. If they aren't placed correctly, they can change the meaning or make the sentence confusing. Let's practice placing them correctly!"

Activity: Misplaced Modifier Fix-It

- Provide students with sentences containing misplaced modifiers.
- Students work in pairs to rewrite the sentences with correct modifier placement.
- Discuss how the meaning changes when the modifier is misplaced.

Example:

- Misplaced: *Running down the street, the dog barked at me.*
- Corrected: *I saw a dog running down the street barking at me.*

Assessment:

Give students five sentences with misplaced modifiers and have them rewrite them correctly.

Part 6

GRAMMAR
IN THE VIRTUAL CLASSROOM

Teaching grammar to **junior high and high school students in a virtual setting** can absolutely be engaging, meaningful, and effective—if it's done with purpose, relevance, and creativity. Below is a structured list of strategies categorized by **instructional approach**, including specific tools, platforms, and examples that work especially well in virtual classrooms.

1. Contextual Grammar Through Writing

Instead of isolated drills, embed grammar into meaningful writing tasks.

How to implement:

- Assign weekly *"grammar in action"* writing prompts. For example:
  "Write a short story using at least three compound sentences with correct semicolon use."
- Use **Google Docs** or **Microsoft OneDrive** for shared editing.
  Comment in real time on misuse of tense, run-ons, or punctuation errors.
- Use **color-coding** for grammar elements (subjects in green, verbs in blue, modifiers in yellow) in a shared document to teach sentence structure.

Why it works:
Grammar becomes part of their writing voice—not just a rule to memorize.

---

2. Gamified Grammar Practice

Turn dry rules into challenges and competitions.

How to implement:

- Use **Kahoot**, **Blooket**, or **Quizizz** to run grammar showdowns (e.g., comma usage, verb tense errors).
- Host virtual **"Grammar Olympics"** using breakout rooms in Zoom or Google Meet:
  - Round 1: Identify sentence types
  - Round 2: Fix comma splices
  - Round 3: Create the best complex sentence using a subordinate clause

Why it works:
Gamification drives engagement and adds friendly competition.

3. Grammar Talks and Peer Teaching

Have students teach grammar concepts to others.

How to implement:

- Assign students grammar rules (e.g., fragments vs. run-ons, semicolon usage).
- Let them record a short **Flipgrid** or **Loom** explainer video teaching the rule and giving examples.
- Post their videos in a shared "Grammar Library" that the class can refer to all year.

Why it works:
Teaching a concept forces students to understand it deeply and builds confidence.

---

4. Digital Grammar Manipulatives

Let students interact with grammar structures in a tactile (yet virtual) way.

How to implement:

- Use **Jamboard** or **Google Slides** with moveable words or sentence pieces. Example:
    - Scrambled sentence: Students drag pieces to form a compound-complex sentence.
    - Parts of speech color sorting: Students match modifiers, nouns, verbs, etc.
- Assign **sentence surgery** where students "cut and correct" sentence fragments or revise passive voice.

Why it works:
These mimic hands-on learning and are highly effective for visual learners.

---

5. Act It Out: Grammar as Drama

Make grammar expressive and interactive—even on Zoom.

How to implement:

- Assign roles to sentence parts and act out clauses. One student is the subject, another is the verb, etc.
- Let students create **skits** or TikTok-style grammar videos using transitions, interjections, or mood changes (subjunctive vs. indicative).

Why it works:
Movement, role-play, and voice variation create stronger memory connections.

---

6. Grammar Lab: Error Analysis

Let students become editors and detectives.

How to implement:

- Post a "Grammar Crime Scene" paragraph with 10 intentional grammar errors. Students must "solve" it and explain their fixes.
- Use **Padlet** or **Nearpod Collaborate Boards** for students to annotate the errors.
- Make it a regular "Fix-It Friday" activity.

Why it works:
Students apply grammar knowledge in realistic, analytical situations.

---

7. Real-World Grammar Applications

Bridge grammar to the outside world and their personal lives.

How to implement:

- Analyze **text messages, memes, or social media posts** for grammar accuracy and effectiveness.
- Create assignments like: "Revise this tweet to be grammatically correct while keeping the same tone."
- Invite them to "edit the internet": find grammar mistakes in ads, reviews, or online articles.

Why it works:
Relevance increases retention. Students see grammar as useful, not useless.

8. Routine Integration: Mini Grammar Bursts

Don't teach grammar in isolation—sprinkle it throughout the week.

How to implement:

- Start each class with a **2-minute grammar warm-up**. Ex: "Fix this sentence," "What's wrong here?"
- Use a **daily sentence challenge** in Google Forms where students correct a line or identify parts of speech.
- Link grammar to the text of the week: "Which punctuation choice best matches the tone of this poem?"

Why it works:
Regular exposure solidifies understanding without overwhelming students.

---

9. Collaborative Grammar Journals

Create a shared space to reflect and grow.

How to implement:

- Each student keeps a **digital grammar journal** in Google Docs.
  - Log grammar concepts learned.
  - Track personal errors in writing and corrections.
  - Reflect on how they'll improve grammar usage going forward.

Why it works:
Grammar becomes individualized and metacognitive, not one-size-fits-all.

---

10. Use the Teach BIG Grammar Framework (if available)

If you're using Teach BIG's *Grammar School* or *Full Circle of Language Arts*:

How to implement virtually:

- Project sentence diagrams, word sorts, or quadrant-specific grammar skills during Zoom sessions.
- Use breakout rooms to analyze and rewrite based on Full Circle grammar integration.

- Use Teach BIG's Grammar Cards or digital versions for error correction, concept review, and sentence construction.

Why it works:
Structured grammar + virtual tools = mastery through consistency and creativity.

Best Practices for virtual learning, specifically designed for junior high and high school students. These techniques focus on engagement, clarity, connection, and cognitive retention—all essential for successful online instruction.

---

1. Set Clear Expectations from Day One

Why it matters: Virtual learning can feel ambiguous. Clarity builds confidence and consistency.

Best practices:

- Post weekly learning goals and assignment checklists.
- Use a consistent structure for all lessons (e.g., warm-up → input → application → recap).
- Include "How to Succeed in This Course" guides with behavior, communication, and tech norms.

---

2. Chunk Content into Mini-Lessons

Why it matters: Attention spans are shorter online—especially for adolescents.

Best practices:

- Break content into **5–10 minute segments** using video, visuals, or direct instruction.
- Alternate between teacher-led instruction and student activity (never talk for 30+ minutes straight).
- Use titles like: "Mini-Lesson 1: What's a Run-On Sentence?" to guide student navigation.

---

3. Use Interactive Tools to Increase Participation

Why it matters: Students learn more when they *do* something—not just watch.

Best practices:

- Use **Jamboard, Padlet, Nearpod, or Pear Deck** for real-time responses.
- Add **live polls, emoji reactions, drag-and-drop**, or short quizzes every 5–10 minutes.
- Let students "vote" on grammar corrections or literary interpretations.

---

4. Implement Retrieval Practice

Why it matters: Learning sticks when students are asked to recall rather than just reread.

Best practices:

- Begin class with a **Quick Recall** activity: "What did we learn yesterday?" or "Define today's key term without looking."
- Use **low-stakes quizzes** and **exit tickets** to reinforce memory.
- Integrate spaced repetition and spiral reviews across weeks.

---

5. Keep Camera Time Purposeful & Flexible

Why it matters: Not every student is comfortable on camera, but human connection is key.

Best practices:

- Encourage cameras during discussion, presentations, or collaborative work.
- Allow off-camera work time with an expectation to check back in visually.
- Use **breakout rooms** for small group interaction and deeper thinking.

---

6. Use Digital Notebooks and Portfolios

Why it matters: Organization promotes independence and reflection.

Best practices:

- Assign each student a **Google Slides or Docs grammar/writing notebook**.
- Use editable templates where they track learning, submit drafts, and revise work.
- Allow students to showcase their best work in a **digital portfolio** at semester's end.

---

7. Build in Movement and Off-Screen Time

Why it matters: Students sitting too long disengage and burn out.

Best practices:

- Give "5-minute unplugged challenges" (e.g., "Find 3 prepositions in your kitchen").

- Use a scavenger hunt or "walk and write" journaling prompt.
- Encourage **stand-up polls** or **whiteboard answers** with pen and paper.

---

8. Model Everything

Why it matters: Clear modeling reduces confusion and builds confidence in students.

Best practices:

- Share your screen to model annotation, grammar fixes, or writing structure.
- Think aloud while solving a problem: "Watch how I find the subject here..."
- Record screencasts using **Loom or Screencastify** for students to rewatch.

---

9. Offer Choices and Student Voice

Why it matters: Autonomy fuels motivation in the virtual setting.

Best practices:

- Let students choose how to show their learning (e.g., video response, infographic, essay).
- Create "Must Do / May Do / Extension" menus for differentiated engagement.
- Use discussion boards to allow students to pose and answer each other's questions.

---

10. Provide Consistent Feedback Loops

Why it matters: Feedback fuels growth—and online learners often feel isolated without it.

Best practices:

- Give timely written or voice comments on submitted work using **Google Classroom, Canvas, or Microsoft Teams**.
- Use **rubrics** with clickable criteria.
- Schedule **virtual office hours** or offer weekly 1:1 or small group conferences.

11. Foster Relationships & Class Culture

Why it matters: Students engage when they feel seen, heard, and valued.

Best practices:

- Start class with 1-minute check-ins, would-you-rather questions, or music-based mood meters.
- Host virtual "coffeehouse" discussions or themed dress-up days.
- Celebrate birthdays, milestones, or even meme-of-the-week to keep joy alive.

---

12. Use Data to Adjust Instruction

Why it matters: Virtual instruction needs to be adaptive.

Best practices:

- Use analytics from tools like **Formative, EdPuzzle, and Google Forms** to track understanding.
- Adjust groupings and reteaching based on quiz or discussion performance.
- Create a "misunderstanding map" to reteach common errors.

Made in the USA
Monee, IL
02 August 2025